Agrarian Life in Awadh

Agrarian Life in Awadh

The Story of Change under Pre-Colonial Regimes (AD 1595-1856)

Saiyid Zaheer Husain Jafri

GYAN

ISBN: 978-81-212-2197-9

Published, 2022

Published by

Gyan Publishing House
5, Ansari Road
Daryaganj, New Delhi-110002
Phone: 011-47034999, 9811692060
www.gyanbooks.com
E-mail: books@gyanbooks.com

Printed at: Gyan Press, Delhi.

To The Memory Of My Mother

Bibi Ayesha

(11th November 1998)

And

To The Memory Of My Father

Hazrat Saiyid Shah Muhammad Husain Jafri

(16th September 1979)

رَبِّ ارْحَمْهُمَا كَمَا رَبَّيَانِي صَغِيرًا ۝

"My Lord! Have mercy on them both
as they did care when I was little!"

Al - Quran, xvii, 24

For

Professor

Dr Syed Shah Naqi Husain Jafri

(d. 9th December 2007)

بجھ گیا وہ شعلہ جو مقصودِ ہر پروانہ تھا

اب کوئی سودائیِ سوزِ تمام آیا تو کیا

&

Assoc. Professor

Dr. Hafiz Syed Shah Wali Husain Jafri

(d. 25th May 2007)

تھا جنھیں ذوقِ تماشا، وہ تو رخصت ہو گئے

لے کے اب تُو وعدۂ دیدارِ عام آیا تو کیا

Contents

Preface

The bulk of the material presented here has appeared earlier in my *Awadh from Mughal to Colonial Rule: Studies in the Anatomy of a Transformation* (2016 & 1998). The sections dealing with the system of land revenue as it operated at the provincial level during the classical period of Mughal Empire, the changes introduced in the system by the Nawab-Wazirs are at least up to AD 1780s, along with a section on the revenue grantees have been added here to provide a complete picture of the agrarian life in Awadh. Perhaps, it was the land revenue system especially during the reign of the fourth Nawab of Awadh, Asafuddaulah (1797) which came under the greedy and watchful eyes of the officials of East India Company for numerous experiments. It was during this period when the resources of Awadh kingdom were milched by the Company officials under various pretexts in a shameless manner. The 'saga' of Bahu Begum and her extensive properties became a memorable chapter in the annals of British parliamentary history during the impeachment proceedings of the then Governor General Warren Hastings. The gross and blatant injustice done to the royal Nawabi family and especially to its ladies has undoubtedly shaken the 'conscience' of British parliamentarians and Liberals. They made memorable speeches but nothing changed at the ground level. The Awadh kingdom continued to be ill-treated and exploited for its resources in the most shameless manner.

The early nineteenth century was even worst for the people of Awadh. With the treaty of AD 1801 more than half of the kingdom was annexed by the British and the Nawab was left with that part of the territory of his kingdom which was described in the chronicles as *mulk-e qadeem,* perhaps the larger part of the Mughal subah of Awadh whose governorship was conferred on Saadat Ali Khan Burhanul Mulk way back in 1722 by Mughal King Muhammad Shah. It was the pressure of the Company officials on the Nawabi regime to keep on changing and experimenting to the various forms of revenue system in the disguise of 'reforms'. Ironically, these suggested changes proved worse for the peasants and paved the way for the increase in resources of rural overlords even the merchants who have entered the lucrative business of zamindari tenure. The institution of talluqadari grew disproportionately in the kingdom that controlled more than half of the territory indirectly. Their armed power and 'fortresses' (*gharis and qilachas*) covered with reserved forests was more than a match for the nawabi forces who could never muster the courage to take on these strongholds of the local landed magnets. The worse sufferers in the match between the administration and these potentates were the helpless peasants. Their conditions can be described only by a reading between the lines.

The conditions of 'anarchy' and 'misrule' due to the British presence and interventions were quite a disaster. It also paved the way for some crooked Company officials of Residency at Lucknow to indulge into their private ventures and avenues like the lucrative bond business which created the flight of capital away from the urban middle class. It has been estimated that large number of people of Awadh were dependent on the interests accruing on the investment in the private business of Company officials. Similarly, the Nawab themselves have invested huge sums of money for the benefit of the religious and ecclesiastical functions/institutions. The officials of the Residency directly remitted such amount to the named beneficiaries. These activities of East India Company had considerably undermined the authority of the sovereign in his own capital. It is worth to recall the testimony of Henry Lawrence in 1845:

> At Lucknow for years the Resident held public *darbar* where the grandees attended and pleaded against their own sovereign and his servants. Thus, were the monarch and his subjects pitted against each other, thus was the sovereign degraded in his own capital.[1]

Consequent upon the agrarian and political instability of the region we see the rise of the armed power of the zamindars and talluqadars in a big way. They were strong enough to threaten the Nawabi establishment while the Nawabs always sought the help of the English forces who controlled these overlords. On their part, the English officials exercised their discretion carefully to accept the request in a selective manner. This further led to the zamindars' capacity to enlist the retainers, maintain the forts etc. The region of Baiswara was the abode of Bais Rajputs and since mid-seventeenth century they have emerged as the powerful block to necessitate the creation of a separate faujdari jurisdiction to have a better imperial control on the zamindars.

1. Henry Lawrence, 'The Kingdom of Oudh', *Calcutta Review*, III, 1845, pp. 414- 15.

During the seventeenth and early eighteenth centuries the region has seen various uprisings by Bais and Kanpuria Rajputs. I feel honoured to reproduce here an unpublished article of my teacher Late Professor Zahiruddin Malik on the 'Problems of Faujdari Jurisdiction in Baiswara' wherein he has used the rare manuscript of *Insha-e Roshan Kalam*, the official letters of the then faujdar of Baiswara to the Mughal Court in around AD 1701. The faujdar has sent numerous petitions to the court about the recalcitrant attitude of the Bais zamindars and the measures he has took to control the lawlessness in his faujdari jurisdiction. Some of the *arzdasht* have been translated by Prof Malik and since his article is a seminal one and cannot be accessed at all, hence, I am reproducing his full article as an appendix to the chapter on armed power of the zamindars.

I consider myself fortunate that I continue to enjoy the benefits of advice and direction from my mentor and guide Professor Irfan Habib. He has thoroughly checked the entire text of the manuscript and I am most grateful to him for his guidance, comments and advice. It was due to his incisive comments that the study has taken a final shape. I am indebted to my teachers especially Professor Shireen Moosvi, Late Professor M Athar Ali, Late Professor Iqbal Husain, Professor Ishtiyaq Ahmad Zilli and Professor Afzal Husain.

For the moral support, advice and help I am thankful to my friends who were working for the thesis at that time. I acknowledge Syed Aslam Ali, Late Dr Iqbal Sabir, Dr. Maqsood Ahmad Khan, Prof Yaqoob Ali Khan, Dr. Arshad Islam, Dr. Iftihar Ahmad Khan, Professor M. Afzal Khan, Prof. Nishat Manzar, Prof. Abha Singh, Mrs. Faiza Simin and Dr. Yusuf Ansari (now working as a surgeon at Jaunpur). I owe my debt to my Persian teacher Mr Habibullah Saheb as well.

Our librarians at the Department Library, Mr Jalal Abbas Abbasi, Mr Mohd Yusuf Siddiqui, Mr Aijaz Mohammad Khan and Raoof Bhai were ever ready to help me with the material. Mr Zahoor Ali Khan, the cartographer and Mr Faiz Habib have drawn all the four maps very meticulously included here. I am thankful to both of them.

I must place on record the affection and kindness always shown to me by my brothers, sisters, nephews and nieces in my work. I can never forget my brothers who always appreciated all my writings; and encouraged me further to take up new themes. With a heavy heart, I remember the departed souls of my two brothers. I pray for the longevity of my brothers, sisters and also wish that our next generation pursue the higher academic career.

I received help from my students Dr. Priyanka Chanana, Dr. Nalini Singh, Dr. Heena Ansari, Dr. Sana Aziz, Dr. Yusra Farooqui, Suman Yadav and Mohd Waseem. At the final stage, Dr. Heena Ansari [now a colleague in the Department of History] shared the major burden by finalizing the manuscript, reading of the proof and other editorial inputs. Once again, I take the opportunity to express my gratitude to my wife, Mrs. Tayyaba Jafri and to my sons Saiyid Naseer Jafri (Tariq), Saiyid Ashraf Jafri (Abbas) and daughter Haleema Sadia Jafri for being considerate, in allowing me to work in the Department up to the late hours.

16th February 2022 **Saiyid Zaheer Husain Jafri**

14th Rajab, AH 1443

Introduction

Awadh has a place in our historical memory owing to its contributions to our composite culture, and the British repeated acts of injustice against it, culminating in the Annexation in 1856. Its institution of the ta'alluqadari tenures came into limelight with the mutiny and Canning's proclamation. The heroic resistance offered by the people of Awadh forms a dramatic part of the Rebellion of 1857.

There would be little support from any physical map for establishing Awadh as a region. The great alluvial plains of the Gangetic basin have no recognised barriers and rivers constitute links rather than obstacles. Yet, historically what came to be the Mughal *suba* of Awadh, with its capital at Awadh (Ayodhya), stretching from the Ganga to the Gandak, had impeccable historical credentials.[1] By and large, it corresponded to the fifteenth century Sharqi kingdom with its capital at Jaunpur on the Gomti,[2] and to the ancient Kosala, with its earlier capital at Sravasti and later at Ayodhya.

Within this region a dialect of Hindi, known as Awadhi, was in vogue in which Kabir, the great monotheist, who lies buried at Maghar, composed his verses and the famous Hindi poet Malik Muhammad of Jais, wrote his *Padmavat* during the sixteenth century. Tulsidas's celebrated *Ramcharitmanas* also is in the same dialect. It could, therefore, be asserted, that the region had a distinct 'cultural personality' as well.

As part of the Mughal Empire, Awadh had little reason to appear prominently in political or military history, after the suppression of the Uzbek rebellion in 1560s, since it did not lie directly on any axis of Mughal expansion and thus remained in political backwaters.[3] As a result, there

---

1. For its exact boundaries in Akbar's time, see Irfan Habib, *An Atlas of the Mughal Empire*. New Delhi, 1982, Sheet, 8A.
2. Jaunpur itself was in the Mughal *suba* of Ilahabad, but became a part of the 18th century principality of Awadh.
3. Cf. M. Athar Ali, 'Provincial Governors under Shah Jahan: An Analysis' *Medieval India - A Miscellany*. III, pp. 80-112, and 'Provincial Governors under Aurangzeb- An Analysis', *Medieval India-A Miscellany*, I, pp. 96-133.

were few nobles of high rank posted in Awadh during the seventeenth century; and this is reflected in the absence of any great Mughal monuments in its cities, after Mun'im Khan's Jaunpur Bridge of the 1560s.

The eighteenth century saw a transformation in the position of Awadh for two different reasons. As the Mughal emperors more or less confined their courts to Delhi from the time of Farrukh Siyar (acc. 1713) onwards, holding possession of adjacent provinces became very important for exerting influence at the Court. Thus, the three successive governors of Awadh, Sa'adat Khan (1722-39), Safdarjung (1739-54) and Shuja'uddaula (1754-75), sought to use their control over Awadh and its resources as springboard for pursuing their ambitions at Delhi. Secondly, as the Mughal Empire began to contract, Awadh became subject to threats from the Afghans, Marathas and, finally, the English. For both these reasons Awadh re-entered and remained in the realm of political annals with a new prominence. Though Muzaffar 'Alam has not drawn attention to these extraneous circumstances for Awadh's rise to importance in his work, *The Crisis of Empire in Mughal North India.* The fact that he singles out Awadh and Punjab as the two key provinces for study underlines the alteration in its status that had now occurred.[4]

A basic shift in the position of Awadh took place with the battle of Buxar (1764), whereafter the centre of power under which Awadh worked became Calcutta, not Delhi. Under the new regime, Awadh became a veritable milch-cow for the British East India Company. One of the major contributions of Richard Barnett's work on Awadh of this period is his study of the resources drained out of Awadh under various forms of tribute and impositions, until the size of the inflow being still judged insufficient, more than half of the area of Awadh was annexed by Wellesley in 1801.[5]

The subordinate principality (designated 'Kingdom' in 1814 with the Ruler of Awadh becoming entitled to the coveted address 'His Majesty' by an unintended stroke of Imperialist humour) was now again in political backwaters. The best Study of its position in the new phase (1801-56) is that by Michael H. Fisher.[6] This was the period when Lucknow became the centre of Urdu culture, a refuge of poets and courtiers from Delhi, as the

---

4. Muzaffar Alam, *The Crisis of Empire in Mughal North: Awadh and the Punjab. 1707-48,* Delhi, 1986, Cf. also Richard B. Barnett, *North India Between Empires: Awadh the Mughals and the British.* Berkeley, 1980, esp. Chapter I (pp. 1-41).

5. Barnett, *op. cit.*, Chapter V (pp. 127-63) and VIII (pp. 223-38).

6. Michael H. Fisher, *A Clash of Cultures : Awadh,* the *British and the Mughals,* New Delhi, 1987, pp. 90-246.

Mughal court found itself bereft of all resources and the Emperor a mere pensioner of the British government after 1803. In the political and economic sphere, Awadh offered an example of abject tutelage, where the British had power but no responsibility. British ambitions, both political and financial grew apace, until Dalhousie enforced the Annexation in 1856, and eliminated a state that, since 1764, had never given any occasion for offence to the Paramount Power.

The annexation led to a short but heroic phase of resistance in the history of Awadh, when during 1857-59 it remained dogged in its support of the great uprising. On this, the main work has been that of Rudrangshu Mukherji. Unluckily, it gives scant attention to Persian and indigenous sources, and this lacuna undoubtedly affects his interpretation.[7]

The three centuries of transformation in the agrarian life and relations from the Mughal occupation of Awadh under Akbar's commanders to the annexation of 1856 is the subject matter of this study. This essentially concerns agrarian and institutional history like the class of zamindars and talluqadars; and the least the institution of jagirdari and ijaradars. The class of the revenue grantees and the revenue grants were spread extensively. They have nurtured the Indo-Islamic culture, Sufic thoughts and the elements of pluralistic ethos in a most imaginative manner. Their changing fortunes due to the policy of resumptions undertaken by the nawab wazirs and the colonial authorities during the Summary Settlement in AD 1856 had practically weakened the basis of the Indo-Islamic learning and have also adversely affected the famous Sufi centers of long standing. In working out these details, much greater use has been made of private documents, including those which have now found their way into official archives, than in most historical studies, which have relied on historical narratives or official correspondence and reports. It is, therefore, hoped that the importance of such material will be underlined by the information brought out by these studies; and it will receive attention from other hands as well.

Finally, the study closes with a description of the agrarian conditions on the eve of annexation and the position of sepoys in the agrarian society of Awadh. It has been shown that the sepoys recruited from Awadh in the Bengal army were a 'nuisance' for their weak landowning neighbours. They could directly approach the British residents at Lucknow for the redressal of any 'grievance' (both real and fabricated) and every matter invariably was decided in their favour. The British officers of the Residency were

7. Rudrangshu Mukherjee, *Awadh in Revolt. 1857-1859. A Study of Popular Resistance.* Delhi, 1984.

running their private ventures in the forms of the 'bond businesses'. It was estimated that around 2-3 million rupees were used by the people of Awadh by purchasing the promissory notes and living the interest of those businesses. The middle class of the city of Lucknow was almost dependent on this source of income. Needless to say that in addition to this 'flight of capital', we also notice that the merchants and bankers from Awadh kingdom have started investing their money in numerous ventures in the adjoining districts under their English control. The industrial growth in the towns of Kanpur, Fatehgarh, Farrukahabad and Allahabad took place in the last decades of the Awadh kingdom. Finally, it has been argued that it is difficult to find much to commend in the kingdom of Awadh during the early nineteenth century. Yet, despite the manifold evils by which it was beset, the Awadh system was not one of the total spoilation or anarchy as has been described by its critics. It's very ineptitude protected the peasants and the *zamindars* of Awadh from the extreme distress which the *mahalwari* system of the colonial rule imposed contemporaneously on the adjoining ceded and conquered provinces.

Note on Sources

The earliest possible initial point for any agrarian history of Awadh is the statistical and topographical information contained in Abul Fazl's *Ain-i Akbari* (completed 1598). Then in the *Ain-i Dahsala,* there are final rates for each locality *(dastur-circle)* (the area with identical revenue rates) within the *suba.* In yet another chapter, 'Account of the Twelve *suba*', there is not only a geographical description of the province, but in a separate statistical table information is provided for measured area *(arazi),* estimated revenue *(naqdi/jama'); suyurghal* (amount alienated in grants) caste of the *zamindars* and the number of their retainers (infantry and cavalry separately stated). The *Ain* stands unique for in the Mughal period, at least, it had no successor.

Subsequent to the *Ain,* we have a number of *Dastur-ul amals,* prepared during the seventeenth and early eighteenth centuries which provide summary statistics and sometimes give *pargana-wise* revenue and, in rare cases area statistics.

The printed Persian chronicles of the Mughal period such as Abul Fazl's *Akbarnama* or Lahori's *Badshahnama* or Kazim's *'Alamgirnama* provide only sporadic information about Awadh, referring to some appointments or to rebellions or expeditions. Similar facts can be abstracted from the *Akhbarat-i Darbari Mu'alla* of Aurangzeb's reign. These sources help in identification of a number of officials referred in various *Insha'* collections and other documents.

Another class of sources consists of collections of letters *(insha)* such as the *Insha-i Roshan Kalam, Munsur-ul Maktubat* and *Ausaf-i Asaf.* Their evidence relates to *zamindars'* rebellions, conditions of law and order, relations of the *zamindars* with the *jagirdars* with some occasional references to the working of the *jagir* system and collection of land revenue.

The historical accounts of *Nawabi Awadh* are rather fewer in number and, with some exceptions, are loaded with political history, and little useful information could be exacted for other aspects of history. The typical representative of this class is Ghulam Ali Naqvi's '*Imadus-Sa'adat* (1808).

A valuable account of the administration of the Awadh kingdom exists in the *Mirat-ul Auza',* penned by a court *waqai-nigar* Lalji during the decade before Annexation (1856). Since the author felt that the details of administration which led to the ruin of the kingdom might not be well received by the Lucknow Court, he kept it secret. Valuable information pertaining to the revenue system, methods of realisation and the armed power of the *ta'alluqadars* is provided here.

The most important sources of information lie in archival material consisting of *farmans, parwanas, sanads, mahzars* (statement of the facts) *chaknamas* (land demarcation papers), sale deeds, judicial decision, and private papers of various kinds. Most of them relate to the seventeenth and eighteenth centuries, and a few to the sixteenth. The principal repositories of these collections are the Research Library Centre of Advanced Study in History, AMU, Aligarh; the Central Record Office, Allahabad; National Archives of India, New Delhi; and the Tagore Library, Lucknow University.

Some ecclesiastical institutions and families enjoying *madad-i ma'ash* grants have preserved the documents relating to their claims as every subsequent confirmation depended on the evidence in support of their fiscal perquisites. *The Historical Documents Purchase Committee* and the *Indian Historical Records Commission* acquired these collections from various individual families. In spite of their success in this venture, a large number of documents still remain with the families connected with the mystic establishments or *qazis'* and other families. Some of them provide ready access to their prized collections, while others need to be persuaded to show these records.

As some of these institutions were involved in long drawn litigation, we come across copies of some of these documents in the records of the judicial and the revenue files preserved in the record rooms of the District Courts and the Board of Revenue Library. These files tell much about the British policy towards the *ma' afidars* after 1857, and the multiplicity of land rights acquired by *ma' afi* holders. Between the Summary Settlement and the First Regular Settlement *(bandobast-i awwal)*, British officers compiled exhaustive reports examining the claims of the *ma' afidars* and the nature of their grants at the time of the annexation. The objects of such enquiries were limited to the terms at which new *sanads* were to be granted. The meticulously prepared *wajib-ul arz* of each village and *rawaj- e a'am* of each *pargana* recorded the customary laws of the then land-owning classes regarding a wide range of matters. Such documents are extremely valuable for giving us a peep into the society of Awadh during the earlier periods as well.

The *sufi* institutions have also 'created' some records having a bearing on a number of vital aspects to understand the inner dynamics of the 'world of spirituality'. The deeds of initiation into discipleship and nomination of successors like *shajra, khilafatnamah,* and *misali khilafat wa janashini* often used to spell out the *sufi* customs and traditions. Since the question of nomination was closely linked to the control of the landed property attached to the institutions by way of *madad-i-ma'ash,* such visualisations ultimately resulted in the change of the character of the grant. The institution of *waqf* was created in such establishments even when the grants were initially made for the personal expenses.[8]

Records of this kind are to be found quite often scattered in the files of the Board of Revenue (records upto AD 1890 have now been transferred to UP State Archives, Lucknow) and in files of judicial proceedings. Many are, of course, still in private hands.

The printed works in English are indispensable for any study of the agrarian life of Awadh during the first half of the nineteenth century. An outstanding source for us is the survey by Donald Buttler of the southern parts of Awadh in 1830s. Though Buttler does not explicitly refer to the official documents of the Awadh government, his detailed survey was hardly possible without some cooperation from local officials. His account appears

8. Recently I have studied some of these aspects using the record from the Board of Revenue to understand the fate of the long standing Sufi institutuions after the revolt of 1857, see my, 'The Mughal-Nawabi Legacy under 'Siege' in the Age of Empire (1860s-1880s): Familial Grants and the Waqf of Khanqah-e Karimia, Salon, India', in Miura Toru ed., *Comparative Study of the Waqf from the East Dynamism of Norm and Practices in Religious and Familial Donations*, Tokyu, 2018, pp. 191-216.

a little biased against the Awadh government and he sometimes offers very severe comments, which are not always well grounded. We find him sharing the views of other British officials, that if Awadh was annexed to the British dominions, the people would be better-off.[9] Buttler, however, offers valuable details of crops, agricultural production, implements, towns, markets and topographical information. Charles Elliott's *Chronicles of Oonao,* deals exclusively with the history of the *zamindar* families of Unao, particularly the Bais clan down to AD 1861. The author consulted a large number of documents in the hands of leading *zamindar* families and also draw upon local traditions. It contains useful informations about the history of revenue farms and the financial administration of the district. But surprisingly he shows little concern with purely economic matters such as the state of agriculture, crop pattern and trade.

Among the travellers' accounts, the most important are those of Heber and Sleeman. Bishop Reginald Heber visited Awadh in 1824, and had some pre-conceived notions.[10] But he revised these after he made his personal observation[11] and also appears to have acquired some sympathy with the *Nawabi* regime. Indeed, he blames the non-cooperative attitude of the Company's officials for the anarchy and misrule of the Kingdom.[12] His judgement about the people is the opposite to that of Buttler, for he argued that "they prefer to be governed by their native *nawabs* rather than to be placed under the rule of the Company."[13]

W.H. Sleeman's diary of his tour of Awadh which he made from December 1849 to February 1850 is now a celebrated historical text. He was the then Resident at Lucknow, and the tour was made to supplement the report which he had presented earlier to Lord Dalhousie.[14] To him, the basic fault in the political set-up of the Kingdom lay in the lack of effective

9. Donald Buttler, *Outlines of the Topography and Statistics of Southern Districts of Oudh and Cantonment of Sultanpur,* Calcutta, 1839, Delhi Reprint, 1982, pp. 50-52.

10. "We have heard much of the mis-governed and desolate state of the Kingdom of Oude", cf Bishop Reginald Heber, *Narrative of a Journey Through the Upper Provinces,* 1824-25, London, 1828, Vol. I, p. 41.

11. "I have been pleased, however and surprised, after all which I have heard of Oude, to find the country so completely under plough, I cannot took that we should witness so considerable population." *Ibid.* p. 49.

12. *Ibid.* pp. 85-86.

13. *Ibid.* pp. 82-83.

14. RD Reeves (ed.), *Sleeman in Oudh,* Cambridge, 1971, see introduction, p. 13.

central government' and the 'maladministration' which resulted from it.[15] Some of Sleeman's observations must be judged in the context of his explicit bias.

Whatever the reasons behind the compilation of Sleeman's diary, it still stands as a treasure house of facts relating to crops, agriculture, local administration etc. *Zamindars, 'ta'alluqadars* and *chakledars* find frequent mention in the diary, and this help us to form an idea of their power and role in local society and administration.

The people of Awadh and particularly the sepoys of the Bengal Army (recruited from Awadh), offered the stiffest resistance to the British during 1857-59. One needs to understand the reasons for the anger and anguish of the sepoys: something which became marked after the annexation of Awadh (on 7th Feb 1856) and soon after the Summary Settlement which put to an end the 'favoured' status which the sepoys of Awadh used to enjoy under the Nawabi regime. Now, they were just ordinary peasants with no special status in agrarian society. Similarly, the artisans, weavers and other entrepreneurs were losing the avenues of employment as the nawabi patronage was no more available to them. The depiction of their distress and hardship has been portrayed quite graphically by the contemporary weekly Urdu newspaper from Lucknow *Tilism*. The substantial data of this newspaper has escaped the attention of the scholars working on this region. It is only of late that Late Prof. Iqbal Husain and Dr. Heena has made use of the data from *Tilism* in a substantive manner.[16] I became aware of the 'neglect' of the indigenous data and almost a total dependence on the English official record while I was working on the biography of Maulavi Ahmadullah Shah, one of the central figures in organising the opposition to British rule.[17] It was possible for me to access material on his activities and career as a leader of the resistance, which has not been explored and analysed in the earlier studies. His versified biography composed by one of his disciples,

---

15. RD Reeves (ed.), *Sleeman in Oudh,* Cambridge, 1971, see introduction, p. 13.
16. Iqbal Husain, 'Lucknow between the Annexation and the Mutiny' originally published in 1983; reproduced in Iqbal Husain, *Religion and Ideology of the Rebels of 1857,* Primus, 2013; Heena, 'Communitarian Relations, Colonial Remodelling and the British in Pre-Mutiny Awadh', in S.Z.H. Jafri ed., *Delhi and Awadh during 1857 Studies, Images and Documents,* Gyan Publications, 2020, pp. 177-206.
17. S.Z.H. Jafri, 'The Profile of a Saintly Rebel: Maulavi Ahmadullah Shah', in Shireen Moosvi ed., *Facets of the Great Revolt 1857,* Tulika Books, Delhi, 2008, pp. 39-50; for an enlarged and revised version see, S.Z.H. Jafri, 'Indigenous Discourse of and Modern Historiography of 1857: The Case of Maulavi Ahmadullah Shah, in Sabyasachi ed., *Rethinking 1857,* Orient Blackswan, 2018, pp. 237-260.

Fateh Mohammad Taib in AD 1861 has been supplemented with the information in the well-known pamphlet *Risala Fath-i Islam* (a representative piece on *Wahabi* ideology whose authorship is now attributed to the group led by Maulavi Ahmadullah Shah). These need to be used with much greater refinement and understanding than has been done, for example by Rudrangshu Mukherjee and Gautam Bhadra. Similarly, Fazl-e Haq Khairabadi's *Al-Sauratul Hindiya,* being the recollections of the chain of events by one of the chief ideologues of the period, has to be used to understand part of the ideological underpinnings of 1857. It is interesting to point out that the Urdu and English translations of this Arabic text became available soon after the independence and partition but none of the scholars working on the field have made any use of this important contemporary evidence. His reading of the events is worth examining. An analysis of such writing along with the proclamations, letters, short notices, memoirs and recollection of the contemporaries will provide much useful information on the 'World of the Vanquished' than has been preserved in the 'Victors' narratives.

Chapter - 1

The Geographical Setting

(a) The Natural Environment

The Mughal province of Awadh extended over the territory entirely consisting of alluvial plains, lying between 79.6° and 84° longitude E, and 26° and 28.4° latitude N. The limits of the *suba* are described by Abul Fazl in his 'Account of Twelve Provinces'. It was bounded on the east by the province of Bihar, and to the north lay the Northern mountains; *sarkar* Manikpur of *suba* Allahabad was situated on the south of the province, while on the western side was *sarkar* of Kannauj of *suba* Agra. The distance from the limits of *sarkar* Gorakhpur to Kannauj was computed at 135 *kos*; while only 115 *kos* were said to separate the northern mountains and the southern boundary of the *suba*.[1]

To some extent, the boundaries of the *suba* took into account the physical features of the Upper Gangetic plains. Besides the Himalayan barrier to the north, the river Ganges separated it from the Mughal province of Agra and the river Sarju fixed the boundary line between *sarkar* Gorakhpur of Awadh and *sarkar* Jaunpur of *suba* Allahabad.

A number of rivers and their tributaries flowed through the province. Abul Fazl lists four principal rivers traversing the plains of the province. These were the Sarju, Ghaghra, Sai and Godi [Gomti].[2] But this list is a very short one. Buttler lists the Ganges, Deoha [Ghaghra], Gomti, Sai, Tons and Lon rivers as the main water channels of the southern districts of Awadh alone. The distinguishing features of each of these rivers are well

1. Abul Fazl, *Ain-i Akbari*, ed. Blockmann, Bibliotheca Indica, Calcutta, 1867-77, Vol. II, p. 78.

2. *Ibid.*

described by him.[3] The Ganges and Deoha had a low bed with an average width of four miles; and alterations occurred in the channels almost annually so much so that within a span of four or five years the rivers considerably shifted their courses. Compared to these rivers, the smaller rivers had almost fixed narrow channels and little change occurred in their courses. Few of these rivers had depth enough to avoid overflow even during the rainy season. The banks of these rivers were made up of high *kankar* (rabble) ridges making them navigable; but it was noticed that as a result of the diminishing of these ridges during the summer, the depth of the rivers was adversely affected. Buttler thought it a duty of the government of *nawab-wazirs* to clear out debris of such fallen ridges to keep the streams navigable.

In importance, the river Gomti, though much smaller, was next only to Ganges and Deoha. Its right bank was made up of solid *kankar* giving the appearance of a mountainous range, while the left bank was low and sandy to the maximum extent of three miles being an arid waste. Beyond this zone, the soil was quite fertile. The water was unfit for drinking because it was heavily loaded with yellowish clay. Fish abounded in all seasons. At some places, the Sai was as broad as the Gomti, but had only half of its depth. The Sai could accommodate boats of 300 mounds during rainy season, but because of its zig-zag course, it was avoided by navigators in favour of the Ganges and Gomti.

The Tons had its source in the Deoha, being essentially an arm of that river. It was shallow, and little navigation could be carried through it. The small river Lon flowed in the western portions of Awadh rising near Shahabad. It joined river Sai near Rae Bareli. During the summer it was of no consequence.

An important feature of the natural geography of Awadh in the 16th-18th centuries was the presence of large forest belts. It is possible to map the main forest tracts by drawing upon diverse sources.[4] We find that the Terai forest spread between the city of Gorakhpur and the Himalayan range as shown in James Rennell's *Bengal Atlas* (1780). Ghulam Hazarat, in his memoir of the Gorakhpur district (1810), tells us that the city of Gorakhpur was surrounded by forests. He says that the *tappas* (Small revenue circle) of *parganas* Anola, Bansi, Silhat, Basti, Maghar and Gorakhpur were desolate owing to the scarcity of peasants, the denseness

3. Donald Buttler, *Outlines of the Topography and Statistics of the Southern Districts of Oudh, and the Cantonment of Sultanpur*, Calcutta, 1839, pp. 10-14.

4. Among the Indian works, only the *Haft Iqlim* seems to refer to forest in Awadh. Cf. Irfan Habib, *An Atlas of the Mughal Empire*, OUP, Delhi, 1982, sheet no. 8A (notes).

of jungle and the inroads of the wild elephants. Owing to the depredations of these elephants, the peasants abstained from cultivation of the sugarcane.[5] Francis Buchanan, who surveyed the district in 1807-11, estimated that out of the total area in the district of 7,438 sq. miles, about 1450 sq. miles were covered with forest.[6] Besides these forests, a number of patches studded with bush and long grass were to be found here and there.[7]

Another category of the forests consisted of jungle situated either on the low land [*kachar*] or on the higher grounds. These were carefully preserved from clearing by the *zamindars* of the area. These offered him a safe place of "asylum from the tyranny and the rapacity of the *chakledar*."[8] The face of the country was level plain, but river Gomti had cut the soil at some places creating ravines to the depth of 50 ft. These ravines were made use of by the *zamindars* who planted trees to create jungles and so made hide-outs for themselves. In the midst of these forests every land-holder of consequence used to build mud-forts (*garhis*) "surrounded by a ditch and dense fence of living bamboos, through which common shot can not penetrate."[9] The *chakledars* were always helpless against such fortifications of the *zamindars*, as the jungles were too green to be set fire to and "being within the range of match-locks from the parapet, they cannot be cut down by the beseiging force."[10] Sleeman laments that such defences could easily be broken down but "Oude force had seldom either the means or the skill for such purpose".[11] Sleeman has listed twenty-four belts of forests in the kingdom of Oudh (1850) which were being used by the *zamindars* to challenge the authority of the government officials. They were spread in all parts of the kingdom, and it was computed that about 886½ sq. miles of area were covered by such forests.[12] Sleeman offers us the figures for the estimated area under forest in the districts of the Awadh kingdom in square miles.[13]

---

5. Mufti Ghulam Hazrat, *Kwaif-i-zila – Gorakhpur*, (1810 A.D.), MS Aligarh Subhan Ullah Collection, 954/12, ff. 12a-b.
6. Francis Buchanan, District Reports, (1807-11) edited and abridged by Mantgomery Martin, *The History, Antiquities, Topography, and Statistics of Eastern India*, 3 volumes, London, 1838: Indian reprint, 1976, 5 volumes. The survey of Gorakhpur is in Martin's abridgement (Volume II), p. 512.
7. *Ibid.*, p. 513.
8. Buttler, *op. cit.*, p. 5.
9. W.H. Sleeman, *A Journey through the Kingdom of Oudh during 1849-50*, 2 volumes, London, 1858, volume II, pp. 279-287.
10. *Ibid.*
11. *Ibid.*
12. *Ibid.*
13. *Ibid.*

Table - I

Sl.No.	*Chakla [District]*	*Forested area [in sq. miles]*
1.	Sultanpur	279 sq. miles
2.	Uldemau	102 sq. miles
3.	Daruabad	76 sq. miles
4.	Dewa-Jahangirabad	64 sq. miles
5.	Bangar	72 sq. miles
6.	Salon	72 sq. miles
7.	Bainswara	30 sq. miles
8.	Hydergarh	7 ½ sq. miles
9.	Khyrabad Muhammadi	150 sq. miles
10.	Baree and Muchreyta	30 sq. miles
	TOTAL	**888 ½ sq. miles**

The mud forts or the *garhis* situated in these belts were said to number about 633.[14]

In order to increase revenue, and perhaps, remove the *zamindars*' hide-outs the clearing of the forests for the purpose of cultivation was generally encouraged by the government. A number of incentives were given to the peasants for carrying the work of reclamation. Forest-land was lightly assessed by the revenue officials of the *Nawab vazirs* free for the first year of occupancy, charged at only two *anna* per *bigha*; the second year, four *anna*; the third year, six *anna*; the fourth year and fifth year, ten *anna*; beyond which, as an encouragement to the settlers, the rent is never raised.[15] In these lands the irrigation facilities were available abundantly as the water table was found just at the depth of 10 feet, and wells and tanks could be dug quite easily. Buttler describes the destruction of a *Chiul jangle* which was twenty miles in length and eight miles broad, situated between Niwurdipur and Manikpur.[16]

However, due to the unremitting destruction of the forest, adverse effects were produced on the general climate. Buttler thought that the annual average rainfall declined and the water-table went down, thus creating difficulties for irrigation. This situation could have certainly been controlled by a "systematic artificial planting to counteract the parching effects produced by the removal

14. Foreign Consultation Number 136/52 dated 31 August 1856, National Archives of India, New Delhi, Cf. A.A. Azmi, "Ta'alluqadars in the kingdom of Awadh, 1814-56". Paper presented at the session of *Indian History Congress*, (Allahabad Session, 1965), but only its summary was published in the Proceedings (page 323). For details, see the cyclostyled paper, p. 16.

15. Buttler, pp. 7-8.

16. *Ibid.*, p. 7.

of these natural protectors of the soil."[17] But reclamation continued unabated. The agricultural statistics of 1885-6 show no forest area in those districts where, as we have Sleeman estimates, forest areas of 888½ sq. miles. It may be assumed, then, that by 1885-6 such extensive tracts of forest comprising about half a million acres had come under cultivation.[18]

Wild animals found their way in these deep and long stretches of green-belts. The *Tarai* forest of *sarkar* Gorakhpur was famous for containing numerous elephants, a menace to cultivation.[19] Tigers, too, were found in great number between the city of Gorakhpur and the mountains, and before the cession of this territory to British their number was still larger. After 1801, due to forest clearing operations, a good many of them were hunted down by British civilians as well as the military officers. These animals lived so largely on cattle that in the year 1769, the year of the great famine, most of 'herbivorous animals' perished. Tigers, for example famished in large numbers.[20] They fell upon the town of Bhewapor in a large hoard and within no time, killed about 400 of its inhabitants. The town remained deserted for a long period.

Wolves and Jackals, too, were very common in these forests, posing a constant threat to the peasants as well as the domestic animals.[21] The wolf was quite a menace in the southern districts of Awadh when Buttler compiled his survey. He says that they carried away a number of children from the small *bazaar* attached to the Cantonment of Sultan. Superstition among the native population precluded their being killed; and their dens were observable along the sides of the 'ravines' throughout the country.[22]

Whether any change in climate occurred in the course of the two hundred and fifty years is a matter on which the information available is rather slight. In 1836, Buttler was convinced of a "great change in the climate"[23] by which he perhaps meant a decline in rainfall. Buttler has appended tables showing the diminishing pattern of the *rabi* as well as the *kharif* crops. At the time of his writing the report (1836 AD) even the 'produce in a good year' was much less than what it was 'before the great change in the climate'.[24]

---

17. Buttler, p. 48.
18. *Agricultural Statistics of British India*, 1885-6, Calcutta.
19. Ghulam Hazrat, *Kwaif-i Gorakhpur*, f. 9a.
20. Martin, *op. cit.*, Vol. II, p. 500.
21. *Ibid.*
22. Buttler, 56.
23. Buttler, *op. cit.*, p. 18.
24. *Ibid.*

Table[25] - II

(I) Kharif Crops, Sown in the Rainy Season					
Sl. No.	*Name of the Crop*	*Sers of Seeds per Bigha*	*Mans of Produce in A Good year*	*Mans of Produce in A Bad year*	*Former Produce in Mans*
1.	Kodo	4	10 to 12	4 or 5	16 or 17
2.	Makra	4	8 to 9	2 or 3	10 or 11
3.	Sanwa	3	8	2 or 3	10 or 12
4.	Asahan *kharif*	30	15	8 or 9	20
(II) Rabi Crops, Sown in the Cold Season					
1.	Chana	30	14 or 15	5 to 8	18 to 20
2.	Genhun	50	14 or 15	7 or 8	20 to 25
3.	Jau	40	20 to 22	10 to 13	20 to 25

The average annual rainfall in Awadh according to him followed very irregular pattern. At the same time it was, 'steadily decreasing on an average of 5 or 6 inches a years'.[26] Buttler attributed such a change to the destruction of the 'sylvan vesture' by the peasants in order to bring more land under the cultivation. It was predicted that the country was under the slow but definite process of becoming 'barren ravines' as there were no forests left 'to ward off' the 'fierce rays of the sun' and 'dew deposition', thus creating 'springs of running water'. The green belts of the region had detained water in meshes, but such land was now 'ploughed into barren ravines'. As a result, the province lost "its springs and perennial streamlets... the distance of water from the earth's increased – and its rainfalls, and the volume of its rivers diminished".[27]

The accompanying map drawn to show the isohytes clearly projects that the annual average rainfall of the province ranges from 54.7 inches to 25 inches.[28] It tends to be heavier as we move towards northwest, and lighter as we go westward. Buttler in 1836 estimated the average annual rainfall in southern Awadh at between "70 to 30 inches within a period of four months in duration; but is, on an average of five or six years, steadily decreasing".[29]

25. *Ibid.*, pp. 57-58. The tables contain information about a number of other crops, but entries are provided against the last column only for the crops listed in our table.

26. *Ibid.*, p. 16.

27. Buttler, p. 9.

28. Gilbert T. Walker, *Memoirs of the Indian Meteorological Department* (From Records up to 1920), Vol. XXIII, pt. VII, Calcutta, 1924.

29. Buttler, p. 16.

The soil of the province was composed of different varieties. On occasions, it contained siliceous and calcareous earth, the latter in the form of *kankar* which occurred in the limited horizontal layers at a depth of six to eight feet. The *kankar* ridges were generally found along the right banks of rivers.[30] At many places *kankar* constituted the surface of the soil as well. The sites of the 'primeval forests of Oudh' and the regions between Ganges and Deoha had the rich and dark soil. In the southern districts of Awadh, the soil of *pargana* Salon, Jayis, Rampur and Manikpur was judged as the best and very productive in different varieties of the grain.[31]

(b) Administrative Divisions

The Mughal province of Awadh came into being in the year 1580, when Akbar superseded the earlier divisions of the Lodi Sultans to make his own administrative arrangements.[32] This set up entailed the formation of provinces (*subas*) with sub-divisions, continuing under the older name of *sarkars*. Each *sarkar* contained a number of *parganas*. All the *sarkars* now included in *suba* Awadh are listed by Babur in his list of Lodi *sarkars*, but with Lucknow as Lakhnau-and-Balkar, and Gorakhpur as Saruar.[33]

The limits of the new territorial divisions were determined by a number of considerations, not all based on physical geography. C.A. Elliot, in his account of Onao district found that the *pargana* boundaries were traced in most irregular fashion, being determined by the proprietary rights of individual clans, formed the basis for fixing the limits of the *mahals* (administrative unit).[34]

The total number of the *parganas* included in the *suba*, as stated in *A'in* is 138, but those actually listed come to 133 *pargana* only.[35] Subsequent to the period when *A'in* was written, many changes occurred in the internal administrative units of the *sarkars*, many new *parganas* were constituted so as to raise the number of the total *mahals* in each *sarkar*. Sometime during the 17th century, *pargana* Kant in *sarkar* Budaun of *suba* Delhi being transferred to *sarkar* Khairabad. But except for this minor adjustment between the limits of *suba* Delhi and Awadh, the territorial limits of the Mughal province of Awadh seem to have remained intact.[36]

30. *Ibid.*, pp. 25-6.
31. *Ibid.*, p. 27.
32. Abul Fazl, *Akbarnamah*, Bibliotheca Indica, Calcutta, 1873-78, Vol. III, p. 412.
33. Babur, *Baburnamah*: English translation by A.S. Beveridges, London, 1921, Vol. II, p. 521.
34. Charles Alfered Elliott, *Chronicles of Oonao*, Allahabad, 1862, p. 149 and notes.
35. Abul Fazl, *A'in-i Akbari*, Vol. II, pp. 78-80.
36. See Add. 6586, f. 95a.

Within the *suba*, the *sarkars* were subject to change, though the changes were perhaps not many. One change was merely of nomenclature. *Sarkar* Gorakhpur was renamed Mu'azzamabad Gorakhpur after Prince Mu'azzam.[37] The *tappa* of *pargana* Pali was made a full-fledge *pargana* by the name Shahabad.

The number of *parganas* in each of the five *sarkars* went on changing. A list showing such changes is worth giving:

Table - III

The Changing Number of *Mahals* in Various *Sarkar* of Awadh Province

Sl. No.	*Sarkar Awadh*	*Sarkar*	*Sarkar Gorakhpur*	*Sarkar Bahraich*	*Sarkar Khairabad*	*Period Lucknow*	*Source*
1.	21	24	11	22	55	1595	*A'in-Akbari* Vol. II, p. 78,
2.	21	31	11	24	55	c, 1656	*Add. 6598*, ff. 118b-19a.
3.	21	35	12	25	56	c. 1720	*Add. 6586*, f. 96b.
4.	21	34	12	24	57	c. 1721	*Chahar Gulshan* (MS Abdus-Salam) ff. 80b-81a.

Awadh remained a relatively trouble-free province of the Empire throughout the 17th century. But things began to change during the second quarter of the 18th century, when Burhanul Mulk Sa'adat Khan was appointed the governor of the *suba* in 1722 A.D. With the general deterioration and slackening of central control, Burhanul Mulk (d. 1739) and later on his two immediate successors Abul Mansur Safdar Jang (1739-56) and Shuja'uddaulah (1756-75) were able to assert their independence from imperial control. However, this was a slow process. In 1739, Sa'adat Khan joined the imperial forces to face Nadir Shah. Safdarjang and Shuja'ud-daulah formally held the office of *wizarat*, and a number of other important posts under the Mughal emperors. The designation of *Nawab-wazir* was applied to them and their successors, at least till 1814, when Ghaziuddin Hyder designated himself King.

Attempts were made by the *nawab-wazirs* to get more and more area under their jurisdiction. By 1728, their area of influence was pushed further

37. *Tappa* Shahabad included in *pargana* Pali was assigned to Diler Khan Afghan in his *al-tamgha jagir* by Emperor Aurangzeb in 1662 (the text of the *farman* has been reproduced by Muzaffar Husain Khan, *Nama-i Muzaffari*, 2 vols. Mujtabai Press Kanpur, 1917 (Vol. I, pp. 174-9), but in 1686, we find in a *Sanad*, Shahabad has been styled a separate *pargana*. *Ibid.*, I, p. 266. See also Add. 6586, f. 95a.

east by the inclusion of fertile regions of Benaras, Ghazipur, Jaunpur and Chunargarh.[38] The western borders of Awadh kingdom were extended upto Kannauj by the use of armed power against the hereditary Rajput chiefs.[39] In 1735, Sa'adat Khan in addition to his duties, was invested with the *faujdari* jurisdiction of *sarkar* Kara Jahanabad to crush the activities of the rebel *zamindar* Bhagwant Singh, who was ultimately killed in a closely contested battle.[40]

Emperor Ahmad Shah conferred upon Safdarjang the office of the *wizarat*, and assigned him the province of Ajmer in 1748, but the *wazir* exchanged his new assignment with *suba* Allahabad, which was contiguous to the province of Awadh; and he now established a hereditary claim over it.[41] The next important addition to the territorial limits of Awadh was made in 1774, when Shuja'uddaulah with the help of East India Company annexed Rohilkhand, much of which formally belonged to *suba* Delhi. In addition, he also controlled Etawah.

From the point of view of the extent, maximum limits were attained by the kingdom under Shuja'uddaulah. It comprised the Mughal province of Awadh, and much of the province of Allahabad (barring, of course, the Bundelkhand region), Rohilkhand and mid-Gangetic Doab including Etawah.[42] This compact region, bordered the Himalayan *Tarai* in the north, the upper course of river Gandak in the north-east, the river Son to the south, and the Yamuna in the south-west. In 1764-65, Shuja'uddaulah joined the armies of Shah Alam II and Mir Qasim in an unsuccessful attempt to invade Bihar and Bengal. After the defeat at Buxar and then at Jajmau, Shuja'uddaulah was compelled to seek terms. Although he was permitted to continue as a ruler of the Mughal *subas* of Awadh and Allahabad, certain areas (notably Allahabad) were transferred to Shah Alam II. The appointment of the British Resident in 1773 and the deployment of various contingents of British forces in the Ruhaela war, whereby Shuja'uddaulah was able to annex Rohilkhand, made the kingdom of Oudh one of the first subsidiary-alliance states in India well before Lord Wellesley.

After the death of Shuja'uddaulah, the situation underwent important changes. A new treaty was concluded with his successor Asafuddaulah

---

38. Essentially these area lay in the *jagir* of one Murtaza Khan, who had leased them out to *nawab* for a payment of Rs 7 lakhs per annum. A.L. Srivastava, *The First Two Nawabs of Oudh*, Lucknow, 1933, pp. 44-5.
39. *Ibid.*, p. 46.
40. *Ibid.*, pp. 49-51.
41. *Ibid.*, pp. 128, 260.
42. A.L. Srivastava, *Shuja'uddaulah*, Vol. II, Lahore, 1945, pp. 312-3.

in 1775. Now the amount of subsidy imposed on Awadh was increased, the *zamindar* of Ghazipur was asked to pay the tribute to the Company instead of *nawab*, and the entire region of Benaras was ceded to the Company. Later, in default of payment of the subsidies, the fort of Allahabad (which had been earlier retransferred from Shah Alam to Shuja'uddaulah) was annexed by the British.

Asafuddaulah died in 1797, and this provided an opportunity to the Company to conclude a new treaty with his successors, first with Wazir'Ali (Sep. 1797 - Jan. 1798) and then with Sa'adat Ali Khan (1798-1814). The treaty concluded in 1801, marks the watershed in the history of relations of the Company with Awadh. Under this treaty the broken crescent formed by Rohilkhand, Farrukhabad, Kara, Kora, Etawah, Fatehgarh, Kalpi, Gorakhpur and Azamgarh, yielding an annual revenue of Rupees 1,35,00,000 was ceded by Awadh to the East India Company.

The limits of Awadh from 1801 AD onwards down to its annexation (1856) remained more or less fixed. The principality was bounded on the north and north-east by Nepal; on the East by the British district of Gorakhpur; on the south-east by British district Allahabad; on the south-west by the Doab including the British districts of Fatehpur, Kanpur, and Farrukhabad and on the north-west by Shahjahanpur. These new limits extended from latitude 29°6 to 25°34, and from longitude 79°45 to 83°. The total area was computed at 23,923 square miles.[43]

With the treaty of 1801, Nawab Sa'adat Ali Khan once more felt that he was the ruler of what territories were left under his control. He started with vigour and enthusiasm to streamline the administration and to introduce the new revenue system. The arrangements entailed a reorganisation of the older administrative divisions by dividing Awadh into *nizamats* and *chaklas*.[44] Of the five Mughal *sarkars*, Gorakhpur had been ceded to the Company. *Sarkar* Bahraich was now too small a unit to continue as a separate division, hence Gonda was added to create the Gonda-Bahraich *nizamat*. The limits of the old *sarkar* Awadh, broadly corresponded to the boundaries of the Sultanpur-Fyzabad *nizamat*, and *sarkar* Khairabad was

43. Buttler, *op. cit.*, p. 1; Masihuddin Ahmad, *Oude:Its Princes and its Government Vindicated*, London, 1857; reprinted as *British Aggression in Awadh* by Safi Ahmad, Meerut, 1969, p. 22; Walter Hamilton, *East India Gazetteer of Hindostan and adjacent countries*, London, 1828, Vol. I, pp. 348-9.

44. Buttler, *op. cit.*, pp. 97-9; C.A. Elliott says that in Oude four large districts, Bahraich, Khairabad, Sultanpur and Bainswara were called *nizamat*, while the smaller ones like Dareeabad, Sandi, Sandila, Meanganj and Rosulabad were called *chakla*, *op. cit.*, p. 131(n).

divided into Khairabad *nizamat* and *chakla* Shah Rah comprising of *parganas* Sandeelah, Sandee, Palee, Shahabad and Bangarmau. Later on the *chakla* of Shah Rah was placed under the jurisdiction of two *chakledars*, having their headquarters at Sandee and Sandeelah. *Sarkar* Lucknow was completely broken up; the Bainswara division was made a separate *nizamat* consisting of a number of *chaklas* namely, Hydergurh, Rae Bareili, Purwa, Meangunj and Rasoolabad.[45]

The *chaklas* were put under the over all charge of the *chakledars* or *nazims*, while the smaller units were looked after by the *faujdar* and the *diwan*, receiving Rs 25 and Rs 15 each respectively as their salaries.[46] While the *chakledars* had no fixed salary, "the difference between the sum, which he has for the year engaged to pay into the public treasury, and the amount, which, with the military power of the state at his command, he can levy from the *zamindars* constituted his official income.[47]

However, sometimes during the last days of Awadh regime, the above arrangements, too, were changed, and while retaining few previous divisions, new units were created for the purpose of revenue administration. The names of the new administrative divisions have not been provided by our authorities.[48]

No further details about the number of the *parganas* included in the new unit are available. It cannot be said as to when the administrative unit described by Buttler were superseded in favour of the new arrangements.

Buttler, writing in 1836, gives the following list of *chaklas* in Awadh.[49]

1. Sultanpur was made up of 6 *parganas*
2. Aldemau had 5 *parganas*
3. Partapgarh had only 3 *parganas*
4. Pachhimrath also had 3 *parganas* only
5. Bainswara contained the largest number, i.e. 13 *parganas*

45. C.A. Elliott, *op. cit.*, pp. 131-32.
46. Buttler, *op. cit.*, p. 99.
47. *Ibid.*
48. *Ibid.*, pp. 97-8.
49. "The fiscal divisions [in Awadh] are arbitrary. Mr Madlock in 1831 showed 24, Dr Buttler in 1837 twelve; we have before us a list of 25 large and small districts, obtaining during the present year". 'The Kingdom of Oudh' *Calcutta Review*, 1845 (part III), pp. 386-7.

6. Salon had 4 *parganas*
7. Ahladgunj too had 4 *parganas*
8. Gonda-Bahraich was divided into 5 *parganas*
9. Khairabad again contained the largest number, i.e. 13 *parganas*
10. Sandee had 4 *parganas*
11. Rasulabad was divided in 5 *parganas*
12. Lucknow was made up of 5 *parganas*.

Maps

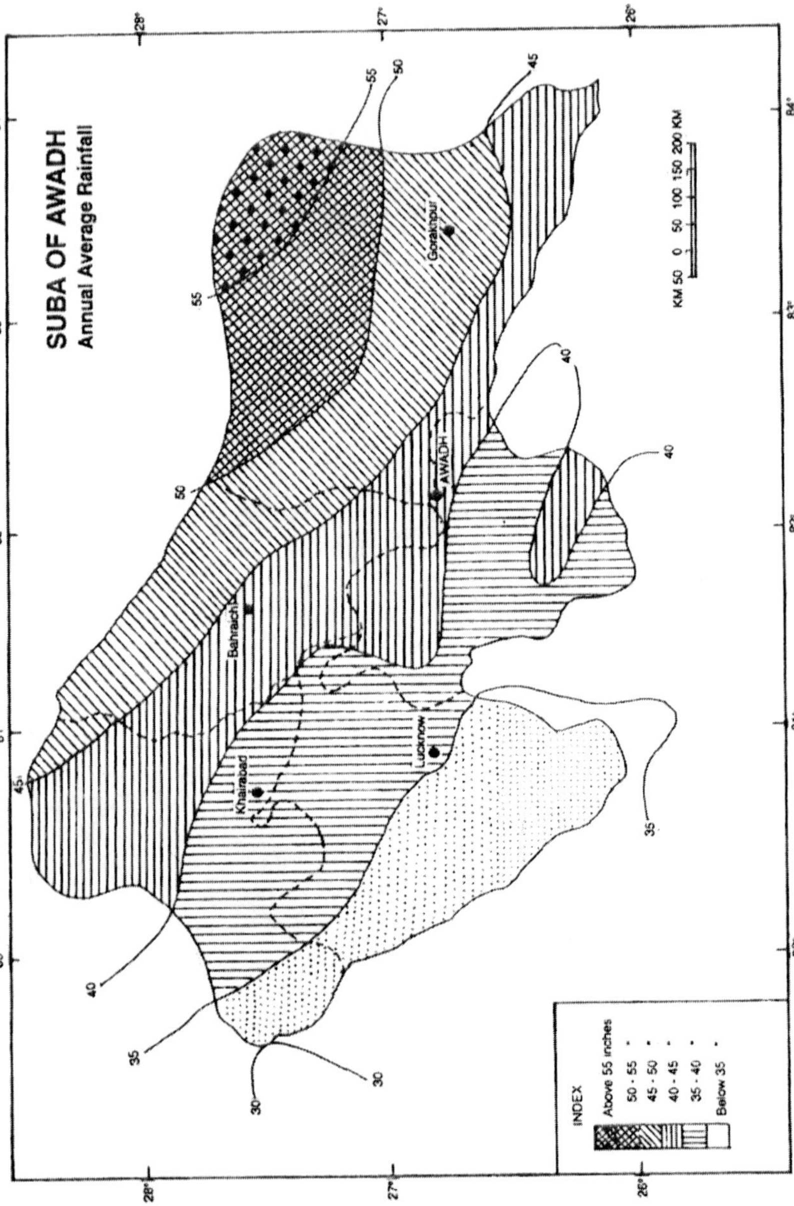
SUBA OF AWADH
Annual Average Rainfall
Gorakhpur
AWADH
Bahraich
Khairabad
Lucknow
KM 50 0 50 100 150 200 KM
INDEX
Above 55 inches
50 - 55
45 - 50
40 - 45
35 - 40
Below 35

AWADH - c. 1595

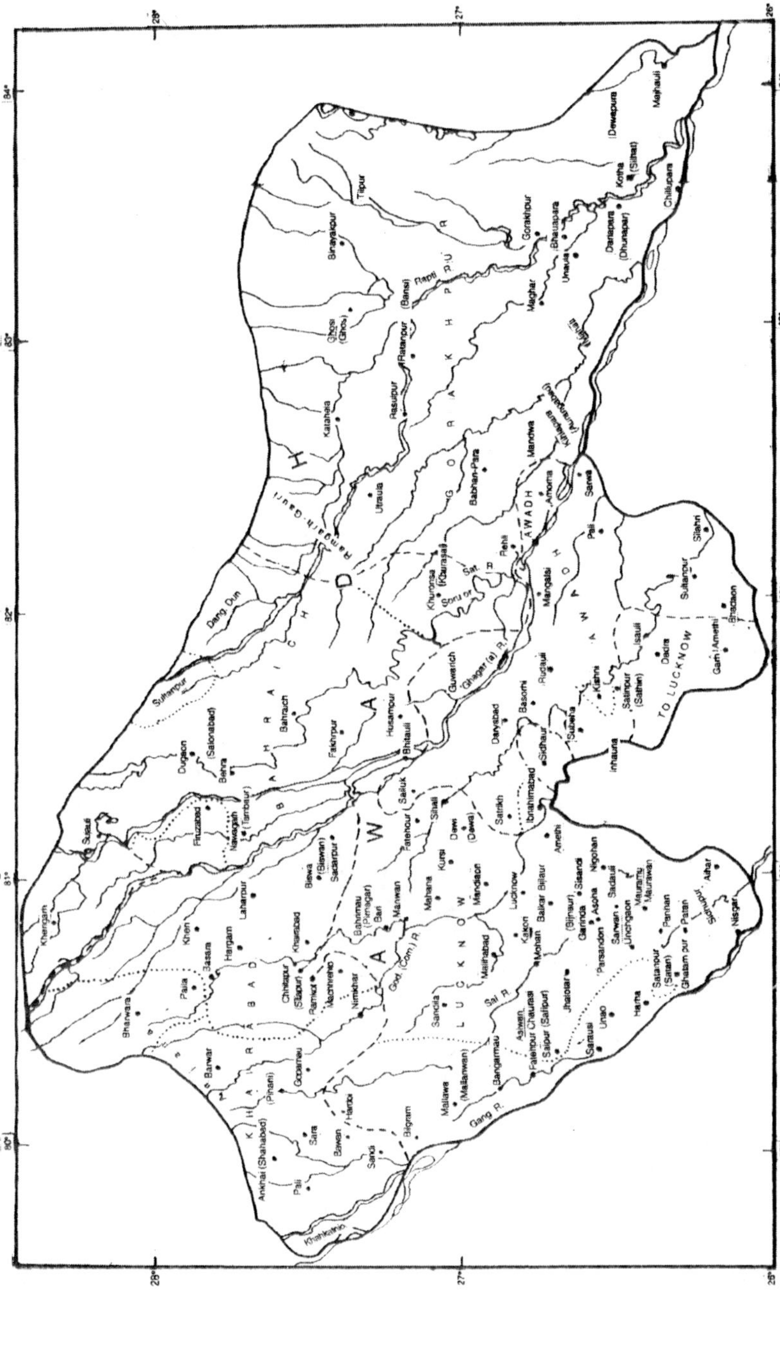

Suba *and* Sarkar *boundaries are based on Irfan Habib* An Attas of the Mughal Empire, *OUP, 1982, see sheet no 8A*

Awadh During the Various Phases of its Expansion C. AD 1720-1774

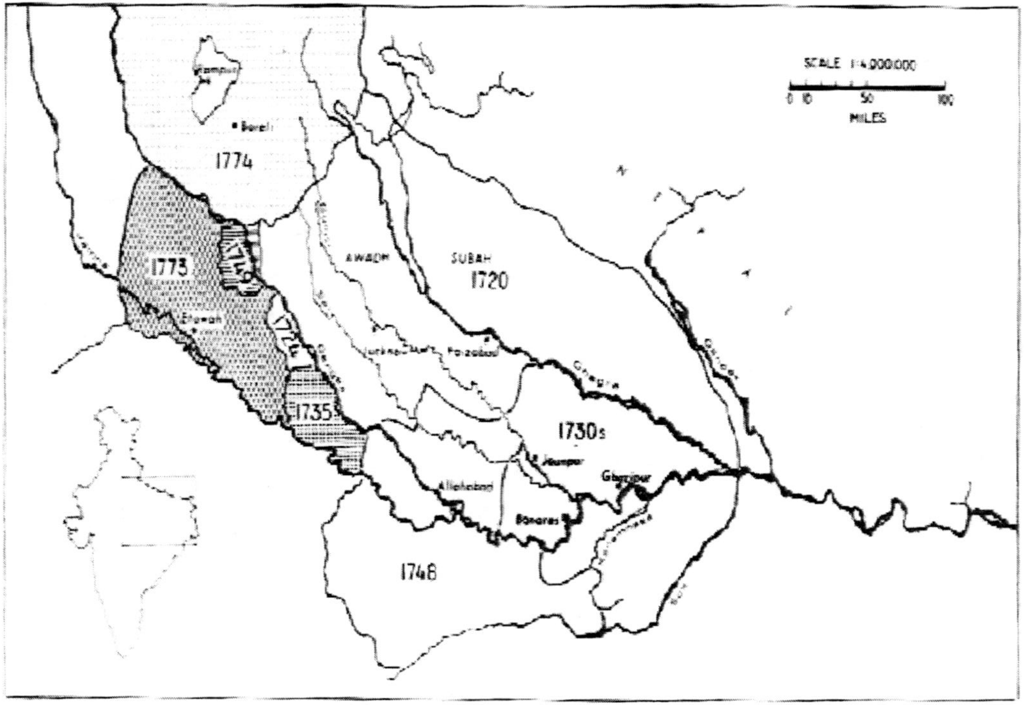

(*Based on Richard B. Barnett's* **North India Between Empires: Awadh, the Mughals and the British, 1720-1801**, ***Barkeley, 1980, p. 24)***

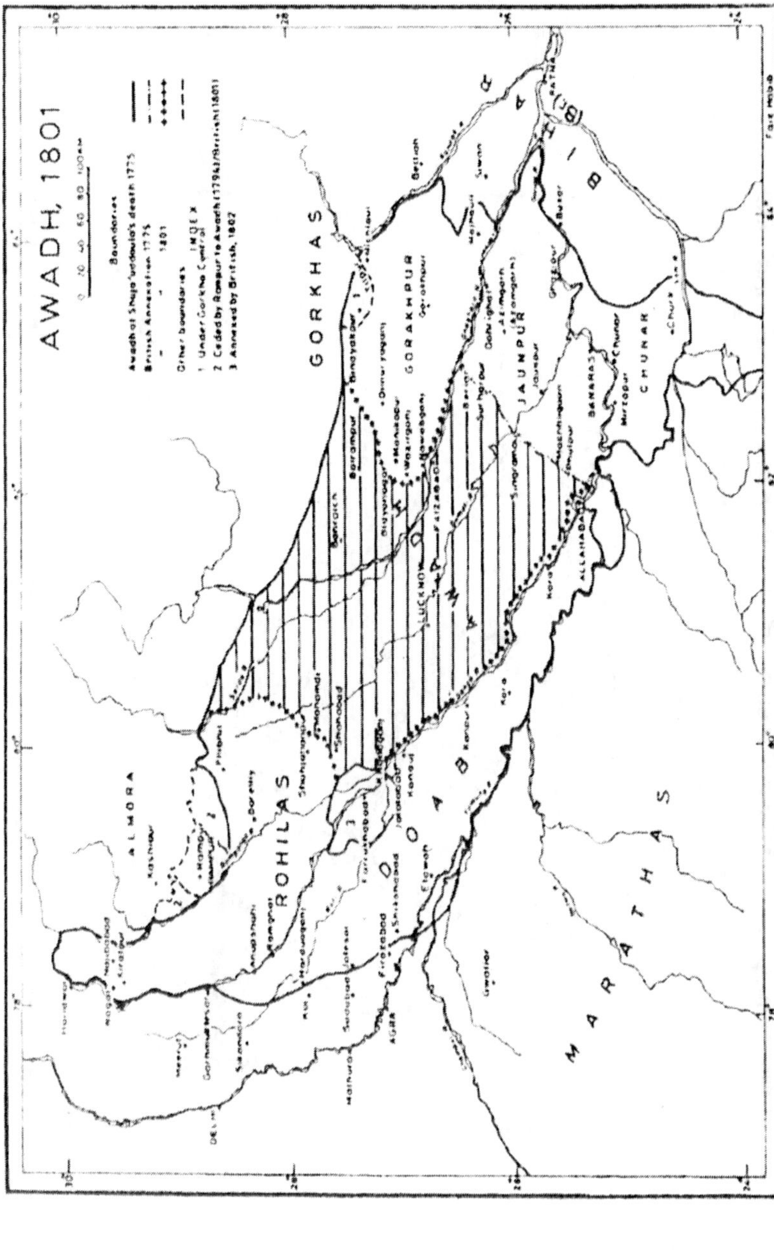

(From Irfan Habib and Faiz Habib, 'Mapping the Dismemberment of Awadh, 1775-1801', *PIHC*, (75th Session, JNU, New Delhi 2014), p. 457)

A Sketch map showing the major administrative divisions of Awadh circa 1850

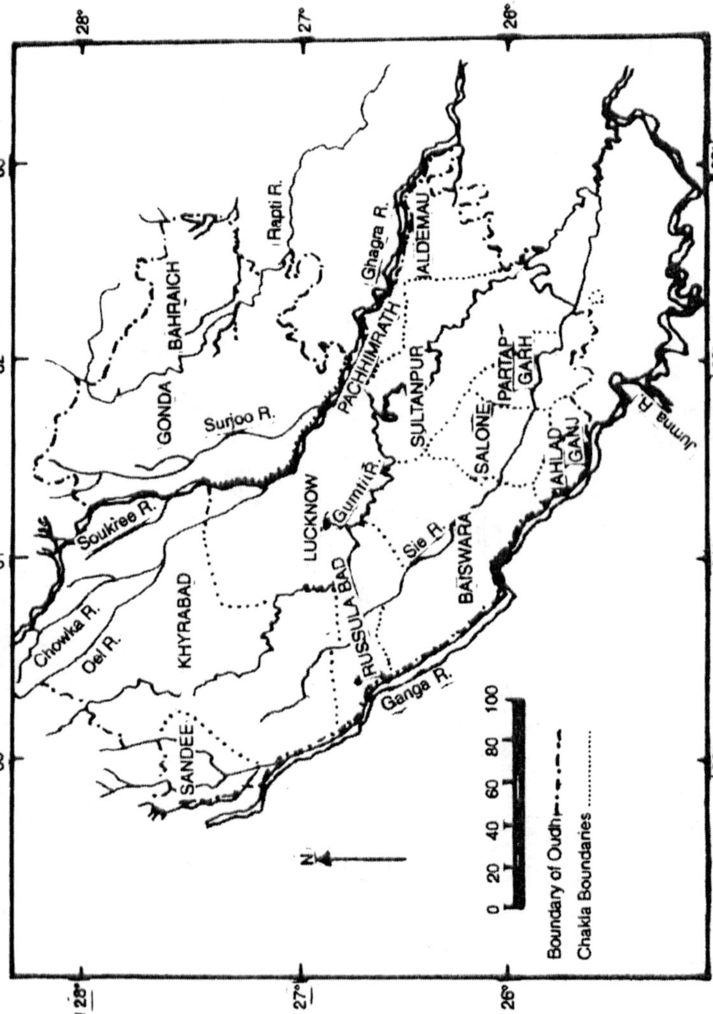

Chakla Boundaries are based on P.D. Reeves' map of Awadh, Ibid. P. 303

Chapter - 2

Extent of Cultivation and Population

(a) Cultivation

The study of the agrarian conditions in Awadh should appropriately begin with an attempt to determine the extent of cultivation in c. 1595 and the subsequent extensions in the area available for the plough down to the extinction of the Awadh kingdom in 1856. These, in the absence of censuses during the period, are also the only indicators we have of population movements. The statistical accounts of Mughal empire contain valuable information about the total *arazi* and the *jama'* of each *sarkar*. An analysis and a comparison of these statistics with data from British-period agricultural statistics may lead to some provisional conclusions.

The interpretation of the figures given under the designation *arazi* in the *A'in* has been a matter of controversy among economic historians. Moreland thought that it represented the cultivated area and equated it with the gross-cropped area of modern statistics. He assumed that such area was fully measured by Akbar's time. This assumption led him to argue in favour of an enormous extension in cultivation in Eastern U.P. between c. 1600 and c. 1900.[1] On the other hand, Irfan Habib thought that, the *arazi* included not only the gross-cropped area, but also current fallows, cultivable waste and some portions of uncultivable waste. This would have the effect of reducing the cultivated extent further, but he also contended that the measurement was complete only in some portions of Akbar's empire, while a very large area remained unsurveyed, notably in the *subah* of Awadh and

1. W.H. Moreland, 'Agricultural Statistics of Akbar's Empire', *JUPHS*, 1919, Vol. II, part I, p. 16.

Allahabad.[2] These conclusions have been collaborated by Shireen Moosvi on the basis of other evidences brought together from different regions of the Mughal Empire.[3]

The *sarkar* boundaries and the pargana headquarters of the province of Awadh have been located by Irfan Habib in *An Atlas of the Mughal Empire*. The total area of each *sarkar* as measured of his maps, and the figures converted into *bigha-i Ilahi* may be compared with the *arazi* of the respective *sarkars* in the *A'in*.

Table - I

Sl. No.		*Measured Area in Bigha-i Ilahi (A)*	*Map Area in Bigha-i Ilahi (B)*	*(A) as % of (B)*
1.	*Sarkar* Awadh	27,95,946	32,38,466	86.33
2.	*Sarkar* Lucknow	33,04,905	61,01,995	54.16
3.	*Sarkar* Bahraich	18,23,435	44,49,800	40.97
4.	*Sarkar* Khairabad	19,80,714	52,98,558	37.38
5.	*Sarkar* Gorakhpur	2,44,681	90,97,370	2.68
	Total	**1,01,49,681**	**2,81,86,198**	**36.00**

The exceptionally low *arazi* figure for *sarkar* Gorakhpur was mainly due to its bordering upon the Himalayas and the large tracts of *Terai* forests and other forest belts spread all over that *sarkar*. Even during the early years of the 19th century, Francis Buchanan informs us that an area of 1450 sq. miles (= 15,45,570 *bigha-i Ilahi*) out of a total 7,483 sq. miles (= 79,81,367 *bigha-i Ilahi*) or 19.36 percent of the whole was covered with dense forests.[4] Similarly, Ghulam Hazrat pointed out in c. 1810 that the city of Gorakhpur itself was surrounded by "forests on two sides and rivers on two sides".[5] If we exclude the map area and *arazi* figures of *sarkar* Gorakhpur, the *arazi* of the rest of the *suba* of Awadh would rise to as high as 51.88 percent of the map-area.

The *arazi* statistics of *sarkar* Gorakhpur in the *A'in* stand alone; subsequent area records of the Mughal period omit them altogether. However, some idea of the extent of cultivation can be formed by reference to the ratio of *jama'* to the map-area. Since the *jama'* represented the estimated income from the area available for cultivation, it should be

2. Irfan Habib, *Agrarian System*, p. 4; *CEHI*, Vol. I, pp. 163-5.
3. Shireen Moosvi, 'The Magnitude of the Land Revenue Demand' *Medieval India – A Miscellany*, Vol. IV, p. 97.
4. Montgomery Martin, *op. cit.*, Vol. II, p.
5. Ghulam Hazrat, *op. cit.*, p. 1a=b.

assumed that with an increase in *jama'*, the area available for cultivation should have increased proportionately. Fortunately, we possess *pargana*-wise *jama'* figures of the Mughal empire in Ethe – 433, 16 *parganas* out of 24 *parganas* of *sarkar* Gorakhpur in the *A'in* are recorded in this manuscript.[6] Still with these limitations, we can proceed to study the increase in *jama'* of these *parganas* within a period of five decades or so. The table below sets out the *pargana*-wise *jama'* in *sarkar* Gorakhpur in this MS, with *A'in*'s figures as base = 100.

Table - II

1.	Stated total for *sarkar* M'azzamabad Gorakhpur	361.52
2.	*Pargana* Utraula	203.58
3.	*Pargana* Unhaula	461.66
4.	*Pargana* Banbhanpura	275.23
5.	*Pargana* Bhaupara	320.71
6.	*Pargana* Tilpur	100.00
7.	*Pargana* Chilaupora	264.56
8.	Rehli	177.50
9.	Rasulpur Ghosi [2 m]	477.32
10.	Gorakhpur ba Haveli or M'azzamabad [2 m]	758.36
11.	Mahauli	205.01
12.	Ramgarh Gori	670.86
13.	Mandwa	340.73
14.	Maghar Ratanpur [2 m]	203.31

Similarly, from the *jama'* figures stated in Br. Mus. Add. 6586 [c. 1707] and *Chahar Gulshan* (c. 1720), it transpires that a constant increase in the total *jama'* of *sarkar* Gorakhpur took place. It can then be assumed quite safely that the area under cultivation should have increased considerably to justify this abnormal increase of *jama'*.

The Table III shows the *jama'* of Awadh taken down into *sarkars*, as given in the Ethe-433, and subsequent documents, indexed to the *A'in*'s figures as = 100.[7] In the last two columns the *sarkar*-wise *arazi* figures in

6. *Ethe* Collection – *433*, ff. 108a-120a [for the *suba* Awadh] Bibliotheca nationale, Paris; M'azzamabad Gorakhpur. See ff. 117b-119a. This hitherto unnoticed work contains valuable information on the total *jama'* of the Mughal empire for the close of Shahjahan's reign, along with the *jama'* and *hasil* figures of Muhammad Shah's reign. The fact, that it provides *pargana*-wise *jama'* (mal and *sa'ir* separately) makes it quite unique (the other known work containing such detailed information in Br. Mus. Add. 6586, (British Museum) but that pertains to c. 1707). Dr Shireen Moosvi has kindly let me use her notes of the manuscript.

7. Summary statistics come down to us from the later part of Aurangzeb's reign. In these returns, the *zamin-i paimuda* (measured land) is recorded for all the *sarkars*

(*Contd...*)

the *Chahar Gulshan* (c. 1720) are compared with the *A'in*'s, and then calculated as percentages of map-area.

Table - III

Suba/sarkar	*Jama' in Ethe-433 c. 1656*	*Jama' in Add. 6586 c. 1707*	*Jama' in Chahar Gulshan*	*Arazi in Chahar Gulshan of Map-Area in Chahar*	*Arazi as Percentage Gulshan*
Suba *Awadh*	*180.72*	*197.89*	*161.21*	*124.80*	*66.45*
Sarkar Awadh	143.40	147.33	122.30	104.37	90.24
Sarkar Bahraich	177.20	161.60	104.45	100.48	41.22
Sarkar Gorakhpur	361.25	368.25	467.03	-	-
Sarkar Lucknow	167.47	197.08	138.59	109.65	59.44
Sarkar Khairabad	204.01	224.90	187.34	219.52	82.36

The fact that the measured area increased substantially during the 17th century is confirmed by the fact that the total number of the villages recorded in Buldian MS Fraser-86 for the *suba* Awadh is 52,691 while 33,842 villages or 64.22 percent of the total number of villages were said to be fully measured.

It would seem that it was largely the heavy rainfall that by defining the forest zone, set limits to the cultivated area. *Sarkar* Khairabad had a small *arazi* during the 16th century, being 37.38 percent of the map-area. But forest clearing must have taken place on extensive scale subsequently, as the *arazi* reached 82.36 percent of the map-area by the beginning of Muhammad Shah's reign (1720).

The agricultural statistics of British India which began to be issued in 1884-5 offers us valuable data for comparing the extent of cultivation during the 19th century with that of Akbar's time. For our purposes the figures for 1885-6 are more appropriate as in the figures the current fallows are separately given and not included in cultivable waste as in the 1884-5 figures. *Sarkar*-wise comparison is of course not possible, as the modern figures are for British districts. For this reason, the statistical returns of all those districts situated within the limits of Mughal *suba* Awadh either wholly or in part have been pooled together. The area units (areas) of the modern returns have been then converted into *bigha-i Ilahi*.

---

of suba (except for Gorakhpur) in *bigha-i daftari which was 3/5th of* bigha-i Ilahi *(cf. Irfan Habib*, op. cit., *pp. 2-3). The above comparison has been made by converting the original figures into bigha-i Ilahi* for keeping uniformity of the units. See Fraser 86, ff...

Table - IV
Map Area and Cultivated Area in 1885-6

Sl. No.	*Districts*	*Map-Area in Bigha-i Ilahi*	*Cultivated Area in bigha-i Ilahi*	*Cultivated as % of Map-Area*
1.	Lucknow	10,42,133	6,09,135	58.45
2.	Unnao	18,57,733	10,88,318	58.77
3.	Barabanki	18,43,200	12,41,416	67.35
4.	Sitapur	23,53,066	16,66,668	70.82
5.	Hardoi	24,38,400	16,35,153	67.70
6.	Kheri	31,49,386	15,17,840	48.14
7.	Fyzabad	17,58,933	11,46,583	65.18
8.	Gonda	28,21,333	15,92,455	56.44
9.	Bahraich	30,12,266	20,40,091	67,72
10.	Rae-Bareili	18,68,800	10,13,588	54.32
11.	Sultanpur	18,14,400	10,26,456	56.57
12.	Partapgarh	15,55,200	8,43,536	54.23
13.	Gorakhpur	49,04,640	32,74,068	66.75
14.	Basti	29,36,320	19,84,300	67.57
15.	Ballia	12,11,733	5,08,178	41.93
16.	Pilibhit	14,64,533	7,63,848	52.15
17.	Farrukhabad	18,33,600	11,67,668	63.68
	Total	**3,78,70,826**	**2,31,19,322**	**61.04**

Compare

A'in (1598)	2,81,86,189	1,01,63,360	36.00
Chahar Gulshan (1707)		1,26,84,872	66.45

The Table shows that the extent of cultivation had dramatically increased in areas of the old *sarkar* of Gorakhpur (districts Gorakhpur, Gonda and Basti). In the district of Mughal *sarkar* Khairabad (notably the districts of Sitapur and Hardoi) too, there was notable extension in cultivation, though Kheri still remained backward in cultivation.

It appears safe to assume that the total span of area under cultivation during the 16th century was appreciably high. It ought to have been about 50 percent of what it was during the 19th century.

It is probable that the extent of cultivation should have been more than 10 percent less in 1856, the year of annexation, than it was in 1885-86. Part of this must have been under forest. The presence of forest, alongside rivers and deep ravines and an open plains of South Awadh are described in details by Buttler in 1836 and by Sleeman in 1849-50, as we have seen in Section I. Since the Agricultural Statistics of 1885-86 do not show any area under forests in these districts, it may be assumed that these were cleared in the thirty or thirty-five years after 1850; and we may then safely allow a margin of 10 percent growth in cultivation during this period.

(b) Population and its Composition

The next question is to determine the average size of the holdings of the peasants during Akbar's time. Moreland thought that the cultivated area per capita to have been the same then as three centuries later. On this assumption he went on to estimate the population of Akbar's empire from 'Multan to Monghyr'.[8] On the contrary, Irfan Habib argued that, given the same technology and the smaller area under cultivation, the Land Man ratio should have been higher earlier. Thus, he assumed that if the extent of cultivation in 1600 was 60 percent of what it was in 1900, one would rather expect the population in 1600 to have been much less than 60 percent of what it was in 1901. It should have been, he suggested, only about half.[9]

For determining the population of Awadh by the method suggested by Irfan Habib some tentative assumptions must be employed. We have just seen that as compared to the map-area, the total *arazi* in Awadh amounted to 36 percent in the end of the 16th century. The cultivated area in 1885-6 was 61 percent of the total map-area. If *arazi* is equated with cultivated area, as by Moreland, it would mean that the extent of cultivation in c. 1600 was about 59% of what it was in 1895-6. But one has to make allowance for certain areas of cultivation escaping measurement under Akbar on one hand, and the inclusion of cultivable waste within *arazi* on the other.[10] Making a rough allowance for this we may say that cultivation in c. 1600 was about half of what it was in 1885-6. The population of districts within the Mughal *suba* of Awadh disclosed by 1881 census was 17.95 millions. If cultivation per capita had not altered markedly after 1600, the population in c. 1600 should have been about 9 millions. If the cultivated land per capita had grown smaller during the three centuries, the population should have been smaller than 9 millions in 1600.

Another method of estimating population of Mughal Empire during 1600 has been suggested by Ashok V. Desai on the basis of the *Ain*'s information. He compares the *Ain*'s data on prices, wages and crop rates with the data relating to 1961. Then he proceeds to establish per capita consumption and per capita agricultural productivity. Finally, he takes

8. W.H. Moreland, *India at the Death of Akbar*, London, 1920, pp. 19-20.
9. Irfan Habib, (ed.), *CEHI*, Vol. I, Cambridge, 1982, p. 165.
10. Irfan Habib, *op. cit.*, pp. 5-6; pp. 11-13.

the *Ain*'s revenue rates on different crops to work out per capita land-revenue. With these figures in hand, he divides the total *jama*' of the Akbar's empire and gets the estimated population in c. 1600.[11] But unfortunately, Desai's method can not be used for determining the population of Mughal Awadh since the prices, wages and yields are not specifically stated for the province. It cannot, therefore, be used to work out the population of Awadh independently, as one can do with Moreland's single method.

The modern population counts of the districts, previously included in the Mughal *suba* Awadh and also the population estimates of the adjacent districts may help us to form some idea of the growth of population during the subsequent period of 250 years.

Unluckily, the comparison can be confused by the numerous territorial adjustments as the result of various treaties between the East India Company and the *nawab-wazirs*. Large portions of *sarkar* Gorakhpur were ceded to the Company as early as in 1801. Portions of *sarkar* Manikpur, *suba* Allahabad came under the administrative control of *nawab*'s government from the days of Safdar Jung (1739-1754). For these reasons, both these regions, notably the districts of Gorakhpur and Basti (in the Mughal *sarkar* Gorakhpur), Partapgarh and Rae Bareli districts (Mughal *sarkar* Manikpur) have been taken by us as belonging to Awadh for purposes of population comparisons.

The pre-census population counts of Awadh were gross under-estimates.[12] Previous to the first all India census in 1872, there were some

---

11. Ashok V. Desai, 'Population and Standards of Living in Akbar's Time' *IESHR*, Vol. IX, part I, 1972, pp. 34-62; Desai's detailed calculations have been criticized by Shireen Moosvi. The criticism relates to the high productivity rates per *bigha* that Desai accepts and to the absence of distinction between *zabti* area and other areas where the revenue rates did not apply at all. As a result she offers a different and much higher estimate of the population of Akbar's empire. See Production, Consumption and Population in Akbar's Time', *IESHR*, Vol. X, part II, 1973, pp. 181-195.

12. The under estimates of the population were made alike by the British officials and the native scholars. Sleeman thought it to be around five millions in 1850. (*A Journey through the kingdom of Oude*, London, 1858, Vol. II, p. 200). The plenipotentiary of the deposed king of Awadh, to the British Crown, Molvi Masihuddin Ahmad gave a similar estimate of the population of the kingdom (*Oude its princes and government vindicated*, p. 22). Indeed surprise was expressed by the British officials at the very large figures revealed by the census of 1869. The confession was made: "we (had) always under estimated it, and nobody imagined that the population was so dense till there was a regular census taken." *Parliamentary Papers, 1871, Colonies : East India*, 19, IUP, p. 98.

fairly reliable census in the North-Western provinces in 1853 and 1865.[13] However, the first census in Awadh was conducted only in 1869. This was conducted carefully and it was accepted as part of the official all-India census of 1872 without any revision.[14]

On the basis of the 1869 census figures, the total population of Awadh can be determined for the year 1856, by sealing it down in the same proportion in which the population had increased in the ceded and conquered districts of the north-west provinces during this period. The total population of the ten selected districts of U.P. encircling and/or touching upon the limits of the *nawab-wazirs* territory in the year 1853 was 1,00,27,145 and 1,10,16,947 by the census of 1872.[15] The compound rate of growth was thus about 0.38 percent per annum. Applying this rate to the growth of population of Awadh in the same period we can work-out the population of Awadh for 1856. The census of 1872 discloses the population of areas within the limits of Mughal Awadh as 1,68,34,564, scaling it down to allow for a rate of growth of 0.38 percent, get a population of 1,56,19,115 for the same territory. Thus, we see that within a period of about 256 years, the population of Mughal Awadh increased from about 9 millions in c. 1600 to 15.6 millions in 1856. The annual rate of growth was, thus, about 0.28 percent. This was rather small in comparison to the per annum rate of growth registered in the adjacent British territories during 1853-72, but is not in itself a disreputable rate.

With the meagre data and a number of other limitations, it would be naïve on our part to attempt an estimation of the relative size of the urban population in Mughal times. But the extent of urbanisation in the pre-annexation Awadh or the 19th century may still be studied. Scholars are sharply divided over this issue. Kessinger assumed that at the time of the annexation, the number of towns in Awadh, apart from Lucknow, were small and it was only with the coming of British control that we see, an expansion of economic activity which led to the rapid growth of the towns.[16] On the other hand, it has been argued that the number of the towns and

---

13. Irfan Habib, "Indian Population, 1800-1872 – A note" cyclostyled proceedings of the Seminar, *The Transformation of the Medieval Economy into Colonial Economy*, Aligarh, 1972, p. 5.

14. *Ibid.*

15. *Census of India*, Vol. XV, 1911. The growth of the population has been determined from the districts of Gorakhpur, Basti, Kanpur, Shahjahanpur, Pilibhit, Bijnore, Aligarh, Bulandshahr, Meerut and Saharanpur.

16. *CEHI*, II, pp. 265-6.

their population in Awadh, sharply declined, "after the territory became subject to the full benefits of British rule".[17]

Donald Buttler's survey of the 'Southern Districts of Oudh' is comprehensive enough to provide us with the details of all the towns, their total population and its religious composition. The total number of the towns having a population of 4000 and above was no less than fifty one only in the southern parts of the kingdom.[18] While the total number of the inhabitants in these towns was counted at between 4,65,000 to 4,75,000, Fyzabad contained as many as 100,000 people, while Ranjitpurwa (in Unao district) contained 50,000 to 60,000 persons.[19] Population estimates of Lucknow are not provided by Buttler, but in 1799, it was said to contain half a million persons.[20] Sleeman, estimated that the population of Lucknow in 1849-50 was around one million[21] while in 1858 it was again estimated to have been at a million's mark. The town was judged to have been larger than Calcutta.[22]

With the British occupation of Awadh, the picture underwent change. The number of towns as well as their population declined considerably as is evident from the successive census. The trend was most notable in case of the larger towns. The respective figures are tabulated below:

Table - V

Sl. No.	*Towns*	*Pre-annexation Estimates*	*1872*	*1881*	*1891*	*1901*
1.	Lucknow	a. Half million (1799) b. One million (1858)	2,84,779	2,61,303	2,73,028	2,64,094
2.	Fyzabad	1,08,000 (1836)	35,817	67,652	74,806	71,179
3.	Ranjitpurwa	50,000=60,000 (1836)	7,286	7,031	7,817	7,994

This decline accompanied by the increase in population of some smaller towns. Tanda and Akbarpur were already famous for the weaving industry in the post-annexation period. A rise in their population may be seen from the following Table:

17. Irfan Habib, 'Studying a Colonial Economy without perceiving colonialism', *Centre of South Asian Studies*, University of Cambridge, 1984, pp. 17-18.
18. Donald Buttler, *op. cit.*, passim.
19. *Ibid.*
20. Tennant, *Indian Recreations*, II, p. 404, Cf. H.R. Nevil, *District Gazetteers of the United Provinces of Agra and Oudh (Lucknow)*, Lucknow, 1922, p. 149.
21. William Howard Russell, *My Indian Diary*, ed. Michael Edward Cf. Irfan Habib, *Studying Colonialism*, p. 16.
22. Sleeman, Vol. I, p. 137 Cf. A.A. Azmi, 'Position of Agriculture in the Economy of Oudh during the Nawabi regime', *PIHC*, (1967), p. 83.

Table - VI

Sl. No.	*Towns*	*Pre-annexation Estimates*	*1872*	*1881*	*1891*	*1901*
1.	Akbarpur	1,000 (1836)	31,000	6,396	7,443	7,116
2.	Tanda	6,000 (1836)	13,543	19,954	19,724	10,835

But in proportion to the decline registered by the large towns, the growth of these new centres was quite insignificant. At the same time we find that the total number of the towns, having a population 4,500 or more declined considerably after the annexation. This may be seen from the following table:

Table - VII

Sl. No.	*Districts*	*Year*	*No. of Towns of and Above*	*Total Population of the Towns*
1.	Rae Bareli	1836	13	96,000
		1868-9	4	29,218
		1811	3	32,680
		1911	4	40,379
2.	Unnao	1836	9	1,03,000 to 1,14,000
		1868-9	5	37,842
		1881	5	38,467
		1911	5	39,809
3.	Partapgarh	1836	11	1,02,000
		1868-9	1	6,240
		1881	1	9,756
		1911	1	16,041
4.	Fyzabad	1836	5	1,34,000
		1868-9	3	55,635
		1881	5	1,05,963
		1911	5	82,549
5.	Sultanpur	1836	5	39,000
		1868-9	1	5,708
		1881	1	9,374
		1911	1	9,574

Thus, we see that the southern portion of *nawab-wazirs* dominion had contained 43 large towns each having a population of 4,500 and above. But the number of such towns declined considerably after annexation, there being in 1868-9 only 14 towns, while in 1911 the number rose slightly 17. Similarly, the total population of these towns in 1836 as estimated by Buttler was between 4,74,000 to 4,85,000 but it declined to 1,34,643 by the 1868-9 census returns, and rose slightly to 1,88,292 in 1911. Even if a large margin of error is assumed for Buttler's estimates, the general tendency is still quite clear.[23] If we derive a converse conclusion, this would be that the total ratio of the urban to the total population in pre-annexation Awadh was probably substantially larger than it was at the close of the 19th century.

23. Irfan Habib, *Studying Colonialism*, p. 19, where the detailed table is also given.

Chapter - 3

Agricultural Production

(a) Crops, Yields and the Productivity

A number of cereal and cash crops were raised in the province of Awadh on "its fertile though light soil".[1] A comparison of the crop-pattern, productivity of the soil and the movement of the prices in relation to these products for a period between c. 1595 and c. 1890, which we attempt in this chapter, suggests a remarkable degree of similarity. No doubt, some new crops were introduced during the 19th century, but as compared with the traditional crops of Awadh, these were only grown over a small area, by the end of the 19th century.[2]

A perusal of the *dastur* rates given in *Ain-i Akbari* shows that 21 *rabi* crops are listed for the six revenue-circles of *sarkar* Awadh and Bahraich, while the crops on which *dasturs* are recorded under *sarkars* Khairabad, Lucknow and Gorakhpur are fewer.[3] Even crops such as wheat, barley and mustard-seed, grown in the localities during the 19th century, have been omitted from the *dastur* lists.[4] Among the twenty-nine *kharif* crops, fourteen have been mentioned in all the twelve *dasturs*, while eleven minor crops are listed in only six *dasturs* of the *sarkar* Awadh and Bahraich. *Arhar* (a pulse) is mentioned in the revenue circles of Bahraich, Kharonsa, Khairabad, and Pali, for the other two, lobiya and carrots, the rates are provided only for one circle (i.e. Ibrahimabad), while *kur* (a wild grain) finds mention in the Ibrahimabad and Bahraich circles.[5]

---

1. W.H. Lawrence, 'The kingdom of Oude', *Calcutta Review*, Part III, 1845, p. 383.
2. *Agricultural Statistics of British India 1885-6.*
3. Abul Fazl, *Ain-i Akbari*, I, pp. 354-6.
4. *Agricultural Statistics*, Government of India – *1885-6.*
5. *Ain-i Akbari*.

The cereal crops cultivated in Awadh can be broadly divided into rice, wheat and millets. A substantial quantity of pulses were also grown in both the *rabi* and *kharif* harvests.

Rice constituted the chief cereal crop of the region, since its cultivation suited the low lying areas subject to inundations. It was cultivated throughout the *Tarai* region and alongside of the courses of major rivers traversing Awadh. The high quality and the common grades of rice find mention in every *dastur* circle. The different varieties of high grade rice namely, *sukhdas, Madhkar* and *jhanwan* were praised for their "whiteness, delicacy, fragrance and wholesomeness". Bahraich was famous for such rice and it was obtained for the imperial kitchen.[6] *Sukhdas* rice continued to be famous throughout the 17th century. Sujan Rae Bhandari asserts that "it (*sukhdas* rice) was of the best kind, the delicacy and fragrance was beyond imagination. The king, nobles and the common men, all appreciated its taste, flavour and delicacy."[7] Another peculiarity of the rice crop in Awadh noted by these writers was that it grew three months earlier than in other parts of Hindustan.[8]

Sometimes during the 18th century, *sarkar* Gorakhpur especially *pargana* Hansi had become quite famous for the high-grade varieties of rice raised there. These were called *bhairni, shamzira, rajhans* and *rat kawal*. In the markets of Faizabad and Lucknow, these varieties sold with the name of *pargana* Hansi.[9] The area under rice cultivation seems to have been much larger than under wheat. *The Agricultural Statistics* of 1885-6 discloses an area of 21,59,424 acres (about 20.5% of the total area) under rice, while under wheat this came to 15,56,198 acres (about 16.5% of the total).[10]

Another major crop of the province was wheat. Its cultivation suited only the higher-grounds and drier areas. The high lands between the rivers was considered especially suitable for the crop. Significantly, Abul Fazl has not recorded the revenue rates for wheat in some of the higher regions such as *sarkar* Khairabad and Lucknow, although during the 19th century these regions were known to raise substantial crops of wheat.[11] Wheat cultivation was not suitable in the low lying areas and the *Terai* as "(it) does not thrive there. It turns yellow and rots. Hoar-frost is extremely

6. *Ain-i Akbari*, I, p. 433.
7. Sujan Rae Bhandari, *Khulasat-ut-Tawarikh*, Delhi, 1918, p. 10.
8. *Ibid.*, p. 45.
9. Mufi Ghulam Hazrat, *Kwaif-i Gorakhpur*, f. 12b.
10. *Agricultural Statistics 1885-6*, p. 26.
11. *Ibid.*

prejudicial to both wheat and barley."[12] In spite of this, a substantial area was under the wheat cultivation in the Mughal *sarkar* Gorakhpur. The *Agricultural Statistics* for the regions covered by Gorakhpur *sarkar* (the districts of Gorakhpur, Basti and Gonda) show that in 1885-6 wheat was cultivated over an area of 7,69,141 acres as compared with 16,72,416 acres under rice cultivation. Daryabad-Rudauli was famous for high-rates of yield during the 19th century. Buttler tells us that it produced around twenty five maunds per *bigha*, while in Bundelkhand the produce of high quality wheat without irrigation was 15 to 16 maunds per *bigha*.[13]

Abul Fazl furnishes us with *dastur* rates for the coarse-grain and most of the pulses in various revenue-circles. But a comparison of the crop-pattern during 16th century with that of the 19th century is not possible, as these cereals have been put under a column headed by 'other food-crops' in the *Agricultural Statistics*. But it is evident that these constituted the bulk of agricultural production during the 19th century, as the 'other food crops' were sown over an area (in Awadh, including *sarkar* Gorakhpur) of 76,27,739 acres as compared with 53,20,822 acres under rice and wheat.[14] Crops like *juwar, lahdara (Bajra), arhar* and *chana* could be raised only on higher grounds, and the cultivation of these crops closely coincided with wheat. In this category, a new crop, maize, was introduced by the end of the 19th century, but as Buttler has not noticed its cultivation in Southern Oudh, it was still sparsely cultivated by 1838.

The chief cash-crops raised in the province were oil-seeds, sugarcane, cotton, indigo and tobacco. The cultivation of the vegetables for markets as well as for the domestic use was also undertaken. It was carried on by the peasants belonging to some special castes.[15]

Abul Fazl has provided the revenue rates for mustard-seed only in six *dastur*-circles. Although oil has been a part of diet of every Indian, it was not considered to be an important crop of Awadh in the Mughal period. The *Agricultural Statistics* of 1885-6 show an area of 4,98,879 acres under oil seeds.[16] Possibly the cultivation of oil-seeds as a cash crop expanded

---

12. Buttler, pp. 59-60.
13. *Ibid.*, p. 60.
14. *Agricultural Statistics 1885-6*, p. 26.
15. The peasants who carried on garden cultivation were mostly*Kachia, Morais, Kunjra* and *Luniya* or *Nuniya*. They raised almost every vegetable on the, 'richest soil immediately around the village, in enclosed and reserved fields'. Garden cultivation needed much manuring; the land around the village was very fertile in having natural manure' provided by human and animal waste. See Buttler, p. 69; Sleeman I, pp. 125-6.
16. *Agricultural Statistics, 1885-6*.

after the annexation owing to European demand, promoted by the construction of railways.[17]

Sugarcane was perhaps the most important cash-crop. The revenue rates for high quality and common sugarcane are provided by *Ain* for all the *dastur* circles of Awadh. Mufti Ghulam Hazrat mentions extensive cultivation of this crop in *sarkar* Gorakhpur, it was of the best kind as compared to the other places for 'its sweetness and delicacy'. In some *parganas* of *sarkar* Gorakhpur, however, its cultivation had to be abandoned due to the menace of the wild elephants.[18]

During the 19th century, Buttler noticed the crop was raised in 'small patches here and there, particularly between the river *Sai* and Ganges; and sugar was made in small quantity is southwest part of Oudh'.[19] Thornton described its cultivation as 'very circumscribed'.[20] However, while passing through the district of Sultanpur, six kinds of sugar-cane were noticed by W.H. Sleeman, and he found its cultivation to be quite extensive there.[21] The *Agricultural Statistics* show as many as 2,40,975 acres under the sugarcane.[22] This large acreage may be due to the subsequent extension in sugarcane cultivation after the Annexation.

Cotton constituted yet another important cash-crop. The '*Ain* provides revenue-rates for the crop in each of the twelve *dastur* circles. It continued to be widely cultivated during the successive centuries. Buttler noticed that cotton was "produced throughout the country and abundantly on the high land along the bank of (river) Sai", it was also "cultivated throughout Bainswara region particularly on its western part". A small amount of cotton was exported to the British districts of Mau and Ghazipur. The remainder was worked up by the cotton corders (*dhuniya*) in the country, particularly at Tanda. The chief markets of the cleaned cotton were said to have been at Salon and Bainswara.[23] But it seems that cotton cultivation declined considerably after Annexation; the *Agricultural Statistics of 1885-6* recorded only 80,248 acres under cotton.[24]

17. Irfan Habib, 'Colonization of Indian Economy', *Social Scientist*, No. 32 (1972).
18. *Kwaif-i Gorakhpur*, f. 12a.
19. Buttler, p. 61.
20. Edward Thornton, *A Gazetteer of the Territories under the Government of the East India Company and of the Native States on the continent of India,* 4 Vols., London, 1954, pp. 28-9.
21. Sleeman, I, pp. 162-3 and pp. 171-2.
22. *Agricultural Statistics, 1885-6.*
23. Buttler, pp. 61-2.
24. *Agricultural Statistics 1885-6.*

The indigo produced and manufactured in the province of Awadh was judged to be inferior even during the 19th century. Perhaps for this reason the European indigo planters were not attracted to the area. Those areas of Awadh kingdom which bordered the British territories such as the districts of Gonda, Fyzabad, Partapgarh and Unao raised indigo in some localities.[25] The *A'in* records that the revenue rate for indigo is only six *dasturs*. The agricultural statistics show an area 19,651 acres under this crop in Awadh, and in the district Gorakhpur to only 14,201 acres were under indigo cultivation.[26]

It seems new crops introduced after the *A'in's* time was tobacco. Buttler noticed it was being raised in a *bigha* or two by the *Kunjra* and *morais* near each village.[27] It seems that even after the annexation; the crop was produced only over a small area. The return of agricultural statistics of 1885-6 show only an area of 17,744 acres under tobacco cultivation.[28]

The cultivation of potatoes does not seem to have made much progress in *Nawabi* Oudh; it was planted by few *kunjras* and *kachis* in the vicinity of Kanpur, Lucknow and Fyzabad. The produce was mainly exported to the nearest British Cantonments. The extension of this crop, in the interior was checked by the prejudice felt by the people, especially the Brahman and Bachgoti Rajputs against eating a new vegetable, especially a root. It also does not seem to have become yet a part of the town and man's diet in Awadh.[29]

Poppy cultivation was noticed by Buttler along the bank of river Gumti by some special castes particularly the *Kachis*. It was mainly exported to the adjacent British districts. The little amount of opium produced on the right bank of the Gumti was consumed inside the country and was also bought to the markets of Lucknow and Fyzabad. Its cultivation seems to have been abandoned in the later period, or it was fully brought under government control, since the *Agricultural Statistics of 1885-6* record no area under the opium cultivation.[30]

---

25. *Agricultural Statistics 1885-6.*
26. *Ibid.*
27. Buttler, p. 69.
28. *Agricultural Statistics 1885-6,*
29. Buttler, p. 76; G. Watt, *The Dictionary of Economic Products of India,* 6 Vols. Landon, 1889, p. 1026.
30. Buttler predicted that, 'the time is not far distant, when the growth of opium will constitute one of the principal sources of the revenue of Oudh' (pp. 60-1), Watt however informs us that in 1905-6, an area of little less than 200,000 acres under opium, *DEP*, p. 851.

A small amount of *Ganja* was also raised in the country. Buttler explicitly asserts that, "no *Ganja* is raised in Bainswara" and he attributes this phenomenon to the, "high tone of the morality" of the inhabitants of the districts.[31]

Quite a large number of other crops were raised in the province. A comprehensive list of these crops has been provided by Abul Fazl in *dastur* rates of the *suba* for both *rabi* as well as *kharif* seasons. But it appears that the peasants of Awadh could not make any improvements in their methods of cultivation during the subsequent period. While describing the rotation of crops, Buttler specifically says that, "the knowledge of the natives .... is very limited", only two systems of crop rotation; suited to high ground and another to the lower ground being followed.[32]

The major cropping seasons of the province were *rabi* and *kharif*. Double-cropping (i.e. raising of both *rabi* and *kharif* crop over the same field) was possible on some parts of cultivated land in Awadh. But even the approximate extent of such area during the Mughal period cannot be determined.[33] However, the agricultural statistics of 1885-6 discloses 29,93,965 acres under double cropping (being about 25% of the total cultivated area).[34] No estimates are provided for the actual seed-yield ratio during the Mughal period. These are given only by Buttler for the southern districts of Oudh (1836). The figures he offers are reproduced below:

Table - I

***Rabi* Crops Sown in the Cold Season**

Sl. No.	*Name of the Crop*	*Sers of Seed Per Bigha*	*Mans of Produce in Good Year*	*Mans of Produce in bad Year*	*Former Produce in Mans*
1.	Chana	30	14 or 15	5 to 8	18 to 20
2.	Geihun (wheat)	51	14 or 15	7 to 8	20 to 25
3.	Jav (Barley)	40	20 to 22	10 to 13	20 to 25
4.	Sarson	¼	1 or 2	½ or ¾	- -
5.	Tisi or Arsi	10	3 to 4	1½ to 2	- -
6.	Masur	30	8 to 10	4 to 5	- -

31. Apart from the above reasons, the soil of Bainswara was dry and irrigation was difficult; and this inhibited the growth of poppy and *ganja*. Cf. Buttler, p. 69.
32. Buttler, p. 63.
33. Sujan Rae Bhandari, *Khulasat-ut Tawarikh*, p. 10.
34. *Agricultural Statistics, 1885-6*.

Table - II
***Kharif* Crops Sown in Hot Season**

Sl. No.	*Name of the Crop*	*Sers of Seed Per Bigha*	*Mans of Produce in Good Year*	*Mans of Produce in bad Year*	*Former Produce in Mans*
1.	Ashan *kharif*	30	15	8 or 9	20
2.	Jarhan	40 for 6 *bigha*	100 from 6 *bigha*	50 or 60 from 6 *bigha*	-
3.	Makai	50	16 or 18	5 or 6	-
4.	Jowar	6	10 or 12	4 or 5	-
5.	Bajra	6	10 or 12	4 or 5	-
6,	Urad	7½	8 or 10	3 or 4	-
7.	Arhar	11/4	8	3 or 4	-

The Table shows a fairly reasonable seed-yield ratios. For wheat, for example, we have 1:11 or 1:12 in good years and about 1:5.6 or 1:6 in a lean year.

Estimates for crop yields and revenue rates per *bigha* are provided by Abul Fazl on the basis of the *rai'* worked out by Sher Shah's administration (1540-5). The yields are given for *polaj* and *parauti* land (the lands continuously under cultivation). Three estimates of yields are furnished for each crop: *gazida*, *'ala* (good or high quality), *miyana* (middling) and *zabun* (low quality). Then an average of yields is given simply by dividing the total by 3. The figure, arrived at, is further divided by 3 to get the amount of produce of each crop that was claimed by the state as land revenue.[35] In the *Agricultural Statistics* from 1892 onwards estimates have been provided separately for irrigated and unirrigated lands in pounds per acre. An attempt could be made to compare the yields of high and middling categories of land during Sher Shah's administration with modern estimated yields for irrigated lands. Similarly, the yields of low category of land in Sher Shah's schedules could be compared with the yield estimates of unirrigated lands of modern statistics. However, a comparison of the yield rates for certain crops in Sher Shah's time with those of modern times will be quite conjectural. The modern reported yields for cotton are those of cleaned cotton, while the *Ain*'s date refer to the raw cotton only. Similarly in case of mustard seeds, the modern statistics has combined it with the

35. The units of area and weight, are to be assumed, are those used during Sher Shah's time. *Man-i Shershahi* was based on a ser equal to 28 *dams* and not of 30 *dams* (as was *man-i Akbari*. Similarly the *bigha* under Sher Shah was based on *gaz-i Sikandari* which was 39/41 of *gaz-i Ilahi* (Irfan Habib, *op cit.*, pp. 367-8 and pp. 353-6). Since both weight and area were smaller by about the same proportion the difference hardly requires conversion of Sher Shahi Units into those of Akbar.

rope seed, while the *Ain*'s information pertains to mustard only. A comparison of the *Ain*'s date for *shali* (paddy) with that of husked rice in modern statistics would seem to be hypothetical. In the accompanying tables a comparison has been offered for the major crops only.[36]

Table - III

Average Yields in *Man-i Akbari/bigha-i Ilahi* of Irrigated Land for c. 1892

Sl. No.	*Districts*	*Wheat*	*Rice*	*Sugarcane*	*Barley*	*Gram*	*Pea*
1.	Sitapur	13.39	10.71	22.32	14.28	9.80	10.32
2.	Hardoi	13.39	-	-	14.28	-	-
3.	Bahraich	13.39	11.29	17.85	13.39	8.92	9.25
4.	Kheri	12.50	-	-	-	-	-
5.	Unao	12.50	10.17	22.32	13.39	-	12.50
6.	Lucknow	12.50	-	-	14.28	10.71	-
7.	Rae Bareli	12.50	-	-	14.28	-	14.28
8.	Sultanpur	13.39	13.19	26.78	14.28	-	14.28
9.	Barabanki	13.39	-	-	14.28	-	-
10.	Partapgarh	13.39	-	22.32	14.28	10.71	14.28
11.	Fyzabad	1	3.39	-	17.85	14.28	- -
12.	Basti	13.39	11.47	22.32	14.28	12.50	12.50
13.	Gonda	13.39	-	17.85	14.28	-	-
14.	Gorakhpur	13.39	11.47	22.32	14.28	12.50	12.50
	Averages	13.15	11.45	20.79	14.16	12.09	12.09
	Ain's average of good and middling lands	15.00	15.10	11.30	9.00	11.30	11.30

Table - IV

Average Yields in *Man-i Akbari/bigha-i Ilahi* of Unirrigated Land for c. 1892

Sl. No.	*Districts*	*Wheat*	*Rice*	*Barley*	*Gram*	*Pea*
1.	Sitapur	8.92	7.36	8.38	6.25	7.14
2.	Hardoi	8.92	7.36	8.92	6.25	-
3.	Bahraich	8.92	8.75	8.38	5.35	6.25
4.	Kheri	7.14	7.36	8.38	5.35	-
5.	Unao	6.25	7.36	7.14	5.35	7.14
6.	Lucknow	6.25	7.36	7.14	5.35	-
7.	Rae Bareli	-	7.36	8.92	6.25	-
8.	Sultanpur	7.14	9.90	8.92	6.25	7.14

(*Contd...*)

36. The comparison is made with uniform units by converting access and British mound into *bigha-i Ilahi* and *man-i Akbari*. (0.6 acre = 1 bigha; 55.32 lb = 1 Akbari mound).

9.	Barabanki	7.14	9.90	8.92	6.25	-
10.	Partapgarh	7.14	8.75	8.92	6.25	-
11.	Fyzabad	8.92	8.75	8.92	6.25	-
12.	Basti	8.92	8.60	8.03	7.59	6.25
13.	Gonda	-	9.90	8.92	6.25	-
14.	Gorakhpur	8.92	8.60	8.03	6.25	-
	Averages	7.75	8.35	8.33	6.03	6.69
	Yields recorded In *Ain* for low Quality land	8.35	9.15	8.15	7.20	8.25

Table - III set out the yields of five major crops (*rabi* and *kharif* both) from the irrigated lands for the districts falling within the limits of Mughal provinces of Awadh (including districts situated on the periphery) along side the averages of Sher Shah's high and 'middling' yields. Table - IV set out the yields of these very crops from the 'unirrigated' land compared with Sher Shah's 'low' yields.

These tables show that the average of *Ain*'s 'good' and 'middling' yields are slightly higher than in 1892 estimates for these crops like wheat, barley and gram, but in the case of coarser grains such as *juwar* and *bajra* the rates of productivity were substantially higher during Sher Shah's time the opposite is the case with peas. The yield of rice and sugarcane in terms of *gur* was certainly higher (about two folds) towards the close of the 19th century as compared to the *Ain*'s time. So far as the increase in the yield of *gur* by the 1890s is concerned, this is understandable in view of the wide-spread use of iron crushers which has resulted in a higher extraction of juice.[37]

The '*Ain* gives us details of the revenue rates on each crop for each *dastur* circle of the Mughal empire. These rates essentially represented the cash value of the portion of produce claimed as land-revenue. In other words, the variation of *dastur* rates from one area to another could be taken as a phenomenon denoting the actual variation in yields or prices or both. In the province of Awadh, for some of the *rabi* crops the final *dasturs* are not recorded for all circles and the rates have been provided only for six circles while the remaining six circles have been left out for unspecified reasons. However, with the rates available, we can study the main trends of these variations.

---

37. J.A. Voelcker, *Report on the improvement of Indian Agriculture*, London, 1893, pp. 276-7. He refers to the wide-use of iron mills by 1893 in the North Western Provinces.

The rates of wheat vary from 54-20 *dams* (in Awadh and Bahraich) to 62-15 *dams* (per *bigha* Ibrahimabad). Rates of barley ranged between 35-20 (Firozabad) to 45-21 (Ibrahimabad again). Notable variations are discernable in the rates for green pea; the highest was 38 *dam* (Ibrahimabad) the lowest 24-15 *dam* (Firozabad). The maximum rate recorded for the high grade dark coloured paddy (*shali*) was 74-20 *dam* (Lucknow) while the lowest was 62-5 *dam* (Bahraich). The rates were generally lower towards the Northeast, and tended to be high towards south and north-west. The cotton rates were high in south-west (93-23 *dam* in Ibrahimabad, Pali, Lucknow and Unam) while lower rates were recorded towards the south-east (83-21 *dam* in Awadh and Bharwara). For *lahdara* the rates seems to have been pretty uniform, the lowest 23-12 *dam* (Bahraich, Gorakhpur and Kharonsa), the highest 25-18 (Ibrahimabad and Unam). Similarly the rates for *juwar* show little variations; the high rate region was the north-east (the rate being 38 *dam* in Ibrahimabad, Kharonsa, Bahraich and Gorakhpur), while low rates were recorded in the western parts (32-15 Pali and Unam). In the case of thick or paund a sugarcane the rates ranged between 240-9 *dam* (Awadh, Bahraich, Kharonsa, Bharwara, and Gorakhpur) and 203-15 *dam* (Firozabad), while the rate of ordinary cane at the minimum was 123- *dam* (Ibrahimabad, Bahraich, Kharonsa and Gorakhpur) and the highest at 190-15 *dam* (Awadh and Bharwara).

No general pattern emerges from the *dastur* rates as to determine high and low yields (and prices) uniformly for all crops.

The modern data for yields gave an almost set pattern for the major crops, with only a few exception. In case of wheat and barley almost a uniform rate of yield is assigned to all the districts of the Mughal *suba* of Awadh. However, in a few pockets of the north-west, the yields were a little low. In these regions, the yield rates of *juwar* and *bajra* are lower than the standard for the region. In case of cotton a decline in yields from the uniform is discernable in eastern districts of Basti and Gorakhpur. The maximum yield blocks of sugarcane (in terms of *gur*) are located in the north-eastern and north-western districts, while the substantially lower levels are recorded for the Bahraich, Fyzabad and Gonda districts. These details show no particular correlation with the *dastur*-variations, probably because the latter were determined not only by yield estimates but also by prices.

(b) Means of Cultivation and Irrigation

Specific details about the practices followed by the peasants of Awadh during the Mughal period are lacking. In the absence of such information, it may yet be assumed that the methods of cultivation and irrigation adopted by them were similar to other peasants of north India. Obviously, these methods, similar as these might have been to those of Europe in the 17th century,[38] tended to become outmoded as two centuries passed by. Thornton thought that in Awadh the "modes of tillage were extremely rude and inefficient. The operation of ploughing was carried out so feebly and unskillfully that it had to be repeated 30 and 40 times for a wheat crop, after that harrowing had to be undertaken seven or eight times.[39] The reasons for such 'feeble operation of ploughing' were not far to seek, as the cattle employed in agriculture were mostly "stunted, broken down and miserable".[40]

In the time of the *A'in* the number of tax-free animals allowed per head of peasant were four bullocks, two cows, and one buffalo. Large grazing grounds, in waste and forest both, were available for the cattle during the Mughal period.[41] The situation underwent a change as the population increased and cultivation expanded. The peasants in Awadh depended on the *siul dhak* and other jungles for the support of their animals. During the 18th and 19th centuries the forests were reclaimed on a large scale to extend the area under cultivation and for the purpose of firewood. The scarcity of the 'grazing ground' led ultimately in fall of the number of animals in relation to the total human population. This deterioration in the south-western districts was so acute that, "people who would formerly have possessed 100 oxen and 50 buffaloes, have now only four or five of them".[42] The animals left with peasants were in no good condition because, "excepting along the Sai and near Faizabad, where there is still a good supply of water and fodder, the oxen are most miserable animals of the kind ... lean, stunted and frequently diseased".[43]

The scarcity of the cattle had also become acute because of the "universal practice of revenue collectors seizing and carrying them away when their owner fell into arrears". The problem had assumed such dimensions that when the fields had to be watered, it was quite common to

38. Cf. *CEHI*, I, p. 214. The use of seed-drill and dibbling were the methods, employed by Indian peasants, were unknown in the contemporary Europe. Cf. *Ibid.*

39. Thornton, pp. 29-30.

40. *Ibid.*

41. *CEHI*, I, pp. 220-1.

42. Buttler, p. 65.

43. *Ibid.*, p. 64.

see, "all members of the family, male and female, working instead of cattle at the well rope".[44] The fall in the number of livestock per capita ultimately raised the price of *ghee*. It was, "formerly sold at 20 *sers* the rupee, is now sold at a *ser* and half."[45]

Manuring was done with the dung of cattle and horses. This was supposed to raise the fertility of land and the productivity of the crop in, 'triple measure'. But one would think that since there was some scarcity of cattle, and reduction in grazing grounds during the 19th century, the dung manure would also have become relatively less plentiful. Moreover, manuring was not done scientifically and Buttler thought that the local peasant had much to learn in this regard.[46]

The peasants seem to have had an accurate idea of the nature of soil and its adaptabilities for particular crops. Separate schedules of tillage were devised for each crop. The fields were especially prepared for wheat cultivation; such fields had to be left fallow in the *kharif* season. In this period of four months, thirty two ploughings were carried out lengthwise (*khara-khara*) and across (*bera-bera*) while the ordinary peasants repeated this course twenty times only. Some diagonal ploughing operations were also carried out. After this much of ploughing, smoothing out of the field was done in order to pulverize the soil. This was done by using a heavy wooden plank called *serawan* eight times; lengthwise and across.[47] The other *rabi* crops such as gram, barley, and juwar needed only two or three double operations of ploughing and smoothing. The fields in which rice was intended to be grown were first filled with water at least a foot deep, and, then, "three or four double ploughings are given and the *serawan* is once passed through the soil, so as to reduce it to the state of soft mud".[48]

Sowing by seed-drill and broad cast has been described by Buttler. No reference is made to dibbling, already noticed in the 17th century.[49]

The agricultural implements used by the peasants of Awadh during the 19th century were judged by Buttler to be "rude and simple in the extreme".[50]

44. Buttler, pp. 65-6.
45. *Ibid.*, p. 64; During the Mughal period, the price of ghee was about 8.75 times its weight in wheat.
46. *Ibid.*, p. 63.
47. *Ibid.*, p. 55.
48. *Ibid.*, p. 55.
49. *Ibid.*, p. 56.
50. *Ibid.*, p. 62.

But as compared to others, the people of Awadh had no, "superstitious prejudice against the introduction of new agricultural implements". The only objection they might had against the use of any new device or implement would be the cost.[51] The following is the list of the implements given by Buttler:

Table - V

Sl.No.	*Name of the Implements*	*Cost*	*Remarks*
1.	Plough (*Har*)	2 annas	
2.	Plough share (*phar*)	8 annas	
3.	Narrow hoe (*kudal*)	8 annas	Its weight was 2½ *ser* or *kacha pasari*
4.	Broad-hoe (*pharua*)	one rupee	
5.	Heavy wooden plank (*serawan*)	2 annas	
6.	Yoke for plank (*machi*)	2 annas	
7.	Big leather bag (*pur*)	1½ rupees	
8.	Small leather bag (*pur*)	one rupee	
9.	Rope, 25 or 30 cubits long	12 annas	
10.	Basket of split bamboos (*dugla*)	2 pice	

The rainfall and the rivers flowing through the province were the major sources of irrigation. Abul Fazl mentions the rivers, Sarju, Ghaghra, Sai and Gomti as the principal streams traversing the province. There is no information about any water lifting devices set upon these rivers. But the floods were very important for rice cultivation. Abul Fazl says, "with the beginning of the dry season it is wonderful how the floods begin from the Saru and Ghaggar; they flood the land before the onset of the monsoon. As the waters rise, the rice stalks also grow and lengthen. Only if the floods take place before the ears grow, is the rice crop destroyed".[52] Similarly over a small area of cultivated land, artificial methods of irrigation were also applied, but in crude forms. Bhandari tells us that, "although at some places cultivation is supported by the wells ... most of the land still depended on rainfall". Earlier the abundance of the rainfall in the province has been praised as it resulted, "in an extension of the cultivation, augmentation of the crop-yields, cheapness of the grains, and the large settlements in *parganas*".[53]

But with the extension of the cultivation through a continuous process of the reclamation of virgin land, the need for having more artificial irrigation

51. *Ibid.*, p. 63.
52. *Ain-I Akbari*, I, p. 433; *Khulasat-ut-Tawarikh*, p. 45.
53. *Khulasat-ut-Tawarikh*, p. 10.

began to be felt. During the 19th century, irrigation was practised throughout the kingdom of Awadh in order to supplement the *mansoon*. The principal sources of artificial irrigation were wells, tanks and lakes.[54] Buttler thought that the need for artificial irrigation had been growing in Awadh because of a possible diminution of rainfall owing to forest clearance. The forest clearing had been carried out very rapidly in north-western parts of the kingdom, and it was not accompanied by any artificial system of planting which might counteract "the parching effects" produced by the removal of the forests.[55]

The most common practice for obtaining water from a river or a lake, when the bank happened to be perpendicular, and close to water, was by means of a basket, woven of split bamboos, called *dugla*. It was manipulated by two men facing each other and holding a rope, tied with the sides of the *dugla*. By applying this method three *bighas* of land could be irrigated in a day by four men, who used to work by turn and raised the water up to six feet.[56] When the river bank was much above the water level, the water was raised by using a leather bag and rope. The rope was either passed over a pulley wheel made of wood or a cylinder made of split bamboos. The rope was pulled either by cattle or manually.[57]

The wells were dug 60 or 70 feet deep. From these wells also the water was raised by using a leather bag (*pur*) pulled by rope. The lever-based *dhenkli* was also used for raising water from the wells of small depth. However, even the digging of the wells alongside the left bank of Gumti was not possible because of the aridity and sterility of the soil. But in 1885-6, the total area irrigated by wells was about 10,63,780 acres, this being 9 percent of the total irrigated area.[58]

The absence of the Persian wheel (*rahat*) was noted by Buttler.[59] It was a labour saving device; that it was not used in Awadh may be ascribed to the relative in efficiency of the wooden machine. The metallic machine came later.

It appears that there was absolutely no canal-irrigation in any part of Awadh. The agricultural statistics of 1885-6 show no returns under the column 'area irrigated by the canal'.

54. Buttler, p. 48.
55. *Ibid.*
56. *Ibid.*, pp. 66-7.
57. *Ibid.*
58. *Agricultural Statistics 1885-6*, p. 32.
59. Buttler, p. 32.

As compared with the cultivated area in 1885-6, the total irrigated area was very small (about 18% of the total cultivated area). There is no reason to believe that the proportion was higher under the Awadh kingdom. Much of the larger area of land was thus left to the mercies of rainfall and riverine inundations.

Chapter - 4

The Land Revenue System Under the Mughals

'Hindustan', according to Abul Fazl, was brought under *zabt* by Sher Shah and Islam Shah. Awadh was apparently a part of this region. Now *zabt* involved the measurement of the area by a standard unit, and assessment of the revenue by the application of cash-rates sanctioned for various crops. Awadh is assigned such rates or *dasturs* from the beginning of Akbar's reign, these being set out in the statistical chapter called *Ain-i Doazdah Sala* in the *Ain-i Akbari*. From the 25th regnal year of Akbar, at any rate, the *suba* came to be divided into a number of circles, within each of which a separate schedule (*dastur-ul 'amal*) was in force. These circles, comprising a varying number of *mahals* had separate schedules of cash-rates sanctioned for various crops, per *bigha-i Ilahi* as measured by the bamboo rod.

The following *dastur* circles were formed within Awadh.[1]

Table - I

Sl. No.	*Name of the Sarkars*	*Name of the Dastur Circles*	*Name of Pargana Included in the Dastur Circles*
1.	*Sarkar* Awadh	(i) Awadh ba Haveli	19 *pargana*
	(21 *mahals*)	(ii) Ibrahimabad	1 *pargana*
		(iii) Kishni	1 *pargana*
2.	*Sarkar* Bahraich	(iv) Bahraich ba Haveli	8 *pargana*
	(11 *mahals*)	(v) Firozabad	2 *pargana*
		(vi) Kharonsa	1 *pargana*

(Contd....)

1. *Ain-i Akbari*, p. 352.

3.	*Sarkar* Khairabad (22 *mahals*)	(vii) Khairabad (viii) Pali (ix) Bhurwara	12 *pargana* 8 *pargana* 2 *pargana*
4.	*Sarkar* Gorakhpur (24 *mahals*)	(x) Gorakhpur	24 *pargana*
5.	*Sarkar* Lucknow (55 *mahals*)	(xi) Lucknow (xii) Onam	47 *pargana* 8 *pargana*

The *dastur* circles were of various sizes, apparently keeping in view the local variations of prices and yield levels of different crops. However, no general pattern emerges. Small *dastur* circles, (Kishni, Ibrahimabad and Kharonsa) are found as isolated blocks in the midst of bigger units like Awadh, Bahraich and Khairabad. It is possible that the fixation of *dastur* rates in such small circles was not made on the basis of the local level of prices and yields, but, "was motivated by some administrative convenience". It has been assumed that, "these *parganas* were included in the *jagir* of some big nobles who held the other circles within their *jagirs* and wished to have identical *dasturs* in the various parts of their *jagirs*".[2]

During the 17th century, the *zabt* system of revenue assessment seems to have continued in Awadh, so far as we can judge from our evidence. Now large tracts of virgin land were brought under measurement and it has been pointed out in Chapter I that as compared to the map area, the total *arazi* in Awadh (excluding *sarkar* Gorakhpur) in 1595 was about 51 percent, and it rose to 66.45 percent during the early years of Aurangzeb's reign. Still about one-third of the total number of the villages were said to be still unmeasured in Aurangzeb's time.

While measurement of the tax-paying land thus continued, we know next to nothing whether the cash revenue rates were set in the same manner as in Akbar's time.

The magnitude of the land-revenue demand under the *zabt* system generally exceeded the formally prescribed limit of the one-third of the total produce, and in practice it rather approximated to a half of the produce.[3] The *Ain* gives us details of the land revenue demand for different crops. It does so far different years of Akbar's reign (6th RY to 24th RY) in the tabular form set out as the *Ain-i Nuzdahsala*. In the attached table eight cereal crops of *rabi* and *kharif* have been selected from the *Ain's* tables. It appears that most of the crops were uniformly rated from 6th to 9th RY throughout

2. Shireen Moosvi, "Formulation of Land Revenue Rates under Akbar", *IHR*, Delhi, Jan. 1978, p. 324.

3. Irfan Habib, *op cit.*, p. 191.

the province. From the 10th RY the rates are entered in pairs of minimum and maximum for most of the crops. Generally these rates are low as compared to the rates sanctioned for the previous years, and the pair suggests a range of different rates in different localities. The revenue rates from the 15th RY to 24th RY, on which the final *dasturs*, too were supposedly based, are given in similar pairs, and again in most cases, they are lower as compared to the rates given for earlier periods.

The 19th RY rates are followed by the final rates. These rates, given in the *Ain-i Deh Sala*, "were permanent and were to be applied each year without any reference to the current yield or prices".[4] These were, however, not the exact averages of the revenue rates sanctioned from the 15th RY to 24th RY, but were much higher. The enhancement was done to adjust the difference necessitated owing to the introduction of the *bigha-i Ilahi*. The new *bigha* was 10.09 percent high in size as compared to the old one.[5] But in actual practice and for the purpose of setting out the revenue rates, the new *bigha* was assumed to be 11.8 percent higher and the *dasturs* too were raised in the same proportion. Shireen Moosvi has reconstructed the conversion schedule which was presumably applied by the Mughal administration. In the revised system 100 *dams* of the old scale now corresponded to 111 *dams* 20 *jitals* and similarly 200 *dams*, now equaled 223 *dams* 15 *jitals*, the increase being exactly 11.8 percent.[6] In fact, most of the rates in the final *dastur* appear to be based on a set conversion schedule.[7]

Table - II

Selected Nineteen-Year Rates (*Rabi*[8] Crop)

RY	*Wheat*	*Gram*	*Barley*	*Mustard*
6th & 7th RY	90	80	70	80
8th RY	90	80	70	80
9th RY	90	80	60	80
10th RY	52 60	48 56	42 50	68 80
11th RY	52 80	48 76	42 60	68 80
12th RY	52 80	48 76	52	68 80
13th RY	52 70	48 64	48 50	68 80
14th RY	46 65	34 58	38 44	54 60
15th RY	48	24 33	28 32	30 33

(*Contd...*)

4. Irfan Habib, *op cit.*, p. 210.
5. *Ibid.*, p. 355.
6. Shireen Moosvi, *op cit.*, pp. 306-9.
7. *Ibid.*, p. 309.
8. British Museum Add. 7652, f. 156b; compare the text, pp. 354-55.

16th RY	42 50	28 33	30 32	28 33
17th RY	50 52	26 33	32 61	28 33
18th RY	33 46	20 27	20 27	22 33
19th RY	33 43	20 28	20½ 28	22 33
20th RY	46½ 58	30 41	29½ 45	25 ?
21st RY	48 72	42 57½	43 62	19 30½
22nd RY	54 74½	30 57½	34 56½	25 31
23rd RY	32 44	19 44	22 30	20 28
24th RY	38 46	21 40	24 40	21 20

Table - III

Selected Nineteen-Year Rates (*Kharif*[9] crop)

RY	*Dark Coloured Paddy*	*Jowar*	*Mash*	*Lahdara*
6th and 7th RY	-	50	48	48
8th RY	-	50	48	48
9th RY	-	60	54	48 50
10th RY	80	48	44	44
11th RY	80	48 60	44 34?	44 50
12th RY	80	48 60	44 50	44 50
13th RY	80 90	48 60	50 54	44 50
14th Ry	68	40	36	40
15th RY	56	26	28	20 70
16th RY	30 68	26 40	28 36	20 40
17th RY	56	26	28	20
18th RY	56 70	26 27	26 28	20
19th RY	50 70	24 26	26 28	20 40
20th RY	54½ 70	23 40	23 35	18 48
21st RY	49½ 68	23 48	28½ 42½	18 48
22nd RY	44 76	25 48	28 34	18 48 1/2
23rd RY	42 76	30 40	19 36	20 40
24th RY	36 60	24 36	17 28	18 30

Revenue incidence per *bigha* could be worked out with the help of the statistical tables included in the account of Twelve *subas*. Appendix 'A' sets out *pargana*-wise information regarding the revenue incidence per *bigha* (*jama'*/*arazi*).

If we divide the *jama'* by *arazi*, as we do in Appendix 'A', we find immense variations. This is to be explained primarily by the fact that the measurement of revenue-paying land had been carried out in a very uneven manner, so that where the proportion of unmeasured land was large

9. British Museum Add. 7652, f. 156a; compared the text, pp. 355-56.

(and the *arazi* small), the revenue incidence per *bigha* of *arazi* is naturally very high. On the other hand low *jama'/arazi* figures would tend to suggest a high level of measurement. Unfortunately, here too it is not clear whether this was the actual revenue incidence, since much unassessed land, e.g. waste, jungle, ravine, habitation, might have been measured and included in the *arazi*.

This brings us to another aspect of the Mughal revenue system. Since measurement was not complete in any *sarkar* of the *suba* Awadh, there should have existed other methods of revenue assessment apart from the *zabt* system. Crop-sharing or *batai*, was often supposed to be the 'best method of revenue collection, since in this system the risks of seasonal variations were shared equally between the cultivators and the authorities'.[10] But from the administrative point of view, it was an expensive method since it required, "a large number of alert watchmen, otherwise the ill-started ones soil their dishonest hands with misappropriation".[11] This attitude of hostility to crop sharing continued to persist under the Nawab Wazirs. A letter included in the *Ausaf-i Asaf* refers to a village, where no cultivation was undertaken since long, and it had been agreed with a *zamindar* that revenue would in future be taken by *batai* if he settled the village afresh. The *zamindar* did so, and distributed seeds and livestock by way of *taqavi*. But when the crops were ripe, the demand was sought to be commuted into a demand in cash of Rs 3 per *bigha* implying measurement, which apparently imposed hardship on the assessee.[12]

A large number of surviving village papers such as *patta, qubuliyat* deeds and *qaul-o-qarar* documents from the various regions of Awadh during the 17th century make it clear that the basic unit of assessment was always the village and not the individual peasants; notwithstanding the officially proclaimed preference to make the assessments upon individual peasants.[13] Such a policy was aimed at avoiding any unjust distribution of the land-revenue burden, but it seems that in actual practice this was not simply possible.[14] In both *khalsa* and *jagirs* the village was assessed as the unit. In *qaul-o-qarar* documents of Saiyed Muhammad i-Arif and his father in *pargana* Hisampur, *sarkar* Bahraich regarding certain villages, included in the jurisdiction of the *jagirdars*, the revenue is invariably assessed on the

10. Irfan Habib, *op. cit.*, pp. 197-8.
11. *Ain*, I, p. 286, Cf. *Ibid.*, p. 197.
12. *Ausaf-i Asaf*, f. 72b, University Collection MS. Also in ff. 105 a-b, Abdul Salam MS.
13. Irfan Habib, *op cit.*, pp. 230-32.
14. *Ibid.*

village.[15] Similarly, in *pargana* Sadarpur *sarkar* Khairabad, one Shaikh Ghulam Ahmad agreed to pay an amount of Rs 1390, annas 9 annually for 21 villages to the imperial treasury in fixed sum (*bil-muqta'*).[16] Again, a *qaul-o-qarar*, relating to *bil-muqta'* arrangements of the *jagir* of Prince 'Azam in *pargana* Sandilah, *sarkar* Lucknow, also treats the village as the unit of assessment.[17] The *ijara* documents for *madad-i ma'ash* holdings also exhibit this feature.[18] The papers concerning the accounts of the revenue-realisation (*tumar-wa waslat*), too were submitted for the entire village;[19] and this practice continued in the days of *nawab-wazirs* as well.[20] The details regarding the distribution of the tax-burden on the individual peasants by the *zamindars* and the *ijaradara* are not furnished in the surviving records from Awadh though they might have been recorded.

We also do not have anything corresponding to the *Ain*'s *dastur* rates for the later periods. The information regarding the total *jama'dami*, however, enables us to form an idea of the change in the total amount of land-revenue in course of time. The available data are tabled below:

Table - IV

***Jama'Dami* of *Suba* Awadh in Different Periods**

Sl. No.	*Source*	*Date*	*Dams*
1.	*Ain-i Akbari*	1595-6	20,17,58,172
2.	*Iqbalnama-i Jahangiri*	1605	22,98,65,014
3.	*Majalisu-s Salatin*	pre-1627	23,22,00,000
4.	*Bayaz-i Khushbu'i*	1628-36	25,97,58,140
5.	*Farhang-i Kardani*	1633-38	25,82,10,000
6.	Add. 16,863	1644-47	26,35,00,565
7.	Lahori	1644-47	30,00,00,000
8.	Sadiq Khan	1646-47	1,00,00,00,000?
9.	Bernier	1638-56	27,32,00,000
10.	Thevenot	1638-56	26,70,00,000
11.	Or. 1840	1638-56	25,82,10,000
12.	*Dastur-al 'Amal-i'Ilm-i Navisindaqi*	1638-56	25,82,00,000
13.	Bodl. 0.390	1638-56	25,82,10,000
14.	Sujan Rai Bhandari	1638-56	26,45,40,000

(Contd...)

15. Allahabad, 1206, and 897.
16. Regional Records Office, Allahabad, 1299 and 1302.
17. Acquired Documents, Oriental Records Division, *National Archives of India*, 1574.
18. Firangi Mahal Document, CAS, Aligarh Muslim University, *FM*-84.
19. Acquired Documents, Oriental Records Division, *National Archives of India*, 1549.
20. Acquired Documents, Oriental Records Division, *National Archives of India*, 1280.

15.	Manucci	1638-56	28,80,00,000
16.	*Farhang-i Kardani-o Kar-amozi*	1638-56	25,82,10,000
17.	*Siyaqnama*	1638-56	27,32,00,000
18.	*Dastur-al 'Amal-i Navisindagi*	c. 1646-56	27,32,00,000
19.	*Dastur-al 'Amal-i 'Alamgiri*	c. 1656	36,39,82,859
*20.	Ethe. 433.	c. 1656	36,39,82,859
21.	*Mirat-al 'Alam*, Add. 7657	c. 1667	32,00,72,193
22.	*Zawabit-i 'Alamgiri*	c. 1687-91	32,13,17,819
23.	Fraser 86	c. 1687-95	32,13,17,819
24.	*Intikhab-i Dastur-al 'Amal-i Padshahi*	c. 1687 ?	32,13,17,819
*25.	*Dastur-al 'Amal-i Shahjahani*	c. 1700	27,95,79,619
*26.	Br. Mus. 6586	c. 1707	39,85,54,135
27.	Jagjiwandas	c. 1709	32,13,17,819
*28.	Ethe-433	c. 1720	33,84,99,340
29.	*Chahar Gulshan*	c. 1720	32,46,80,247
30.	Uny. Coll.-FA-73 Aligarh	c. 1759	37,46,74,559

It seems that a revision of the *jama'dami* was undertaken after the compilation of the *Ain-i Akbari*; and by the close of Akbar's reign itself there was considerable increase in the total *jama'* of the *suba*. During Jahangir's reign the *jama'dami* was again enhanced, but as compared to the earlier revision, this was only marginal. Under Shah Jahan, the *jama'* of the province was raised considerably through periodic revisions. Before the war of succession, the total *jama'dami* of the province was about 145 percent of *Ain*'s time. But partly perhaps as a result of the devastation caused by the war of succession and partly owing to agrarian distress of the early years of Aurangzeb's reign, the total *jama'* of province decreased during the early phase of Emperor Aurangzeb and remained so during the 17th century. But in the last decade of his long reign, it again rose to a level 197.5 percent of what it was in 1595. In the post-Aurangzeb period, the total *jama'dami* again seems to have undergone a decline.

In some of our sources a *sarkar*-wise break up of the total *jama'dami* has also been given. In the following table, these figures have been indexed with the figures of *Ain* as = 100. The figures are put in a chronological order.

We find that in *sarkar* Gorakhpur the *jama'dami* increased five times, while in *sarkar* of Khairabad and Lucknow, it became double of what it was in 1595. The *sarkars* of Awadh and Bahraich on the other hand, do not record a high increase by 1707. In these *sarkars*, as can be seen in Appendix 'A', the revenue incidence per unit of map area was the lowest at the time of the *Ain*.

Table - V

***Sarkar*-Wise Break-up of the Total *Jama'Dami* of *Suba* Awadh**

Sarkar	*Br.Mues. Add.6588*	*Ethe-433*	*Br.Mues. Add.6598*	*Ain = 100 Br.Mues. Add.6586*	*Chahar Gulshan*	*Uniy. Coll. F.A.73*
Suba Total	138.81	180.72	180.73	138.81	161.21	191.00
Sarkar Awadh	127.04	143.40	143.40	147.33	122.30	143.35
Sarkar Bahraich	115.60	177.20	177.43	161.60	104.45	177.20
Sarkar Gorakhpur	204.09	361.25	361.52	386.25	467.03	363.46
Sarkar Khairabad	134.43	167.47	167.47	197.08	138.59	179.85
Sarkar Lucknow	160.90	204.01	224.90	224.90	187.34	203.98

Hasil or *hasil-i ausat* figures are also provided in some of these statistical accounts. In general the ordinary *hasil* are considerably lower than the *jama'* figures in the same statistics: this is what is to be expected, since the actual realisation seldom reached the level of the *jama'* ('twelve-monthly') in the Mughal Empire.

The distance between *jama'* and *hasil* is illustrated in a *farman* of Aurangzeb's time relating to a village situated at the boundary of Awadh. The *zimn* of the *farman* to Shaikh Muhammad Ashraf issued on 18th Jamad I, 22nd R.Y. contains *hasil* figure (from 4th to 17th R.Y.) of the village Singhwal in *sarkar* Manikpur, *suba* Allahabad.[21] It fluctuated between rupees twenty-one to rupees ninety-six while the total *jama'* of the village was rupees 802½ or 32,000 *dams*.

The picture is otherwise with the *hasil-i kamil* or the maximum revenue ever realised. This uniformly exceeds the *jama'*.

Table - VI

***Jama'* and *Hasil-i Kamil* Statistics of the *Suba* (Awadh)**

Sl. No.	*Source*	*Year*	*A Jama'*	*B hasil-i kamil (dams)*	*B as %* of A
1.	Fraser-86	XVIIIth RY	32,13,17,819	39,54,30,814	123.78
2.	Fraser-86	1687-91	32,13,17,819	36,88,26,340	114.78
3.	*Zawabit-i* Alamgiri	1687-91	32,13,17,819	36,48,22,040	113.53
4.	Jagjiwandas	c. 1709	32,13,17,819	36,40,26,040	113.29
5.	Br.Mues.Add.6586	1707	39,85,54,135	39,65,33,360	99.49
6.	Uny. Coll.,FA-73	1759	38,46,74,559	33,77,68,480	87.88

(*Contd...*)

21. See my paper, Proceedings Indian History Congress, 1979, pp. 302-14.

7.	Br.Mues.Add.6588	?	27,95,79,619	33,57,58,800	120.89
8.	*Chahar Gulshan*	c. 1720	32,46,80,247	33,24,33,660	102.38
9.	BM Add.22831	?	28,95,79,619	33,41,79,120	115.48

It is, however, of some interest that this exceptionally high level of *hasil-i kamil* is a peculiar feature of Awadh. In none of the other provinces does the amount of *hasil-i kamil* exceed the total *jama'dami*, with the exception of Delhi. The actual significance of this peculiarity of *suba* Awadh is, however, hard to grasp ; it can only be noted here (see Appendix 'B').

Appendix 'A'

(*Jama'/Arazi* Per *Bigha* in 1595)
***Sarkar* Awadh**

Sl. No.	*Pargana*	*Jama'/Arazi*
1.	Awadh ba Haveli	52.37
2.	Ambodha	6.98
3.	Ibrahimabad	23.03
4.	Inhauna	17.12
5.	Pachhimrath	14.69
6.	Bithori	51.44
7.	Basodhi	16.20
8.	Thana Bhadaon	49.12
9.	Baktha	8.67
10.	Daryabad	11.02
11.	Rudauli	9.24
12.	Sailuk	8.27
13.	Sultanpur	50.44
14.	Satinpur	20.71
15.	Subeha	15.35
16.	Sarwapali	20.66
17.	Satrikh	30.40
18.	Guorich	47.65
19.	Kishni	52.16
20.	Mangalsi	11.69
21.	Naipur	51.49
	***Sarkar* Total**	**14.62**

***Sarkar* Bahraich**

Sl. No.	*Pargana*	*Jama'/Arazi*
1.	Bahraich ba Haveli	13.07
2.	Behra	40.10
3.	Husampur	44.19

(Contd...)

4.	Dangdun	5.21
5.	Rajhat	41.03
6.	Sujauli	7.02
7.	Sultanpur	2.85
8.	Fakharpur	16.47
9.	Firozabad	17.79
10.	Qila Nawabgarh	5.12
11.	Khuraunsa	46.15
	***Sarkar* Total**	**13.21**

Sarkar Khairabad

1.	Barwar Anjana	54.28
2.	Biswa	26.24
3.	Pali	12.78
4.	Bawan	20.67
5.	Basrah	16.41
6.	Bharwara	12.69
7.	Basora	12.69
8.	Paila	48.90
9.	Chhitapur	27.28
10.	Khairabad ba Haveli	13.58
11.	Sandi	14.42
12.	Sara	30.39
13.	Sadarpur	6.88
14.	Gopamau	52.34
15.	Kheri	12.49
16.	Kherigarh	42.49
17.	Karkhaila	29.95
18.	Khan-Khatmau	76.36
19.	Laharpur	13.21
20.	Machhrehta	29.72
21.	Nimkhar	60.67
22.	Hargaon	2.98
	***Sarkar* Total**	**21.95**

Sarkar Gorakhpur

1.	Utraula	43.59
2.	Unhaula	48.88
3.	Binayakpur	43.29
4.	Babhanpara	50.20
5.	Bhanapara	50.20
6.	Tilpur	44.41
7.	Chilaupara	44.25
8.	Dariyapur	48.45

(Contd...)

9.	Dewapara Kalta (2m)	44.32
10.	Rehli	48.76
11.	Rasulpur wa Gori (2m)	43.80
12.	Ramgarh wa Gori (2m)	45.72
13.	Gorakhpur ba Haveli	44.83
14.	Katehla	44.44
15.	Kihlapara	40.12
16.	Mahauli	245.02
17.	Mandwa	48.06
18.	Mandla	40.81
19.	Maghar-wa Ratanpur (2m)	51.89
	***Sarkar* Total**	**48.82**

***Sarkar* Lucknow**

1.	Amethi	26.20
2.	Unam	32.95
3.	Isauli	45.85
4.	Asiyun	14.38
5.	Asoha	20.36
6.	Unchagaon	12.61
7.	Bilgiram	26.57
8.	Bangarmau	15.69
9.	Bijlaur	31.08
10.	Bari	15.94
11.	Bahriman	30.47
12.	Nigawan	12.11
13.	Bhitauli	16.42
14.	Panhan	29.93
15.	Parsandan	26.07
16.	Patan	38.11
17.	Tara Singhaur	17.47
18.	Jhalotar	18.18
19.	Dewi	21.81
20.	Deorakh	51.68
21.	Dadra	6.83
22.	Ranharpur	32.13
23.	Ramkot	27.38
24.	Sandila	26.98
25.	Saipur	67.17
26.	Sarasi	482.17
27.	Satanpur	16.97
28.	Sahali	53.17
29.	Sidhapur	47.27
30.	Sidhpur	53.89

(Contd...)

31.	Sisandi	49.93
32.	Sarwan	37.71
33.	Fatehpur	15.94
34.	Fatehpur Chaurasi	8.58
35.	Garh Amethi	38.00
36.	Kursi	20.95
37.	Kakori	45.43
38.	Kahanjara	36.70
39.	Ghatampur	20.17
40.	Kachhando	19.51
41.	Gorinda	22.61
42.	Kumbhi	29.93
43.	Lucknow ba Haveli	19.04
44.	Laskar	9.97
45.	Malihabad	26.46
46.	Mallanwan	43.34
47.	Mohan	32.73
48.	Mauranwan	24.66
49.	Manchiaon	22.99
50.	Mahona	19.21
51.	Manwi	26.18
52.	Makraid	32.06
53.	Hadha	15.01
54.	Hardoi	30.65
55.	Aihar	25.15
	***Sarkar* Total**	**24.44**

Appendix 'B'

Jama' and _Hasil-i Kamil_ of the _Zabti_ Provinces and Mughal Deccan

Scubas	*Zawabit-i Alamgiri*	*Br. Mues. Add.6598*	*Fraser-8*		*Jagjiwandas's Muntakhabut Tawarikh, Add.26253*	
	Jama	*Hasil-i Kamil*	*Jama'*	*Hasil-i Kamil*	*Jama'*	*Hasil-i Kamil*
-A-						
1. Awadh	32,13,17,199	36,50,20,440	32,13,17,819	36,90,23,640	32,13,17,119	36,50,26,040
2. Akbarabad	1,14,17,00,157	82,78,94,840	1,14,17,60,157	80,28,44,120	1,14,17,60,057	52,38,94,840
3. Shahjahanabad	1,22,29,50,177	1,24,04,86,160	1,22,29,50,137	1,24,04,86,160	1,22,29,50,658	27,39,64,400
4. Allahabad	45,65,43,278	42,39,06,840	45,65,43,248	42,38,93,640	45,65,43,248	42,39,34,840
5. Lahore	89,89,32,170	66,82,55,440	89,81,32,170	74,81,75,320	89,81,32,107	74,81,75,320
-B-						
1. Aurangabad	-	-	40,20,40,000	1,00,49,65,000	40,20,40,000	
2. Berar	-	-	38,46,52,360	81,40,25,000	36,06,56,160	
3. Khandesh	-	-	16,34,68,760	34,86,30,200	14,24,00,760	
4. Bedar	-	-	12,40,00,000	37,29,74,407	-	

Chapter - 5

Land Revenue System Under The Nawab Wazirs

Land revenue formed the major source of state income under the Nawab Wazirs. Its size varied according to circumstances such as the yields at particular harvests, fluctuations in prices and the effectiveness of the collection machinery. Buttler observed, "..... there are no fixed limits to the land-revenue or rent, which he (the king) levies from its occupants, save their inability or unwillingness to pay".[1]

We have no information regarding the magnitude of the land-revenue demand in relation to the produce of the land or in relation to the surplus generated by the peasant. What we get are only the rates of land-revenue per *bigha* in rupees. By taking the prices of the agricultural products prevalent in Awadh or in the adjacent territories under the East India Company, one can then perhaps have some idea about the size of the revenue in terms of the grain.

Buttler informs us that, "During that sovereign's (Saadat Ali, 1798-1814) life, the rent of good land varied from one to one and half rupee per *bigha*, now (c. 1836) the assessment is 2, 3 or 4 rupees per *bigha*, and can seldom be fully levied without the ruin, both to *rai'yat* and the *zamindar*".[2] At another place he praises the good and judicious administration of Saadat Ali and adds, "Since the death of Nawab Saadat Ali ... rent is fixed at such a rate ... generally 50 percent above that of former times".[3] But Heber

1. Buttler, *op. cit.*, p. 48. British officials saw the land-revenue or the rent; and the king was considered to be the actual proprietor of the land; "the sovereign is, agreeably to established Indian rule, the only acknowledged proprietor of the soil". Buttler, (p. 48). However, I have not found any native statement to this effect from Awadh.
2. Buttler, *op. cit.*, p. 54.
3. *Ibid.*

who toured the kingdom during 1825-27 says: "I asked (the *gumashta*) the rent per *bigha* of the land. He said, generally 4 rupees, but sometimes 6; and sometimes the peasant had all taken from him".[4] It appears that he had spoken to some one who had exaggerated the matter. The revenue rates prevalent in Tiloin Raj during 1836 indicate the extent of the exaggeration. In the Chattari estate of Tiloin, "the assessment (was) allowed to remain at the old standard of 2 rupees per *bigha* of old arable soil and one rupee for newly reclaimed land ...."[5]

Buttler tells us that revenue rates per *bigha* in Southern Awadh varied from 2 to 4 rupees; the latter rates, he deems to be rather harsh and difficult of realisation without the ruin of the payers.[6] At another place we come across the statement that because of the high revenue rates the peasants were left with little for their subsistance. They had not even been left with the resources to carry on cultivation and were forced to borrow seeds from the village bankers.[7] Bishop Heber wondered how under such extremely oppressive conditions the peasants could still carry on cultivation. Thereupon he was told, "what can they (the cultivators) do ? ... ... they must eat; and when they have put the seeds in the ground, they must wait till it comes up, and then take what they can get of it".[8]

Moreover, the peasants were obliged to pay certain other fiscal dues, which in turn formed the amount of recognised perquisites of the *zamindars*. Thus, the *faujdar* was, "authorised to levy for his own benefit a rupee from every *zamindar* ... this gratuity is called *bhent*".[9] The additional fiscal obligations claimed by the superior right holders from the peasants are discussed elsewhere.[10]

---

4. Heber, *op. cit.*, pp. 102-3.
5. For a detailed description of the administrative arrangements in Tiloin Raj see Buttler, pp. 109-114.
6. *Ibid.*, p. 54. As far as the size of the *bigha* is concerned, some local variations are noted by Buttler. But it seems that the revenue-rates and the productivity of the soil had been recorded in the standard unit of the pakka *bigha* (20 *lathas* x 20 *lathas*; each *latha* being of 100 inches). It would be unreasonable to think that the revenue rate or the productivity of the soil was recorded anywhere in *kacha bigha* which was only 40% of the former. However, the methods by which the revenue officials dealt with the local variation in the unit are not known. Buttler, pp. 82-83.
7. *Ibid.*, p. 49.
8. Heber, pp. 102-3.
9. Buttler, *op. cit.*
10. See the Chapters on the Nature of the Rights of the *Zamindars* and of the 'Revenue Grantees'.

Charles Elliott in his *Chronicles of Oonao* has given figures of land-revenue settled in that district by the 'Native Government' in 1855 and by the British in 1861. The figures suggest that the revenue levied by the Awadh authorities, at least in the first half of the 19th century, was not by any means more onerous than that levied by the British authorities, particularly since by 1861 the ravages of the mutiny and the subsequent scarcities had taken their toll. Elliott's figures are:[11]

Table - I

	Parganas	*1855 (in rupees)*	*1861 (in rupees)*
(i)	Bangarmau, etc. 3 *parganas*	2,99,240	2,99,033
(ii)	Fatehpur *Chaurasi* etc. 4 *parganas*	2,96,274	2,77,049
(iii)	Hurha, etc. 7 *parganas*	3,68,416	4,67,377
	Total	**9,63,930**	**10,33,364**

The Nawab Wazirs inherited the Mughal system of revenue assessment and collection and this seems to have been largely retained by them till at least 1765. After the battle of Buxar, Shuj'auddaulah was forced to sign a treaty with the British East India Company at Jajmau, near Kanpur. Apart from the political implications of the treaty, the most important financial clauses of the treaty stipulated a drastic reduction of the Nawab's army and the payment of large amounts to the Company for keeping its forces in Awadh. In spite of this new financial pressure, the traditional financial structure was maintained under Shujauddaulah. But his death in 1775 marks the turning point in the history of Awadh as the British got a fresh opportunity of imposing new demands upon his successor Asafuddaulah. Under these pressures the system of *mansab* and *jagir* inherited from the Mughal empire was abandoned, and the Awadh government had to make arrangements for direct collection of taxation everywhere.[12]

The system of the assessment was known as *tashkhis* while its collection from the payers bore the name *tahsil*. The amount of land revenue was assessed separately for *kharif* and *rabi* harvests. The revenue for the autumn crops was divided into five monthly instalments (*qist*), while for the spring

11. Elliott, p. 104. Jagdish Raj says, "Had this state of affairs continued (the one prevailing under the *nawab-wazirs*) much longer a general desolution of the country must have followed" [*JESHO*, 1958, p. 104]. This is open to question since he makes no comparisons with the revenue rates prevailing in Awadh before the annexation and immediately after it.

12. See especially Richard B. Barnett, *North India Between the Empire*, Berkley 1980, pp. 166-192; for a discussion on the methods of assessment and collection of the land-revenue system of the Nawabs of Oudh', *JESHO*, 1954, pp. 96-104; Purnendu Basu, *Oudh and the East India Company*, Lucknow, 1943, pp. 100-133.

crops the payment was demanded in four.[13] These nine instalments in total were payable at the new moons, between 11th September and 12th June of the succeeding year. This rule was followed very strictly by the officials. In case of the inability of the *zamindars* to pay the whole amount before the last lunar month (12th June) an invasion of his village was sanctioned by the *faujdar* and soldiers were sent to attach and sell away the entire property of the defaulting land-holders and *zamindars*.[14]

The key point in determining the amount of taxation was that it should be in confirmity with the previous year's assessment. The actual settlement with the *zamindars* took place in the month of December, as by that time the *rabi* crops were well forward, and an estimate could be made about the quality of the expected harvest. The *chakledar* ordered the *tahsildar* to gather the land-owners of his *pargana*, along with the village accountants and *qanungo* by a certain date, when the *chakledar* encamped on the spot to receive them. The scene in the tent of the *chakledar* is described in detail by Elliott. First of all the village accountant (*patwari*) used to give information as to how large an area of land of such and such crop was under cultivation. The *qanungo*, by his personal knowledge of the condition of the crops, would confirm the report of *patwari*. The *tahsildar* reported on the actual realisation made from the village during the previous year. At the same time he gave his opinion as to whether the amount of the land-revenue should be raised this year or not. Most often suggestion with some land-holder, who might be interested in taking the particular village on farm were also taken. Naturally, such suggestion were contested vehemently by the actual owners of that village who insisted that they were already ruined men and could not pay as much as had been paid last year. But in case the original owner wished to retain his village, he had to agree to make some settlement with the *chakledar* with some enhancement over the last year's figure. Otherwise the village was "settled" with the new land-holder who agrees to raise the amount of the tax. The trick often was that next year the *tehsildar* would report that the village had been very much over assessed, and recommend that the amount of demand be reduced to the original one, or even less than the actual realisation of the previous year.[15]

We get little information as regards the determination of the share of the burden placed on the individual peasant. Since the village was assessed

13. Elliott, *op. cit.*, pp. 137-9.
14. Buttler, *op. cit.*, pp. 100-101.
15. Elliott, *op. cit.*, pp. 137-9.

as a unit, there is every reason to believe that the distribution of taxes among individual peasants could have been very unequal and unjust. Moreover the system gave full liberty to the land-holders to deal with the peasantry as they thought fit.

Buttler informs us that the land-revenue was fixed on the basis of the actual cultivated area in *bigha*.[16] According to him, the reign of Nawab Sa'adat Ali (1798-1814) marked the watershed in the agrarian history of Awadh. With him departed, "the permanent prosperity of the country". This was now "sacrificed to the exigencies of the year, to the supineness and extravagance of the ruling powers, and to the rapacity of the temporary local authority. During that sovereign's life, the rent of good land varied from one to one and half rupee per *bigha*: now (1836) the assessment is 2, 3, or 4 rupees per *bigha* and can seldom be fully levied, without ruin, both to *ra'iyat* and *zamindar*".[17]

Apart from the relatively low revenue rates then prevailing, the peasants enjoyed some security of tenures under Sa'adat Ali Khan. The leases and acceptance were executed to run from 3 to 5 years.[18] These fiscal documents were signed, put under the seal, and verified by the various revenue officials such as the *zamindars, qanungos, diwan, faujdar* and *chakledar*.[19] But after the death of Sa'adat Ali in 1814 the entire picture underwent a change, as thereafter, "No lease has been granted for more than a year and rent is fixed at such a rate generally 50 percent above that of former times as to leave the farmer (peasants) little, beyond a bare subsistence".[20]

The Government officials most often made the revenue-settlements with the local Chieftains and the community brotherhoods. The local magnates remitted a fixed sum to the treasury, while it was left to them to assess and collect the amount from the other members of the communities. The most notable example of this class has been provided by Buttler in connection with the family of the *Chattari* Rajputs established at Tiloin in *chakla* Salon. The head of the brotherhood was Shankar Singh, styled Raja. He had to pay Rs 7,50,000 as land-revenue on behalf of the whole brotherhood. Each member of the fraternity paid his share of the land-revenue to him. The *chakledar* received this amount without any difficult. The peasants of the Tiloin estate were assessed very lightly, i.e. the rate of

16. Buttler, *op. cit.*, p. 54 and pp. 109-114.
17. Heber, *op. cit.*, pp. 102-3.
18. Buttler, *op. cit.*, p. 54.
19. *Ibid.*, p. 49.
20. Heber, pp. 100-1.

the arable land was Rs 2 per *bigha*, while one rupee was charged for newly reclaimed land. As a matter of fact it seems that since such estates had some hereditary interests, a fairly good and judicious system of revenue administration here prevailed. Buttler describes Tiloin as, "one pleasing oasis amidst this wide-spread social waste."[21] Probably because of the existence of such estates "the district of Salon has long enjoyed a degree of tranquility unknown to any other part of Oudh…".[22]

When the *nawab-wazirs* made arrangements for direct revenue collection through their own officials, they appointed the *'amils, nazims, chakledars* and *tehsildars*. These officials were expected to remit to the treasury whatever amount they could collect. No sum was specified as such. The system was known as *amanee* (trust management).

The revenue officers under the *amanee* system were almost free of any constraints of paying the specified sum in the public treasury. They could often enrich themselves at the expenses of both the *nawabs* and the land-holders. The only thing these were expected to do, was to pay large bribes to the court officials, so as to be sure that their accounts would be dealt with leniently. However, the history of Awadh, under the *amanee* system, to quote an English official, was, "a disgraceful tale of the shameless spoilation of the *ra'iyat* by all classes, from the minister, who stood behind the throne, to the lowest peon who served a process on the *zamindar*".[23] The system was so designed as to succeed only if the revenue officials worked honestly and were vigilantly supervised by the minister in charge of the revenue department. But in actual fact, if any minister ever tried to know anything, he could get no information as the, "news writers are in the pay of the *'amils* (being) generally their servants."[24] The system had to be given up in despair, as it impoverished the state while it had substantially increased the wealth of the revenue collectors. An idea could be gathered from the fact that as per testimony of an English official, Maddock, "the *nazrana* received by one minister (Mahmud-ud Daulah) amount(ed) to more than 17 lacs of rupees"; and he estimated that "the *'amil*'s share among them nearly 50 lacs of rupees yearly".[25] This state of affairs continued for long, and Lalji, protests at the unseemly behaviour of the *'amils* and the ineptitude of the high officials to cope with them. "The *'amils* of different

21. Buttler, pp. 109-114.
22. *Ibid.*
23. Montgomery, R., *Administrative Report of Oudh 1858-9*, p. 55, cited in *JESHO*, 1958, p. 101.
24. 'Kingdom of Oudh' *Calcutta Review*, Vol. III, 1845, p. 387.
25. *Ibid.*, p. 387.

area (misappropriate) lakhs of the rupees and (show) it under heads of the various proper and improper items of expenditure, while the authorities of the revenue department (in collusion with them) deal leniently with their accounts, and write-off the amount (as irrecoverable)."[26] Thus, the kingdom of Awadh was thus robbed of its resources by its own officials.

The visit of the *chakledar* in any area for the purpose of revenue collection was most dreaded by the *zamindars* as well as the peasants. For with him, "the work of plunder and devastation commences with the uproofing of the neighbouring villages, to supply temporary huts for his troops."[27] When the *chakledar* contemplated any move to raise the amount of land-revenue, it was usually resisted by the land-holders, "the *zamindars* and their immediate adherents at the same time"[28] took flight to the dense forests and mud forts, "surrounded by a ditch and dence fence of living bamboos, through which cannon shot cannot penetrate."[29] Buttler cites the example of the *zamindars* of Nain in *pargana* Salon. The *zamindar* Isri Singh punctually remitted a sum of Rs 1 lac as the land-revenue, still he thought it fit to maintain 3,000 men for collecting the land-revenue and fighting the *chakledar* when the necessity arose. The peasants were light assessed and held extensive farms varying from 20 to 100 *bighas*. In 1837, the *chakledar* Kunnanlal enhanced the demand by ten thousand rupees. Isri Singh, not agreeing to pay the enhanced rates, mustered his troops and held the village against the *chakledar*, until the approach of newly raised brigade of Colonel Roberts. The *zamindars* were now forced to retire to the neighbouring jungal, and his house was burnt down by the *chakledar*. On occasions, the refuges *zamindars* were forced to remain in jungals for years.[30]

The military element in the process of the revenue collection seems to have been always very important. Regular forces had to be maintained to ensure the realisation of the stipulated amount, these forces being known as the *mut'aiyanah*. In case these forces were thought insufficient at the time of the harvesting season, additional troops were recruited to assist the revenue collectors and revenue farmers. These additional recruits being called *sehbandi*.[31] The *sehbandi* troops were employed by the '*amils*

26. Lalji, *Miratul Auza*.
27. Buttler, *op. cit.*, pp. 51-54.
28. *Ibid.*
29. Sleeman, *op. cit.*, p. 267.
30. Buttler, *op. cit.*, p. 57.
31. Barnett, *op. cit.*, pp. 166-192.

as well as the agents of the *jagirdar* in the earlier period, at the approach of every harvesting season. A *qubuliyat* executed by the *ijaradar* for a *jagir* in *pargana* Sandilah in 1708, excludes the cost of maintaining the *sehbandi* troops from the total amount to be paid to the *jagirdar*.[32] In a document of Asaf-ud Daulah's reign, we find the revenue-collector saying that, "the *rabi* harvest is approaching and the (number) of the *sehbandi* troops in not adequate; so it is requested that one *taman* (contingent) be sent with Khwaja Bahman for the necessary work; when the *sehbandi* (troops) are recruited, the said *taman* will be returned".[33]

When Sleeman passed through the district of Sandilah in the course of his tour, he found the '*amil* of the district possessing a considerable force. The district was put under the *amanee* system and the '*amil* Husain Bakhsh had three regiments of *najibs* and twelve guns. The soldiers of these battalions, says Sleeman, "are a terrible scourge to the country – by for the worst that the country suffers under".[34] Although the soldiers were always expected to accompany the '*amils*, and there was hardly any occasion when their services were not needed in collection of the revenue, yet the troops and artillery was never kept in a working condition. The bullocks employed to carry the guns carriages were utterly useless, so much so that when Sleeman passed from the district, the '*amil* had to, "hire a few flough bullocks from the cultivators to draw out two guns to my camp to fire the salute".[35] With the help of such unorganised force, the revenue was collected with the utmost harshness, and in doing so all the limits were crossed. Revenue collection, it was said, "resembles rather the levying of tribute in a hostile country, than the enforcement of the claims of a lawful sovereign upon his own subjects".[36]

During the mid 19th century Awadh, Sleeman as well as Lalji are unequivocal in declaring the '*amils* and other revenue collection to be responsible for increase in banditry. The reasons for the ravages and the depredation of the country, says Lalji, "are that the settlement of the revenue upon those who pay it, is not made in accordance with their portions and

32. *NAI – 1487.*

33. Inamullah Raghib, *Ausaf-I Asaf*, MS. Abdul Salam Collection, Maulana Azad Library, AMU, ff. 72a-b.

34. Sleeman, *op. cit.*, p. 182.

35. Sleeman, *op. cit.*, p.

36. Edward Thornton, *A Gazetteer of the territories under the Government of the East India Company and the native states on the Continent of India*, London, 1854, p. 37.

shares in this country ... the '*amils* and the revenue contractors never respected the agreement and having the temptation to raise the amount, they never allowed the due share to the share holder".[37] At another place Lalji says that peace would have prevailed, "if the '*amil* had given half share to the rebel ...".[38] Sleeman too cited an instance from the district of Muhammadi, where the " '*amil* Khwaja Muhammad wanted to increase the rate of the government demand on the village from 400 to 450 – that they (the owners) refused to pay"[39] while another *talluqadar* of the locality agreed to pay the enhanced rate of revenue; and this led to the depredation and lawlessness in the area. The followers of one land-holder "attached, plundered and burnt down the village and killed his (the previous owner's) brother with his two sons".[40]

The revenue collectors had been held responsible on a number of occasions for their negligence in performing the duties, and giving a free hand to depredators, and highway robbers. Sleeman indeed charges the '*amil* of Dureeabad Girdhara Singh for his, "notoriously conniving at these crimes (gang-robbery) from a consciousness of utter inability to contend with the land-holders who commit them".[41] At the same time, we are informed that he had a big force at his disposal, "sufficient to keep in order a district five times as large".[42] His forces included one *jannisar* battalion, *zulfiqar* battalion, and the *jadeed* battalion. Nine guns and a squadron of horses were also kept by him.[43]

The fact was that the '*amils* and other revenue officials were often in collusion with the leaders of the robber-gangs. In the course of his tour Sleeman found, at many places that, "ruffians residing in the same or the neighbouring village", were to be found in the camp of '*amil*".[44] Even if the '*amils* were not in league with such elements, they "get their (robbers ?) aid in punishing defaulters or the pretended defaulters among the land-holders".[45] The support extended by them to the '*amils*, helped the latter to

37. The third section of the chapter two of *Mirat-ul-Auza* is entitled, "A description of the occurrences of depredations and murder as a result of the arbitrary manner of the '*amils* and revenue collectors", ff. 118-228.

38. *Ibid.*, f. 13a.

39. Sleeman, Vol. II, pp. 221-2.

40. *Ibid.*

41. *Ibid.*

42. *Ibid.*

43. *Ibid.*

44. *Ibid.*

45. *Ibid.*

realise the land-revenue with little difficulty; and in reward of this, he shut his eyes to their activities. The '*amil* of Dureeabad Raja Girdhara Singh, says Sleeman, "acquieces in all the atrocities committed by these robbers, and is in consequence, able to collect his revenues and secure the favours of the court".[46]

The revenue collectors used to make conciliatory gestures towards the big land-holders so as to make them agree to pay the land-revenue. They even went to the extent of giving an absolute increase in their share of *nankar*, which was quite contrary to the royal orders. They bribed the high and influential officials at the court to get sanction for the increased share of the *nankar*. In case, it was not sanctioned, the offending land-holder "takes to the *jungles* and declares that he will resist till his permanent right to the increase (of the *nankar*) be acknowledged".[47]

Misuse of the military force by the revenue-collectors was common occurrence. The land-holders of even unoffending villages could be attacked by the powerful '*amils* in order to reduce their forts. In case of any difficulty in quelling these *zamindars*, the revenue officers were at liberty to ask the commandant of the English forces for, "sending him the aid of two battalions and heavy artillery".[48] The English civil and military officers were advised to exercise the utmost caution before they complied "with the requisition of the *aumil*".[49] The English resident to the court of Awadh lord Baillie informed the governor general in 1808 that, "he sanctioned it (use of British troops) after a careful and minute investigation of each and every case".[50] Yet British arms and troops were employed so indiscriminately by the '*amils* in punishing the 'pretended rebels' and devastating the country that it was suggested by Paton in 1833 that such assistance be discontinued altogether.[51]

An off-shoot of the *amanee* system was the *qabz* system. The *nazim* used to assign a portion of the land from his estate to the commandant of the troops in order to collect the revenue and pay salaries to his troops. Since the soldiers know it to be their only means of livelihood, they used to collect the amount with the utmost harshness.[52] Sleeman describes, in detail,

46. Sleeman, Vol. II, pp. 221-2.
47. *Ibid.*
48. *Foreign Secret Consultations* (iii), 8th Jan. 1778, *NAI*, Delhi.
49. *Ibid.*
50. *JESHO*, 1958, p. 101.
51. *Ibid.*
52. Sleeman, *op. cit.*, pp. 140-1.

the *Lakulame qabz* (pledge to collect and pay a certain sum, for which the estate is held liable; the Persian term being presumably *la-kalami qabz*) and the *wasuli qabz* (pledge to pay the collector or troops a sum which the commandant may be able to collect). In the second method the work of revenue collection was carried out by the commandant and his soldiers. Sleeman observes, "if they can't collect it from the sale of all the crops of the season, they seize and sell the stock and the property of all kinds to be found on the estate; and if this will not suffice, they will not scruple to seize and sell the women and children".[53] Still quite strangely this system was thought to be less oppressive to the peasantry than the actual collection of the land-revenue by the *nazim* of that area himself.[54] Lalji explains, the actual mechanism of the *qabz* system:

If any "Officer" (*afsar*) of the military forces posted in the area had amounts outstanding for payment of the salaries of the troops, he would submit the *qabz* for one lac of rupees before the '*amil*.

Lalji says that if an officer of the artillery had a sum of Rs 10,000-15,000 outstanding, he would make a claim for one lac of rupees and take control of an area with that *jama*' by submitting a *qabz* for one lac. With his taking charge the oppression of the *raiyat* would commence as instead of one rupee, one and half would be demanded from them. The *zamindars* and *taalluqdars* were also penalised in various ways. A number of perquisites were levied by the commandant under various excuses, such as *rusum-i qabzana, residana, talbana* and *sazawalana*. The officers alone were the beneficiaries of these arrangements, says Lalji, the troops were to remain satisfied with their pay, and that too on occasions remained unpaid for 6 months or so for a year. Sometimes the entire amount was kept by the officers, and the soldiers got nothing.[55]

W.H. Sleeman cited an example from the district of Sultanpur regarding the *qabz* system. The *nazim* Wajid Ali assisted one lady Bibi Sughra, the head of the Munuapur estate. Although she remitted Rs 50,000 regularly to the Government, she was made to enter into agreement with a body of the troops to pay them 10 months pay out of the revenue-collections of the ensuing year. The troops were to give the receipts for the full amount of the arrears of their pay. These receipts, in turn, were to be forwarded to the *darbar* as the *nazim* Wajid Ali might get credit for the amount in his previous

53. Sleeman, *op. cit.*, pp. 140-1.

54. *Ibid.*

55. Lalji, *op. cit.*, ff. 43a-44b.

years accounts. As Sughra could collect only Rs 15,000 from the tenants since their crops were destroyed by these troops, she was put into confinement and was subjected to most cruel indignities.

It should not be assumed that this was a solitary instance; such practices were a common phenomenon among the *nazims* of the district. They borrowed large sums on the basis of the revenues of the ensuing year. The work of revenue-collection was entrusted to the troops whose pay claims had fallen into the arrears. It was common for these troops either to destroy the crops or to extract the double amount from the debtors. This practice was said to be "the source of much evil".[56]

The *qabz* system was introduced only when the *mustajirs* and '*amils* were unable to enforce payment in any way. The commandants of the troops, when taking possession of their assignment, appropriated the whole produce for themselves. They had little regard for the rights of the *zamindars* or the peasants. As the side-effect of the system, the troops were rendered unfit for any sort of military service as all their time was consumed in making arrangements in their respective 'estates'. The soldiers as well as the officers were converted into "manorial under stewards of the worst possible description".[57] They used to extract every possible penny from the payment that might become due to them within the course of time. Out of these collections only a portion was remitted to the Government, the rest was consumed by the troops and their officers. In spite of the number of evils with which the *qabz* system was beset, it was very common in the kingdom of Awadh and was getting even more widespread during the 19th century.[58]

It should not be assumed that the *amanee* system of revenue-administration had such inbuilt defects as to inhibit its operation everywhere. The experiment made by Mir Hasan 'Londoni' working at the Residency, to implement this system in *pargana* Bijnore was quite successful, at least for a year and is worth recording. During the reign of Amjad 'Ali Shah, he complained of the mis-management of the kingdom. Hearing of this, Nawab Aminuddaulah, the prime minister, suggested to him that he should take the assignment of an area and implement the proposed reforms there. He agreed to the proposal on the condition, that there should be no interference from any quarter. Accordingly, he was entrusted the '*ilaqa* of Bijnore.

56. Sleeman, Vol. I, p. 86.

57. *Ibid.*, Vol. I, p. 86.

58. *Ibid.*, Vol. I, pp. 84-86.

Although its total *jama'* was about one lac of rupees, its villages had been ruined through oppression, and the total realisation from the area never exceeded Rs 50,000. Mir Hasan himself made a tour of the area, contrary to the practice of sending only the revenue officials, and executed *qubuliyats* with the *zamindars* and the *ijaradars*, wherever the latter held farms. Hearing this, these hereditary *zamindars*, who had abandoned their villages as a result of the rapacity of the previous *'amils*, returned and entered into agreements with Mir Hasan. He established such a judicious system of the revenue collection in the area, that the *zamindars* used to send the revenue to the treasury without any demand or *talbana* being sent to them. At the end of the year Mir Hasan was able to deposit Rs 70,000 in the *nawab*'s treasury after meeting all the expenses incurred in the administrative arrangements. The peasants of the area became quite prosperous and acts of banditary and bloodshed became fewer. The outstanding success achieved by Mir Hasan was taken as a challenge to their authority by the officials and the court favourites. Hence he was relieved of his assignment and new officials were appointed in his place. Under the new officials the territory returned to the situation in which Mir Hasan had found it.[59]

The working of the *amanee* system was directly controlled by the high officials of the Nawab. The *amalguzars* were appointed by these '*amils* with the consent of these officials. They were expected to collect the revenue as per village papers; and at the end of the year whatever collection could be made was remitted to the treasury of the *nawab*. If any amount was left to be realised, it was debited to the account of these *malguzars*. Apart from collecting of the revenue, they were expected to make customary gifts to the '*amils* and his establishment.

During the later period of the Awadh administration the *amanee* system became subject to as many evils as the *ijara* system. When the authorities used to assign an area to the '*amil* under this system, they used to take an *iqrarnamah* from him, just as the *mustajirs* used to give *qubuliyat*. The '*amil*'s *iqrarnamah* was the effect that a stipulated amount of *jama'* would be paid to the treasury at the end of the year and in case of his failure to discharge the obligation, he was to be held responsible for the default. The *nawabi* establishment attached to the *amani* district had little say in the affairs of the '*amil*. The '*amil* used to realise large amount of customary gifts which were above to the amount stated in *iqrarnamah*. Thus, large fortunes might be made by '*amils* from such extra levies. After the appointment of the '*amil* to an *amani* district, he would show large amounts

59. Sleeman, ff. 16b-19a.

of deductions on account of the expeditions sent against the *ta'allugadass*; similarly a number of fictitious accounts were submitted to the court. On occasion the slackness of the state's supervision over the activities of these '*amils*, emboldened them so much that they realised the revenues of an '*ilaqa*, but did not pay anything into the *nawab*'s treasury. Induced Lalji laments that the *riaya* suffer more hardship in the hands of these '*amils*, than by the revenue collectors of the *mustajirs*."[60]

Often revenue arrangements were made with large community-brotherhoods in the areas where caste ties were strong. Their chiefs, styled Rajas, in their turn made agreements with the heads of their minor branches. Areas, where such arrangements existed, were free from the interference of the *chakledars* and '*amils*, that the peasants enjoyed some security of tenures. The rate of assessment, too, remained as we have already seen in one case, "at the old standard of 2 Rs Per *bigha* of old arable soil and 1 Re Per *bigha* for newly reclaimed land; generally, the rates in such estates was about two-thirds of what prevailed elsewhere.[61] Francis Buchanan in his survey of the Mughal *sarkar* of Gorakhpur found that the hereditary chiefs pay revenues to the treasury or the '*amils* as the case might be, while they "managed their estates by letting each *mauza* or *deh* to a *birtia* or *Sikmi*."[62] These *birties* were the hereditary chiefs of their brotherhoods, and the arrangement was made with the brotherhoods rather than with the individual chiefs, as the ablest member of the brotherhood was chosen by the members themselves to represent their interest with the *raja*. In case of his discharging the duties dishonestly, his dismissal could be procured by other members of the brotherhood. In case the *raja* was dissatisfied with the conduct of the *birtia*, he would appoint a *mahto* from the same clan to perform duties in place of the dismissed *birtia*. In such arrangements the proprietary rights of the peasants were not protected as they could be evicted at the will of the *raja*, and the *qubuliyats*, if made, ran for a short period. Still since most of the cultivators were the members of the same brotherhood, and the *raja* had to depend upon their support at times of emergency, oppression of the peasants in respect of tenure and assessment was often avoided. In course of time, due to the internal conflicts and laxity of caste-ties and the effects of indebtedness, the power of the local chiefs (*rajas*) faded away. This process, in turn, offered an opportunity to the '*amils* and revenue officials of the *nawab-wazir* to assert their authority over the chieftains in demanding

60. Sleeman, ff. 22b-25a.

61. Buttler, pp. 109-114.

62. Martin, *op. cit.*, p. 546.

regular payment of the revenues. The situation was supposedly tolerable under Shuja'uddaula, but Asafuddaulah farmed out the entire region to one Col. Hanny, on the recommendation of the Governor General. This gentleman adapted such "violent measures in the collection, as to depopulate the country". The traces of such destruction of the country's agriculture were to be perceived even after a number of years.[63]

The system of making arrangements with the local chieftains seems to have continued in the southern districts of Awadh during the first half of the 19th c. Buttler, while describing the unique administration of the Tiloin estate of Salon district, says that the chief of the *chattari* family was one Shankar Singh, who was styled Raja of Tiloin. He used to pay Rs 7,50,000 for the whole Tiloin *zamindari* to the *chakledar*. The payment was made regularly without giving any pretence to the *chakledar* for making any attempt at undue exaction. The five brothers of Shankar Singh were also courteously styled *rajas*, while his nephews were called *Thakurs*, they remitted the specified revenues of their share to Shankar Singh punctually. In case the sub-*zamindars* showed any defiance, he was, "left to be dealt with by the *chakledar*, who puts him in fetters, and levies the rent from the *ra'iyat*". The *zamindar* was not released, "until he (gave) security for the future regular payment".[64] Apart from such occasions, the *chakledar* could never make any undue demand from the *zamindars*. This being known to the neighbouring *zamindar* as well, "they sometimes make successful appeals at Lucknow, against the *chakledars*' exactions".[65]

Besides the above revenue arrangements, the chief method employed under the *nawab-wazirs* for the purpose of revenue collection was the *ijara* or contract system. By employing this method, the *nawabi* Government ensured a fixed amount for treasury establishment. Under this system the *muta'iynah* and the *sehbandi* troops were maintained and paid for by the revenue farmers themselves.[66] Even the hereditary officers serving in the *ijara* villages were also paid their salaries by the revenue-contractors.[67]

63. Martin, pp. 546-48.

64. Buttler, pp. 109-114.

65. *Ibid.*, p. 114.

66. A *qubuliyat* deed executed in 1116F/1708, by one Diler Khan for a *jagir* in *pargana* Sandila, stipulates a payment of Rs 22,000 to the *jagirdar*. This excluded the cost of maintaining *she-bandi* troops and *peshkash* to *faujdar*. *NAI-1487* (1116/1708).

67. *NAI-1287* (1254/1838). This *parwana* was issued to the *chakledar* of Sandila to enquire the complaint of a village *patwari* regarding his pay claims against the *mustajir*.

The system had become so popular that the land-grantees (*a'immadars*) started making farming arrangements with the *mustajirs* in the villages of their grants.[68] The *ijaradars* had of course, no salary or land grant in view of the services performed by him but as Buttler put it, "the difference between the sum, which he has for the year engaged to pay into the public treasury", and the amount which, with the military power of the state at his command he can levy from the *zamindar*, constituted his income.[69] In case of the natural calamities the *ijaradar* could be provided some relief by allowing a deduction, and by not insisting for the full amount for which the contract had been made.

In theory the contractors could have an interest in improving the lot of the peasantry and raising the productivity of the soil, thus to generate a larger peasant's surplus. The tenure of the contract was for a number of years and an increase in capacity of the peasants would have benefited the contractors themselves. But this was not so in practice. Wajid Ali, the *nazim* of Partapgarh, under whose *ijara* lay the *ta'alluqa* of Mundone in *pargana* Nawabgunj, discouraged the cultivation of the district in the hope that none else should venture to farm the revenues of the district with such a scanty tillage and so he would go on retaining the contract on more favourable terms.[70] The treasury incurred heavy losses on account of the oppressions of these contractors, but the high officials of the state too were a party in such designs. Wajid Ali, the *nazim*, had a balance of Rs 12 lacs, when he was replaced by another *nazim*; but says Sleeman, he would get the balance written-off from his name by paying Rs 2 lacs in bribe to the minister and other influential persons at the court, and just paying Rs one lac to the treasury. Ironically, there was no bar imposed upon his getting a contract for some other district subsequently.[71]

During the last quarter of the eighteeth century about 85 percent of the total *jama'* of the kingdom of Awadh was formed out to the revenue contractors. About c. 1780 there were 18 big and small contractors, but the bulk of the territory was in the hands of four revenue farmers controlling 65 percent of the total *jama'*. These were Almas Ali Khan, 'Ainuddin Khan,

68. *FM-84* (4th R.Y. of Farrukhsiyar). The village in question belonged to Mulla Nizamuddin and was situated in *sarkar* Bahraich, while the grantee's headquarters happened to be at Lucknow. (Firangi Mahal papers are preserved in the Department of History, AMU, Aligarh).

69. Buttler, p. 99.

70. Sleeman, pp. 114-5.

71. *Ibid.*

Bhawani Singh and Ghulam Husain Khan. The table prepared by R.B. Barnett is reproduced here (as table - II) to show the relative position of the contractors and the deductions claimed by these revenue farmers in c. 1780. Since most of the columns are self explanatory, they need no comments. However, it should not be assumed that the cost of the collection (25.2% of the total *jama*' collected) and the deductions (12.9% of the total *jama*' collected) claimed by the contractor had in any way increased during this period.[72] There exists a *qubuliyat* dead executed in 1116F/1708 by one Dilawar for a *jagir* in *pargana* Sandilah, having a *jama*' of 41 lacs *dams* (= Rs 1,02,500). In all, excluding the cost of maintaining the *sebhandi* troops and *peshkash* to *faujdar*, Rs 22001 were to be paid to the *jagirdar* in two instalments[73] - here, therefore, the 'military' expenses amounted to well above 20 percent.

Buchanan in his survey of Gorakhpur points out that the '*amils* appointed by the *nawab*'s government generally took the revenues on farm from the government. They then made their own settlements with the land-holders for the period of their tenure. But these agreements were hardly ever respected as the intentions of the contracting parties were contradictory; the '*amils* wanted to establish their authority over the chieftains by pretending a settlement, while the land-holders sought to procure the help of the '*amil* against their adversaries. Although the '*amils* dealt with these chiefs quite firmly, they did not wish generally as to lower their prestige and status. Such a policy on part of the '*amils* had created such conditions that the actual amount of the revenue was ... quite unconnected with the settlement."[74] Often, it was that "some governors ('*amils*) were unable to collect as much revenue as they paid to the nawab".[75] But generally, the '*amils* used to accumulate a great deal of wealth and power during the tenure of their contract of which they were often deprived of all on their return to the capital.[76]

During the first half of the nineteenth century, the *nazims* and *chakledars* generally held entire districts on contract, all the big and small estates of the district falling under their jurisdictions. These officers enjoyed practically unlimited powers in their dealings with the *ta'alluqadars*. Indeed, the visit of the *chakledar* to a village of the land-holders was thought to be a natural calamity, and the *zamindars* used often to prepare for battle

72. R.B. Barnett, pp. 181-191.
73. *NAI-1487*.
74. Martin, Vol. II, p. 549.
75. *Ibid*.
76. *Ibid*.

at the news of the approach of an oppressive *chakledar*. Generally, the *zamindar* retired to the neighbouring jungal with his family and immediate retainers after making a summary levy of the revenues from the cultivators. But on such occasions the *chakledar*, too, used to realise the Government dues from the poor peasants, who had already paid the levy to the *zamindars*.[77]

Table - II

Revenue farmers in c. 1780, and the cost of collecting the land revenues and deduction allowed to the contractors.

			1		*2*	
Sl. No.	*Farmer's name*	*Ijara*	*Gross jama' in Rs*	*Percent of of the Total Jama'*	*Deductions in 1779-80 of Jama' in Rs*	*Percent*
1.	Almas 'All Khan	Kara Shara	64,60,831	23.2	500,000	7.7
2.	'Ainuddin Khan	Bareili	50,00,000	17.9	575,000	11.5
3.	Bhawani Singh	Bainswara	38,78,748	13.9	301,089	7.8
4.	Muhammad Husain Khan	Gorakhpur/ Bahraich	21,82,904	7.8	810,904	37.1
5.	Mirza Ali Raza	Khairabad	10,50,371	3.8	100,317	9.6
6.	Maiku Singh	Dalmau, Bareili	8,34,891	3.0	129,151	15.5
7.	Ismail Beg Khan	Allahabad	7,06,000	2.5	59,000	8.4
8.	Mirza Nur Beg	Azamgarh/ Mahaul	6,64,864	2.4	139,063	20.9
9.	Mirza Mehdi	Sandila/ Malihabad	5,17,161	1.9	158,301	30.6
10.	Nawab Muzaffar Jang	Farrukhabad	4,50,000	1.6	—	—
11.	Jhau Lal	Sansi	3,67,800	1.3	67,800	18.4
12.	Amber Ali Khan	Anhuna/ Sandila	3,28,280	1.2	—	—
13.	Mir Nahim Khan	Kursi	3,24,326	1.2	146,821	45.3
14.	Khahim Khan	Pali	2,25,776	0.8	—	—
15.	Chait Singh	Khairagarh	2,00,000	0.7	—	—
16.	Isma'il Beg Khan	Mahmuda	1,50,000	0.5	—	—
17.	Kewal Ram	Manalari	1,20,000	0.4	38,895	32.4
18.	Mir Ali Khan	Mahaur	49,578	0.2	—	—
	Total		**2,35,11,565**	**84.3**	**30,26,396**	**12.9**

77. Buttler, pp. 50-1.

Reserved Asaf's Account	***Reserved, Company's Account***	***Mughal Charges, Transport, Crops etc.***	***Percent of Jama'***	***Percent of Jama or Actually Collected***
5,00,000	26,00,000	19,99,669	30.9	61.3
-	25,00,000	6,37,141	12.7	75.8
8,74,004	13,00,000	11,10,393	28.7	63.6
-	10,00,000	4,76,553	21.8	40.1
-	3,32,000	5,85,170	55.7	34.7
4,04,796	-	2,54,695	30.5	54.0
-	3,50,000	1,61,313	22.8	68.8
-	1,50,000	3,92,285	59.0	20.1
-	2,00,000	1,46,016	28.2	41.2
-	5,50,000*	61,276	13.6	86.4
1,69,355	-	1,04,860	27.9	53.7
2,55,357	-	69,712	21.2	78.8
66,048	-	None**	—	54.7
4,75,776+++	-	None++	—	?
-	2,00,000	4,890	2.4	96.9
1,50,000	-	None++	—	?
81,105	-	None++	—	67.6
-	-	6,196	12.5	87.3
29,76,620 (10.7% of the total *Jama*')	1,06,62,000 (45.4% of all forms)	59,30,274	25.2	61.9

* Includes increase of Rs 2,50,000 over the previous year

† Includes unpaid balance from previous year

‡ Apparently under *huzūr* (direct) collection.

Chapter - 6

The *Zamindars*

(a) *Zamindari* Rights and their Nature

The zamindars formed a hereditary class of superior rights holders. There were a number of local synonyms used to designate the holders of these rights in Awadh. For example, the term *satarhi* appears in our documents as an interchangeable word for *zamindari* under the formula, '*zamindari* known as *satarhi*.[1] In the earliest available sale-deed from Akbar's reign (988/1580 AD) we find a group of 13 *muqqaddams* selling jointly their *satarhi* known as *biswi*' in the village of Manchankapur in *pargana* Sandila.[2] In another sale-deed (994/1586 AD), the term *milk* has been used for *satarhi* so that the right alienated is styled '*milk-dar-imlak-e-satarhi*'.[3] In yet another sale-deed of the 17th century, the word *milkiyat* has been put as an equivalent for *satarhi*, but the papers from the subsequent century (c. 1763) use the same formula with the addition of a conjunction viz., '*milkiyat* and *zamindari* known as *satarhi*', thus seemingly making *milkiyat* and *zamindari* into two distinct rights.[4] A sale-deed (c. 1720) speaks of '*milkiyat* rights, in *satarhi*' and other *zamindari* rights as two different things.[5] The Persian word *haftdehi* (one-seventeenth) is also found as a literal equivalent of the word *satarhi* during the later period.[6]

---

1. *Allahabad 310* (1198/1783) and *415* (1198/1783).
2. *RAA-1165* (968/1580 AD).
3. *Allahabad-317* (994/1585) by this deed, some Brahmans had sold their, *milk-dar-imlak-e-satarhi and sai*' of the ten villages to one Miyan Aman for a consideration of 1560 *sikka-e-muradi*. The rights and the privileges transferred by way of this deed were numerous.
4. *Allahabad-435* (1110/1698).
5. *Bilgiram-40*.
6. *Allahabad-199*.

Another set of sale-deeds from *pargana* Bilgram, *sarkar* Lucknow, give the formula *milk-i-khoti* (proprietary right in *khoti*) to designate the superior rights in village. The earliest of these documents (c. 1540) sets out the sale *milk-i-khoti* of a certain village for 100 *tanka 'Adli.* These rights included control over trees, streams, ponds and water channels.[7] Again in two 18th century transactions, the term *milk* had been applied to denote fiscal perquisites. These included rights over trees, streams, ponds, *mahat* and *khaildari* water and jungle rights (*jalkar* and *bankar*).[8]

Eighteenth century sale-deeds from *pargana* Sandila, *sarkar* Lucknow lead us to infer that *milkiyat* rights derived from *satarhi* and other superior rights were quite different from the right to appropriate the land-revenue (*haqq-e-akhaz-e-kharaj*) as these two rights over the same village could be sold separately. In 1759, one Shah Muhammad Akbar Ali sold his *milkiyat* right derived from *satarhi* and other *zamindari* rights over two *bighas* of land in village Khajurpati, *pargana* Sandila, for the sum of Rs 6. But the right to appropriate the land-revenue over the same land was not sold then. This was subsequently transferred in exchange for a plot of the residential land in 1763. But in the same year this plot of residential land too was sold in consideration of the sum of Rs 15.[9] From these figures, we may take it that, assuming these prices to represent the capitalised values, the *zamindar*'s income from his own rights was about two-fifth of the land-revenue. Surely, it was not an insubstantial amount.

As for the substance of the *zamindari* rights the documents from Sandila, Bilgiram and Khairabad established the fact that possession of village ponds, and water channels,[10] including water products such as *Shali-e-abi-Khudrau*

7. *Sharaif-e-'Usmani*, p. 120.

8. The sale-deed (c. 1716) records that the 17 *biswa mata*' of village Posinda and 15 *biswa mata*' of village Shaikhanpur was in *haqq-wa-milk* of the executants by virtue of the inheritance. These rights were sold in consideration of Rs 650 only. See *Ibid.*, p. 82. While in another deed (c. 1741) 6 *biswa mata*' of village Bhanknapur was mortgaged for Rs 77. The buyer was to enjoy the benefits of *malikana* from crops, *mehat, khaildari, jalkar* and *bankar* till he gets back the amount of mortgage. *Bilgiram-64* (1154-1741).

9. *Allahabad-355* (c. 1759), *439* (c. 1763) and *443* (1763). Of course there are other cases as well, where the *zamindari* rights and the right to appropriate the land-revenue were sold separately. But as a result of gaps in the chain of the documents a comparison with the capitalised value of the *zamindari* rights could not be attempted. In 1760 one Ain-ud-din sold the *zamindari* rights over one *bigha* for Rs 3 excluding the right to appropriate the land revenue, which was subsequently sold in exchange of a residential plot of land. See *Allahabad-432* (1760) and *444* (1766).

10. In every deed selling the *zamindari* rights in Awadh for these three centuries always

(*Contd...*)

('self-grown' paddy crop in water) and *mahigiri* (fishing rights) flowed from the possession of superior right over the village. A sale-deed of c. 1580, which we have referred to earlier also, specifically speaks of the sale of the right to collect the self-grown paddy crop in water, alongwith *satarhi* rights of village Manchanchapur.[11] Similarly, another sale-deed (c. 1769) records the sale of '*milkiyat-wa-zamindari* known as *satarhi*, 'of the village Tamorkha alongwith the fiscal-claims over *Shali-e-abi* (water paddy) and *Mahigiri* (fishing).[12] If members of the menial caste trespassed on this perquisite of the superior-right holders, they were obliged to pay some fine in addition to the *malikana* perquisites. A *ba'inama* executed by a group of *kahars* (c. 1638) of *pargana* Sandila contains a pledge to pay Rs 18 in cash and 35 mounds of *Shali-e-abi* on account of their unauthorised poaching in the Jatar Tank in village Mahsona. They further undertook to pay annually Rs 7 and 35 mounds of the said crop to the heirs of the Qazi. In case of default, the heirs were at liberty to evict the *kahars* from the pond.[13] Fishermen were similarly required to pay a fixed amount by way of *malikana* to the holders of the superior rights in case they made use of the ponds and tanks situated in their villages. A *parwana* issued to the *gumashta* (agent) of the *jagirdars* of Sandila (c. 1612) records that since the time the village of Mahsona had been made over to Qazi Abdul Razzaq and his brothers, one Sita *mehtar* along with his group of fishermen had been fishing in the ponds of the said village without paying any amount by way of *haqq-e-malikana* to the Qazi. It was ordered that the trespassers be directed to use the ponds only with the permission of the Qazi and should pay him the amount of *malikana* for the use of the ponds on the previous occasions as well.[14] From a *hukmnamah* (c. 1846), it appears that even a legal remedy was available to the superior right holders against any encroachment upon such perquisites.[15]

At the same time separate proprietary rights over water-use could also exist. Indeed an imperial *farman* of Shahjahan (c. 1629) forbids the *shiqdar* of the village *pargana* Sandila from dismissing one Asi, a *kahar* by caste,

---

contained a recitation regarding the sale of wells, pond, tanks and likewise other things. Indeed in some documents wells, ponds, and tanks are styled as the 'necessary paraphernilia of the village (.............)', *NAI-2125* (c. 1667).

11. *RAA-1165* (c. 1580). In this deed the sale of the 'Wells streams and the paddy crop grown in water' has been listed alongwith a number of other rights.

12. *Ibid.*

13. *NAI-1454.*

14. *NAI-1596.*

15. *NAI-1398.*

from the office of the *muqqadami* (headship) of the said village. It also purports to recognise the hereditary right of the said *muqqadam* over the village. He was permitted to carry on cultivation of the water paddy in the pond-bed on the usual payment of Rs 30. No enhancement in the amount of the *salana* as demanded by the *shiqdar* was allowed.[16] In a letter of agreement from Bilgiram (c. 1715) one party gave up every claim of using the tank and its water for all time to come. The claim was recognised as the exclusive right of the other party who was to use it for irrigating his *khud-kashta* land.[17] In case the other peasants utilised this facility, they had to pay a fixed rate or *haqq-e-dastur* to the *zamindar*. In a statement of facts presented by the *zamindar* (c. 1858) it is alleged that a rate of one *ser* (of produce) per *bigha* from everyone selling up a *nova* (boat like scoop) to water their fields from the tank of village Panwaria, *pargana* Khairabad used to had been realised by the petitioning *mutawalli*.[18]

In addition to land-revenue, the peasants were required to pay some amount in cash as well as in kind to the superior-right holders under the name of *dami* and *satarhi*. In a letter of agreement executed by a group of *karindas* (cultivators) of the village Korna (*pargana* Sandila) (c. 1746) it was agreed that 10 *sers* (of produce) per *bigha* and on account of *dami*, 1 *fulus* (a copper coin) per *bigha* would be paid on account of *satarhi*. The *karinda* also agreed to deliver 50 maunds of grain and 7 rupees in cash annually to the claimants of these rights.[19]

Other perquisites of the *zamindars* extended to fruit bearing and non-fruit bearing trees. "Orchards, wells, tanks etc." were designated as "the assets of a village" (*lawazima-i deh*) in *pargana* Unao in 1667.[20] If a fort or a *garhi* existed in any village, it also fell under the jurisdiction of these

16. *NAI-1646*, Here '*muqqadami*' had been recognised as, hereditary property' (*milk*) of the complainants. It is not clear that whether the pond in question was attached to the office of the *muqqadami* or it was in the other hereditary possession.

17. *Bilgiram-71* (c. 1715), The parties to the agreement seem to have been members of the religious class. It is quite possible that the tank in question was acquired through some *aimma* grant.

18. *Khairabad-9* (c. 1858), Iqbal Husain, 'A calendar of Khairabad documents: 16th-19th centuries, *Islamic Culture*, Vol. LIII (I) & (ii), Hyd. 1979.

19. *RAA-442* (c. 1746), The total amount of the grain to be delivered was fixed at 50 *mans* for the whole year. In the *kharif harvest it came to 25* mans; *10 maunds of rice, 10 maunds of millets and* mash *5 maunds. Of the 25 maunds to be delivered from* rabi *crop, the claim from wheat was 7* maunds; gram 8 maunds; and barley 9 maunds. As for cash Rs 7 were to be paid in the whole year, half of the amount at cash harvest. See also Irfan Habib, *Agrarian System*, p. 145.

20. *NAI-2125* (c. 1667).

proprietors. We notice in a 16th century sale-deed that a fort was also sold by the *zamindars* along with their *satarhi* rights of a village in *pargana* Sandila.[21]

The income from these various claims amounted to a fairly substantial sum, so that when a *zamindar* was by-passed by the revenue authorities, he was deemed to be entitled to some compensation. Thus, *malikana* was defined as, "a right of the *zamindar*, when the (authorities) convert his land into *sir*, and give him (something) on account of his being *malik* out of every hundred *bighas* or every hundred *mans* of grain".[22] If the *zamindars* himself happened to be the revenue payer (and that land was converted into *sir*) he was allowed only *nankar* instead of *malikana*.[23] The rates of the *malikana*, when made in cash, was 10 percent of the total revenue collected, and if land was to be allotted on the said account, it came to two *biswas* in every *bigha* or again 10 percent of the land. A *sanad* (c. 1595) records the grant of 29 *bighas* land to a group of persons on account of *malikana*, in a village when revenue had been remitted (*ma'af*) to the grantees.[24]

The *zamindars* on account of their rendering service' in collecting the land revenue from the peasants and remitting the same to the state treasury, used to get an authorised share known as *nankar*. Either the *zamindar* was allowed a deduction of 10 percent of the total collection or he was assigned some land revenue-free. Surely such grants would have been made in proportion to the claims of the *zamindars*.[25] The concept of *zamindari* as *Khidmat* (service) and *nankar* as *haqq-ul*-khidmat brings the entire right closer to the office of Chaudhari. The latter official too, helped the administration in the same sphere. On this account this allowance payable to the *chaudharies* was also known as *nankar*.[26] In a *parwana* (c. 1650) in *pargana* Bilgiram, a *chaudhari* is assigned one village as his *nankar* on account of his *khidmat*. He was further called upon to serve well and be loyal.[27] Again in 1731, a *parwana* was issued to grant one village in *nankar* to some *Chaudhari*. It states that his two *nankar* villages had been resumed

---

21. *RAA-1165* (c. 1580).
22. *Add-6603*, f. 79a, also Patna Private ff. 110b-111a.
23. *Add-6603*, f. 61b.
24. *Allahabad-294* (c. 1595).
25. *Zamindar* addressing a revenue official declares that he is ready for the proper official service, "if the *jama* of the *ta'alluqa*" was assessed according to the statement of the last ten years with deduction of one tenth as *nankar*. "Bekas, f-52b cf. Irfan Habib, *Agrarian System*, p. 174n.
26. *Ibid.*
27. *Bilgiram-49*. Since other *chaudharis* held their wajh-e-nankar *in the* pargana *Bilgiram, and the present assignee* had nothing of that sort. Hence village Pewandi was assigned to him to meet out his *nankar* claims.

and included in *khalisa* so as to enhance the income of the state. In lieu of this resumption, a fresh grant was being made.[28] Similarly 18th century documents from *pargana* Bilgiram contain a number of *parwanas* making *nankar* grants in cash.[29] In a very interesting *parwana* from *sarkar* Khairabad (c. 1824) it is recorded that two villages were granted to some Karam Ahmad and Rauf Ahmad as *wajh-e-nankar* in *al-tamgha*. The grant was made in perpetuity.[30] In another *parwana* (c. 1830) a *nankar* grant of Rs 50 was made as the grantee was a *khairkhwah* (well-wisher) of the state.[31] Nawab Wajid Ali Shah through a royal *farman* (c. 1848) bestowed an amount of Rs 200 and 55 *bigha* of cultivated land in *nankar* to a lady named Lado. Again the grant was made on hereditary basis. It is, however, not clear in lieu of what service the grant was being made. There is hardly any need to point out that in 19th century the entire concept of *nankar* grants had undergone a considerable change in Awadh, often becoming a kind of simple grant.

During the first half of the 19th century, with the weakening of the administrative machinery of the kingdom of Awadh, the revenue-farmers and the big *zamindars* increased their power tremendously. They were able to obtain a much larger share of the total land-revenue as their *nankar*. W.H. Sleeman aptly remarked that, "the (*nankar*) could be 10 percent, 20 percent or 100% upon the rent-roll of the estate".[32] It appears, that the difference between the claim of the *malikana* and *nankar* had practically disappeared, the general designation *nankar* applying to both allowances; Sleeman says:

> "The *nankar* is a portion of the recognised rent-roll, acknowledged by the rulers to be due to the land-holders for the risk, cost and the trouble of the management and for his perquisites as hereditary proprietors of the soil, when the management is confined to another."[33]

Sleeman explained how the amount of the *nankar* could be manipulated by the *zamindars* and the revenue-farmers. He cites an instance from the district of Sandila (c. 1849) where the '*amil* was weak and the *zamindars*

---

28. *Bilgiram-9*, The *nankar* villages of Khormi and Pewandi belonging to Sayyed Qubul Alam *Chaudhari* were included in *khalisa*. In lieu, he was allotted the other villages the *Chaudhari* was required to get the villages inhabited and to meet out his needs out of its revenues.
29. *Khairabad-7*.
30. *NAI-1563*.
31. *NAI-1416*.
32. W.H. Sleeman, *op. cit.*, pp. 121-2.
33. *Ibid.*

very strong. They refused to pay the dues on the plea of a bad season. The man who had to pay Rs 10,000 in revenue could not be induced to pay Rs 5,000. He enjoyed an acknowledged *nankar* of Rs 2,000 upon a recognised rent-roll of Rs 12,000 and to induce him to pay the *'amil* increased *nankar* to Rs 3,000, and reduced the revenue to Rs 9,000. At another place Sleeman observed that "the amount of *nankar* once recognised, remains the same till a new rate is recognised by the government".[34] That is, not the rate, but the sum remained constant, whatever the actual revenue.

During the first half of the 19th century, no sanctity seems to have been attached to the total percentage of the revenue allowed to be retained as *nankar*.

> To quote Donald Buttler (c. 1836), "In Baiswara, the largest *zamindari* is *Dundiakhera* held by Rambaksh Singh and in past sublet by him to his relations. It is in extent, 30 miles from east to west and 20 miles from north to south and pays an annual revenue of 300,000 rupees. In ordinary years, the amount of *nankar*, or allowance for management is 45,000 rupees ... but in favourable years, he obtains an additional profit, amounting to 100,000 or 150,000 rupees."[35]

Sleeman's diary, too, contains a number of specific instances about the enormous income obtained by the *zamindars* on this account. The returns of *pargana* Nawabgunj, Munkapur and Bahana Paer gave the following figures:[36]

Table - I

S. No.	*Pargana*	*A. Rent-Roll*	*B. Nankar*	*C. Cost-demand*
1.	Nawab Gunj, Wazir **Gunj, Mahadeva**	**1,08,000**	**32,000**	**76,000**
2.	Munkapur	40,000	12,000	28,000
3.	Bahana Paer	12,000	4,000	8,000

Again while giving a description of the estate of Seo Buksh Singh of Laharpur district Khairabad, Sleeman, says, "Its rent is now estimated ... at Rs 54,640 out of which is deducted a *nankar* or 17,587 leaving a government demand of only Rs 37,053".[37] The revenue-contractors and

34. Sleeman, *op. cit.*, p. 207.

35. Buttler, *op. cit.*, pp. 53-4.

36. Sleeman, *op. cit.*, p. 123. These *parganas* were transferred to the East India Company as per terms of the treaty of 1801, but were retransferred to the Awadh Kingdom in 1816.

37. Sleeman, *op. cit.*, p. 253.

talluqadars were also entitled to *nankar*. It is not clear that in such areas what amount was allowed to the hereditary *zamindari.*

Rent-free villages continued to be granted in *nankar* claims. One Muhammad Husain Khan of Bharwara district Khairabad, "held twelve villages, rent-free as *nankar* and pays revenue for all the rest that compose his share of the great estate. The heads of families, who hold the other shares enjoy, in the same manner, one or more villages, rent free, as *nankar*".[38] On such *nankar* villages the *zamindar* had apparently no obligation to pay anything to the government.

Apart from the *nankar*, another major source of the *zamindars* during the 19th century came to be the *seer* lands. These lands were those which the landholders and their families tilled themselves. Such lands were not entered at all in the rent-roll, and were shared among the heirs as hereditary possession.[39]

It should not be assumed that the administration was just a silent spectator to the destruction of its own income. Attempts were made to put restrictions on the claims of the intermediaries. An order was issued to the revenue officials, directing them not to acknowledge any increase in the amount or percentage of *nankar*, acquired after 1814 AD, the year of Nawab Saadat Ali Khan's death. But the evil was so deep-rooted that the measure proved abortive:

> "The increase to the *nankar* and the alienation in rent-free tenure of lands liable to assessment in 1814, by local authorities and influential persons at court are supposed to amount, in all Oude, to forty lakhs of rupees a year. None of them have been formally recognised by the court, but a great part of them has been tacitly acquired in by the minister and diwan for the time being. They can not enforce the order for reverting to the *nankar* of 1814; and if attempt to do so, the whole country will be in disorder. Indeed, the minister knows, his own weakness too well, to think seriously of ever making such an attempt."[40]

The things were manipulated by the big land owners in collusion with the *mustajirs* at great loss to the public treasury. Describing the conditions in the Baiswara district, Sleeman tells us that Dharupur yielded Rs 1,74,000 in annual amount of revenue when the estate was put under the direct management of Raja Durshan Singh as revenue-contractor. A deduction of Rs 20,000 was allowed as *nankar*. But in 1849, the government could not

38. Sleeman, *op. cit.*, p. 242.
39. *Ibid.*, p. 199.
40. Sleeman, *op. cit.*, p. 199.

persuade Raja Himmat Singh, the hereditary owner of the same estate to pay Rs 1,30,000 as per rent-roll, while the deduction by way of *nankar* was allowed at Rs 40,000. When the land owner was threatened with royal vengeance, "he looks, we are told, at their military force and smiles".[41] This was not a solitary case but there was a general realisation on the part of every *ta'alluqadar* of consequence about their armed strength and of relative weakness of the government. The officials, too, were afraid and hence they behaved very feebly in dealing with such potentates. At the same time their cruelty and oppression knew no bounds when they came to deal with a weak or small land-holder.[42]

Apart from the major items of the perquisites and the privileges enjoyed by the *zamindars*, we find a number of fiscal dues and obligations claimed by them by virtue of their being superior right holders. The nature, denomination and the amount of these claims varied from area to area. A set of documents from *sarkar* Khairabad shows that within a span of hundred years or so even small *milk* holders had enlarged their fiscal claims. In 1658, one Shaikh Daim was allotted five *bighas* of land in village Panwaria as *milk* for establishing a mosque and *Khanqah* and for the maintenance of the tombs.[43] Within two hundred years the right had been grossly enlarged. In 1858 his descendant presented a statement of facts with the attestation of the thirty persons of every class of village Panwaria. It was now alleged that he and his predecessors held the *zamindari* rights over village Panwaria and hence anyone laying the foundation of his house, was under an obligation to pay one *tanka* and offer some sweetmeats by way of *bhent* to pay *dastur-e-haqq-e-zamindari* on cultivable land and a rate of one *ser* (of produce) per *bigha* from everyone setting up a *nova* (boat like scoop) to water their field from the tank of the village.[44]

Salt and Saltpetre were extensively made in almost every district of Awadh. These were extracted from nitrous soils by a special caste of people known as *nuniyas* or *luniyas*.[45] The nitrous soil was found in every locality; and Buttler tells us that, "when *Luniyas* or the salt-manufacturers pitch upon a spot where they think salt water likely to be found, they obtained the *zamindar*'s permission to sink a well, by engaging to pay him annually 50 rupees for the water".[46]

41. Sleeman, *op. cit.*, p. 143.
42. *Ibid.*, p. 143.
43. *Khairabad-3*.
44. *Khairabad-9*, Iqbal Husain, *op. cit.*
45. The Chief occupation of the *nuniyas* or *luniyas*, was making of the salt and saltpetre. There population in every district of Awadh was quite considerable. W. Crooke, *The Tribes and Castes of North Western India*, Vol. III, pp. 386-95.
46. Buttler, *op. cit.*, p. 73.

Another source of income of the *zamindars* was the collections made by them in markets and fairs held within the limits of their *zamindaris*, who annually paid a fixed amount to the *zamindars*. These *Chaudharies* in turn enjoyed some concessions from the *zamindars*. In 1666, Diler Khan, *jagirdar* of *pargana* Pali, issued a *sanad* to one Maiku, *Chaudhari* of the market, granting him fifty *bighas* of barren land as *inam*. The grantee was asked to treat the peasants (*riaya*) gently as to attract them to these settlements.[47] Similarly in 1688 the office of the *Chaudhari* of Dilergunj (*bazar*) and its ferries was given over to a new incumbent. The newly appointed person was asked to look at the general welfare of the population, the bankers, the big traders and *kasibs* in such a way to enable the population of the place should increase.[48] Buttler (c. 1836) says of the *hat* (market) of Karahya *bazar*, that it was the greatest *hat* of the *chakla* Salon, and was attended by about one lakh people. This *hat* was managed by a *Chaudhari* who resides on the spot and pays Rs 8000 a year to the *zamindar*.[49]

The *zamindari* right was a freely saleable article of property. A number of surviving sale-deeds and mortgage deeds from the various *pargana* of the province of Awadh are strong evidence of this. A full scale market in *zamindari* rights (not property perhaps a land market) had developed here at least from the sixteeth century if not earlier.

The *zamindari* rights were usually represented in terms of *biswas* or twentieth shares in a village. The share in the *zamindari* of a village is thus stated in the number of *biswas*, the *biswa* here having nothing to do with the land-measure of that name.

The earliest known sale-deeds of these superior rights from *pargana* Bilgiram (c. 1542) and *pargana* Sandila (c. 1585) show transfers of rights from one class of persons to another. A group of land owner hitherto unknown in an area, could establish their sway over it by buying up *zamindari*. In 1852, a group of Janwar Rajput land owners told their rights on a village in *pargana* Bilgiram for a consideration of 300 silver *tanka-e-'adli* to a Qazi or Muslim judge.[50] Similarly in 1585, Brahman *zamindars* of *pargana* Sandilah had sold their proprietory rights over the ten villages for 1560 *sikka-e-muradi*.[51] It appears that by 1595, the Janwar Rajput and the Brahman proprietors were reduced to the status of the under proprietors

47. *Nama-e-Muzaffari*, Vol. I, p. 191.
48. *Ibid.*, p. 268.
49. Buttler, *op. cit.*, p. 92.
50. *Sharaif-e-Usmani*, p. 80.
51. *Allahabad-317.*

in these *parganas* respectively, for Abul Fazl does not record them as the dominant *zamindar* caste.[52]

A number of sale-deeds of eighteeth century from *sarkar* Khairabad give the impression that even *jagirdars* in their *al-tamgha* or *watan*-assignments were tempted to acquire *zamindari* rights. One Rae Siroman Das son of Alam Chand held on *inam-al-tamgha jagir* in *pargana* Sandi. It consisted of 30,000 dams, being the revenue of 500 *bighas* (60 *dams* per *bigha*). The grant was made to him with the specific purpose of settling people and orchards. The grantee was exempted from all revenue obligations and cesses like *begar*, *khanashumari* and *sardarakhti wa zer-darakhti*. In the period subsequent to this grant, we find that he had purchased *zamindari* rights in a number of villages from Rajput land owners. Thus, he came to enjoy an important position in the landed aristocracy of the *pargana*. The details of his acquisitions are given in the following table:

Table - II

Sl. No.	*Year of Transaction*	*Area Involved*	*Description of the Sellers/ Castes*	*Price paid*	*Reference*
1.	1124/ 1715	*qasba* Saroman nagar *pargana* Sirsa, Khairabad	Jeet son of Sultan *zamindar* of the said *qasba*	Rs 500/- being Rs 25/ per *biswa* for 20 *biswa*.	RAA-2
2.	1141F/ 1737	Village Baqar Nagar, *tappa* Honsipur, *sarkar* Khairabad	Santokh son of Pratap Sahi etc. *zamindars*	Rs 271/4 *annas* for 5 *biswa* & 10 *biswansi*	ALL-224
3.	1144F/ 1740	Village Baqar Nagar and Sarjospur *tappa*, Honsipur, *sarkar* Khairabad	Himmat Singh S/o Har Singh and Maha Singh Sahi *zamindar*	Rs 546/- for 7 *biswas* and 15 *biswansi*	ALL-225
4.	1200/ 1785 (date of the seal)	Village Sikandar-pur, *pargana* Sirrah, *tappa* Rasulabad	*Zamindars* of the Rajputs Chamar Kaur tribe	Rs 202/- 8 *annas* for 6¾ *biswa*	RAA-382
5.	-do-	-do-	-do-	Rs 375/- for 13 *biswas* in various villages	RAA-12

Similarly we find two sale-deeds dealing with the transactions between the Gaur Rajput *zamindars* of *pargana* Sirrah and Muhammad Sardar Khan, grandson of a well known noble of Aurangzeb, Diler Khan. We know from the other sources that Sardar Khan held a large *inam-al-tamgha* grant of 7 lac dams in the adjacent *pargana* Pali (afterwards Shahabad) as hereditary

52. *Ain-i-Akbari*, 'Ain-e-Dawazdeh Suba, Suba of Awadh', Vol. II.

jagir.[53] This enabled him to purchase a large number of *zamindari* villages from their owners. The details of these transactions are given in the following table:[54]

Table - III

Sl. No.	*Year of the Trans-action*	*Area Involved*	*Description of the Sellers/ Castes*	*Amount of Consideration*	*Reference*
1.	1141/ 1728	Rampur Ghalib etc. *pargana* Sirrah, *sarkar* Khairabad	*Zamindars* of the Rajput Gaur Caste	Rs 1124/- 12 *annas*	ALL-228
2.	1141/ 1728	-do-	-do-	Rs 560/-	ALL-229

Two sale-deeds from *pargana* Lucknow record the sale of considerable portions of the superior rights by the hereditary Rajput landowners of Janwar clan to one Sayyid Muhammad Yasin. One transaction involved half (10 out of the 20 portions) of the village Bharasa for a consideration of Rs 581 in 1694.[55] While the other sale-deed relates to 1½ portion of the same village purchased for Rs 46 in 1702.[56] This suggests the ability of the outsiders to obtain a favourable price once he had established himself in the village for at the latter rate the original acquisition should have cost only Rs 307. We have seen how Saiyyed Muhammad Arif in *pargana* Hisampur *sarkar* Bahraich, purchased from Rajput *zamindars* a number of the shares in the Pasanjat group of the villages,[57] all the portions of the village Debidaspur and one-fourth shares of the village Inchapur between the years 1672 to 1688.[58] We know from other papers that originally Arif was a *madad-e-ma'ash* holder,[59] and subsequently he contracted to collect and to pay the revenues of *jagirs* in *pargana* Hisampur.[60]

53. *Nama-e-Muzzaffari*, Vol. I, pp. 316-17.
54. *Allahabad-228 and 229*. These sale deeds were executed on the same date in 1728 AD. The earlier one was executed for the sale of 19 portions in the 4 villages for a consideration of Rs 1124 by the Gaur Rajput owners, while another deed involved the sale of 16 portions in the same villages by the owners of same caste for a consideration of Rs 560.
55. *NAI-141.*
56. *NAI-143..*
57. See the Chapter on The Revenue Grants, Section II.
58. See the sale-deeds of Regional Records Office, *Allahabad especially numbers, 1196, 1221, 1222, 1224, 1216, 1215 and 1205.*
59. *RRA-849, 853, 860, 864, 866, 879, 861 and 939.*
60. *RRA-867.*

Such examples of outsiders entering the zamindar class could be multiplied. But the point at issue is that, to an extent, the saleability of the superior rights in land had been instrumental in altering the general pattern of the land holding classes. The new masters of soil were often former salaried bureaucrats, revenue contractors and the holders of grants. Holders of tax grants (*a'imma* or *ma'afi*) inevitably tended to combine these, if they could, with superior or *zamindari* rights. A sale deed from Bilgiram (1723) clubs the *muqqadami* and *malikana* rights with the *madad-e-ma'ash* rights, all of which had been previously mortgaged. A description of these rights shows that these included the headmens' and *zamindari* perquisites such as *mehat, khaildari, adhetra, pachotra, mustajiri,* alongwith *mahsul-e a'imma* or revenue from the land-grant.[61] Another interesting petition from *pargana* Sandila shows one Ghulam Haider and others representing before the *qazi* of the *pargana* that the *milkiyat-i-zamindari* known as *satarhi* of the village Kondwa was purchased by their predecessors and that their ancestors also held *madad-e-ma'ash* rights over the said village. It was alleged that one Shah Muhammad Akbar, a co-sharer of these rights had now mortgaged his share of those rights in view of his poverty, with some Rajput *zamindars* for a consideration of 1½ maund of cereals. Although the price of the grain had been paid to these *zamindars*, they had not returned the mortgage papers of the said village, so far, to the petitioners.[62]

Most frequently the grantees (*a'immadars*) sought to obtain *malikana* and *muqqadami* rights over their *a'imma* lands. An *iqrarnamah*, executed in 1697 stipulates that an *a'imma* village having been mortgaged for Rs 476 in *sarkar* Lucknow, it was agreed that Malik 'Abdul Karim, the *a'immadar*, be paid Rs 48 and 24 *bighas* 7 *biswa* of land be reserved for him in view of his *malikana* and *muqqadami* rights.[63] Apparently he had only mortgaged his grant, and not his superior rights. Similarly, the Khairabad documents show that in village Panwariya Shaikh Daim held a land grant of 5 *bigha* for maintaining a *Khanqah*, mosque etc., but afterwards his descendants Shaikh Aminuddin, claimed that all the *zamindari* rights in the said village had been acquired by his predecessors since long and that he too enjoyed all such perquisites.[64]

Elsewhere the fortunes of the family of the mystics established at Salon had been discussed at some length. They had a humble beginning as holders

61. *Bilgiram-60.*

62. *Allahabad-362.*

63. *NAI-144.*

64. *Khairabad-3 and 9.*

of the *madad-e-ma'ash* rights over 200 *bighas* of uncultivated land in 1679, but subsequently their possessions were greatly expanded so that by 1761 they held 44 villages 21 *chaks* and a substantial number of the *bighas* of cultivated land. These included the *zamindari* "Lambordari" (sic) as well as the *madad-e-ma'ash* rights. The proprietary rights of the establishment were so firmly established that Buttler in 1836 was led to conclude that, "he (the head of the family) also is called a *faqir*, though the *malik* (proprietor) of Salon".[65]

(b) Changes in Composition of the *Zamindar* Class

Superior rights in land have been linked in Awadh, as elsewhere, with the domination of a particular clan, or caste, over an area. As we have seen these rights could originate quite independently of any royal action. The association of caste with more or less well defined tracts of country was so conspicuous in Awadh that C.A. Elliott was led to conclude that *pargana* boundaries were fixed on the basis of the "possession of an undivided clan".[66] However, in so far as these superior or *zamindari* rights were fully alienable, the territorial hegemony of a clan or caste was open to the dissolving effects of money. It could also be disturbed by the deliberate policy of Government to dislodge a clan from an area and install some other group in its place.

A study of the position of various land-holding clans, their share in the agricultural surplus and the changes which came in their fortunes during the period 1595-1900 can be extremely fascinating. One such study has been attempted by Bernard S. Cohn for the Benaras region. After comparing the data for circa 1595 with those for circa 1900 he concluded that, "the rise of one group or class did not necessarily mean the concomitant fall of another".[67] A similar study has been attempted by K.K. Trivedi for Western Uttar Pradesh. His conclusions are quite different from Cohn's. He has shown that changes in land holding classes were quite substantial and that a large number of castes recorded in the *Ain* had been largely eliminated from various localities, being supplanted by others. In most cases the

65. For a detailed discussion of the rise of this family of the mystics see the chapter on Revenue Grants, Section II.

66. C.A. Elliott. *Chronicles of Onao*, Allahabad, 1862, p. 149. He argues that since the boundaries of the *mahals* were not fixed in accordance with the physical or geographical features of the country, the only reason, "for their irregular tracing seems to be proprietary rights."

67. Bernard S. Cohn. "Structural Changes in Rural Society" *Land Control and Social Structure in Indian History*, ed. R.E. Frykinberg, London, 1969.

money-lending castes which replaced them are not even recorded as *zamindars* in the *Ain* but they appear with sizeable holdings by 1900.[68]

The study of the *zamindar* clans of Awadh must obviously begin with the rich information in the *A'in-i Akbari.* Abul Fazl has given us a detailed census of the dominant caste in each *pargana* along with the *naqdi* (*jama*') figures assessed upon it. Very often more than one caste is recorded for a *pargana.* We have therefore divided the amount of *naqdi* accordingly in order to determine the share payable by one caste from the *pargana* in question.

A cursory glance at Table IV (prepared with the help of the data provided by *A'in*)[69] will show that more than 75 percent of the total *jama*' of the *parganas* recorded in the *A'in* was from lands under the various Rajput clans-Bais, 18.50 percent; Bachhils 5.22 percent; Ghelots 5.11 percent; Bachgotis 4.73 percent; Bisins 4.13 percent; others 3.42 percent; undifferentiated, 25.64 percent. The Brahmans and Muslims trailed for behind accounting for only 6.42 percent and 10.86 percent shares in the total *jama*' of the *suba.* The reminder was controlled by other minor clans and some of which are unidentifiable.

The Bais Rajputs are recorded as *zamindars* of 27 *parganas* in Awadh by Abul Fazl. In the *sarkar* of Awadh, they are co-sharers in 3 *parganas* holding 6 percent of the total *naqdi* of the *sarkar* and one *pargana* each in *sarkar* Bahraich, Khairabad and Gorakhpur, while in *sarkar* Lucknow they possessed 15 *parganas* singly and 6 *parganas* as co-sharers. In all they controlled 18.22 percent of the total *naqdi* of the *suba.* These *mahals* formed a contiguous block. The tract acquired the name of Baiswara in the 17th century; the first occurrence of the name appears to be in Shahjahan's time, when the recalcitrance of the Bais *zamindars* caused the creation of a special *faujdari* jurisdiction of Baiswara,[70] "consisting of many *mahals*, that are the native places of the seditious *zamindars* of the caste of Bais".[71]

---

68. K.K. Trivedi. "Changes in caste composition of the *zamindari* clans in Western Uttar Pradesh, c. 1595-1900", *Indian Historical Review*, Vol. II, No. 1, Delhi, 1975, pp. 47-67.

69. Abul Fazl Allami. *Ain-i Akbari*, Persian Text edited by W.H. Blochmann (Bib. Ind. Series), Vol. I, pp. 71-84.

70. Abul Hameed Lahori. *Badshah Namah*, Bib. Indica (I), pp. 243, 278. The *sarkar* of Lucknow and district of Bainswara were under one *faujdari*; subsequently Bainswara became a separate *faujdari.* Also see Zahiruddin Malik, "Problems of *faujdari* jurisdictions in Bainswara", *PIHCI*, 1973, (Chandigarh Session). For a note on Bais zamindars see my paper in the cyclostyled papers of the members of the Department of History, AMU, presented at 42nd session of *Indian History Congress*, Bodh-Gaya, 1981.

71. *Insha-i Roshan Kalam*. MS Azad Library, AMU, Aligarh, f. 7a.

They supported the rebellion of Bahadur the Bachgoti chief in Aurangzeb's first R.Y.[72] and apparently lent aid to the Chauhans of *pargana* Shahpur in or about 1700 AD. The disturbances were suppressed with some difficulty and Ra'd Andaz Khan, the faujdar of Bainswara reported his successes with much satisfaction.[73] C.A. Elliott provides us with detailed information on the settlements of the Bais Rajputs in the Baiswara region from their traditional settlement till about 1860.[74] We are told that there were 22 *parganas* in all, under the dominance of this clan:

Table - IV

Sl. No.	*District (According to Present Distribution)*	*Pargana*
1.	Rae Bareili	(a) Dundiakhera (b) Unchagaon (c) Kombhi (d) Bar (e) Kehengur (f) Ghatampur (g) Serhapur (h) Mukrid (i) Dalmau (j) Bihar (k) Pathan (l) Punhan (m) Rae Bareili (n) Hurha
2.	Onnao	(o) Satanpur (o) Purwa (p) Maurawan (q) Serwan (r) Asoha (s) Gorinda (t) Pursundan
3.	Lucknow	(u) Bijnor

"The Banswara Nizamat included very little more than the *parganas* in the above list".[75]

The Bais *zamindars* seem to have extended their possessions in *parganas* Dalmau and Bijnor, since Abul Fazl has recorded the former under 'Turkmans', and the latter under the Chauhan Rajputs.[76] On the other hand,

72. Muhammad Kazim, *Alamgir Namah*, Bib. Ind., Calcutta, 1873, Vol. I, p. 450.
73. *Insha-i Roshan Kalam*, f. 3a.
74. C.A. Elliott, *op. cit.*, pp. 67-68.
75. C.A. Elliott, *op. cit.*, pp. 67-68.
76. Abul Fazl, *op. cit.*, pp. 71-84. However, *Insha-i Roshan Kalam* records the

(*Contd...*)

after the suppression of the Mutiny some Bais proprietor's lost their possessions. The most notable loser was Raja Beni Madho Singh of Shankarpur whose large estate was confiscated for his involvement in the Mutiny. The final picture with regard to the land holdings of Bais clan suggests that by and large all the *mahals* recorded in the *Ain* were kept intact by them but only a few new additions were made to the land holdings of this clan by C. 1900. It appears then that the possessions of Bais Rajput at least did not, on the balance, suffer any contraction over the three hundred years spanning 1600 and 1800.

The Bachgoti Rajputs are recorded as the exclusive zamindars of 6 *parganas* and jointly of one in *sarkar* Awadh where they thus seem to have accounted for 18.85 percent of the total *jama*'. In *sarkar* Lucknow they held only a share in a *pargana* and 2.6 percent of the total *jama*' of the *suba* Awadh their *parganas* were assigned 4.87 percent. All the *parganas* were assigned 4.87 percent. All the *parganas* except one, formed a contiguous block of territory in the south-eastern portion of Awadh in 1595. The Bachgoti *zamindars* raised considerable disturbance in 1070 AH/1660 AD. Their leader Bahadur recruited a large number of followers from amongst the local, '*qanwars*', the 'turbulent Bais' and other 'bad characters of the area'. The banner of revolt was raised in the Bainswara division. He devastated a considerable area. Such were the dimensions of the revolt that an imperial force was deputed under the command of Bahadur Khan.[77] The rebellion was suppressed and peace was restored in the area.[78] Subsequently we hear little of this clan. But they largely retained their *zamindaris*, and held on to almost all the *parganas* against which they are entered in the *Ain*. The famous Khanazad house of Hasanpur (Muslim Bachgotis) and their latter branches of Maniarpur and Gangeo had their large *ta'alluqadari* possessions in the present district of Sultanpur and Fyzabad.[79] We know that 5 of the Bachgoti *parganas* of the *Ain* lay in Sultanpur district, while one each lay in the districts Fyzabad and Barabanki, the *pargana* Baktha is yet to be identified.[80] Other notable possessions of

mahal of Bijnor under the Bais *zamindars* (f. 7). They have been called as *zamindaran-i zor-talab*. While Nevill informs us the *pargana* of Dalmau was possessed by Bais Rajputs. See H.R. Nevill, *District Gazetteers of the United Provinces of Agra and Oudh*, (hereafter as *DG*), Vol. 39, pp. 168-69.

77. Lahori, *op. cit.*, Vol. I(I), pp. 243 & 278.
78. Muhammad Kazim, *Alamgir Namah*, Vol. I, p. 450.
79. *DG*, Vol. 46, pp. 88-93.
80. Irfan Habib, *An Atlas of the Mughal Empire*, Oxford Press, 1982, Sheet No. 8A, p. 29 (notes).

the Bachgotis lay in the *ta'alluqa* of Kurwar, Samrautha and Khajurahat, the Rajkumars had the estates of Dera, Pirpur, Meopur Dharua and Nanemau.[81] We find that in addition to their old possessions some new 'estates' were also acquired by them. The *ta'alluqa* of Khajurahat was established during the time of Shujauddaulah and the house of Bhiti came into existence during the first half of the nineteenth century. Most of the villages of these *ta'alluqa* lay in the *Ain*'s *pargana* of Pachhimrath and *Haveli* Awadh, where the Bachgotis are not recorded as *zamindars*.

The Chauhan Rajputs held one *pargana* each in the *sarkars* of Khairabad, Awadh and Lucknow. In two *parganas* of Awadh they are recorded as the co-sharers, and so they controlled areas yielding 4.33 percent of the total *jama*' of the *suba*. These *zamindars* had grown strong enough, subsequently, to cause trouble and harassment to the imperial authority at the close of the Aurangzeb's reign. It was reported by the deputy *faujdar* of the Bainswara division, Sher Andaz Khan, that these 'troublesome' people had collected a force of their kinsmen consisting of about 8 or 9,000 persons and gone into rebellion. The usual allegation, namely, refusal to pay the land revenue was also levelled against them. As a result of the successful operation carried out by the imperial forces against the rebels, 12 strong fortresses and about 1500 captives captured by the army. Also we come across the recommendation of the *faujdar* to confer the *zamindari* rights of the area over one Syed Muzaffar who helped imperial forces with all possible means.[82]

Comparing the relative position of the Chauhan possessions between 1595 and 1900, it appears that some of their old possessions had been lost to their powerful neighbours while they had themselves established their sway in areas where they are not recorded in the *Ain*. The *pargana* of Daryabad and Sara had almost completely passed out of their hands. *Pargana* Inhauna was kept intact by Chauhan Khanazads (Muslims). In *pargana* Rudauli and Bijnor they are only recorded as the inhabitants, but not as the proprietors of the land; they might have been under proprietors for which unfortunately we possess no information.[83] Their new acquisition lay in the District of Kheri. The large *talluqas* of Oel, Mahewa and Kaimahra consisted of 326 villages and 28 *pattis*, assessed at Rs 1,89,744. Originally,

---

81. For a detailed description of the rise of these *ta'alluqas*, see *District Gazetteer*, Vols. 39, 43 & 46.

82. For a detailed description of the nature and the dimension of this revolt see *Insha-i Roshan Kalam*, f. 3.

83. *DG*, Vol. 48, 37.

it was a Janwar possession; the Chauhans got it as a 'dowry gifts' since their predecessor had no one to succeed them. The Jangre Rajputs, a branch of the Chauhans also possessed the large estate of Bhur, Isanagar and Ramnagar in Kheri District. Their total possessions consisted of 161 villages and 14 *pattis* and it was assessed at Rs 1,54,745.[84] It appears that on balance the Chauhans did not suffer, though there were some territorial changes.

The *zamindari* possessions of Raikwar and Janwar Rajputs display striking similarity with that of Chauhans in 1595, their most numerous possessions lay in *sarkar* Bahraich, where they held 6 *parganas* and paid 24.67 percent of the total assessed *jama*'. In *sarkar* Awadh, the Raikwar held 3 *parganas* as co-sharers with 19.34 percent in the total *jama*'. One *pargana* belonging to the Janwars, lay in *sarkar* Khairabad. In the *jama*' of the *suba* their share amounted to 7.10 percent. A comparison with the relative size of their land-holdings in 1900 suggests that the Raikwars had lost a good deal of their possessions while some of the Janwar houses had acquired very large estates in those areas where they are mentioned as *zamindar* caste by Abul Fazl.[85]

The Raikwars lost hold of the *parganas* Gumarich and Daryabad; the *parganas* of Siluk was kept intact by them. In *pargana* Fakharpur and Hisampur they retained at least some landed possession. The Janwars also lost some of their old possessions. First of all, the entire *pargana* of Rajhat and large tracts in *pargana* Sujauli and Sultanpur were transferred to Nepal in 1860. From the *pargana* Sadarpur they were expelled during the Nawabi period. *Pargana* Dangoi was included in the *ta'aluqas* of Ayodhya and Nanpara. As against these losses, the new estates acquired by them are of some interest. The estates of Balrampur and Payagpur were now owned by Janwars while Mallanpur and Ramnagar constituted the possessions of the Raikwars. By taking into account their *ta'alluqadari* possessions and revenue obligations, some idea can be formed of their position about 1900. In 1900, the Janwar possessions in Gonda and Bahraich districts consisted of 1189 villages and *pattis* 52, assessed at Rs 8,47,388, while the Raikwar possessions in these districts consisted of 413 villages and 126 *pattis*, assessed at Rs 3,37,089.[86]

The Bisin Rajputs were the most dominant clan in the Gorakhpur *sarkar*. They were *zamindars* in 9 *parganas* forming a contiguous block of the

84. *DG*, Vol. 42, pp. 85-7.

85. *DG*, Vol. 44, pp. 81-5; Vol. 45, pp. 81-3.

86. *DG*, Vols. 44, 45.

territory in the south-western portion of the *sarkar*, and these *parganas* accounted for 45.66 percent of the total *jama*'. In *sarkar* Khairabad they were co-sharers in two *parganas* while one *pargana* each of their *zamindari* lay in *sarkar* of Bahraich and Lucknow. In the total *jama*' of the *suba* their share amounted to about 4.13 percent. Comparing these data with 1900, it appears that there had been quite drastic changes in the fortunes of this clan. With the close of the tenure of one Qazi Khalilur Rehman (1680-1707),[87] there was a spontaneous rise in the power of the local chieftains. There were constant conflicts among local *zamindars*. During the eighteenth century the Banjaras acquired considerable power in the north-eastern regions in the *sarkar* of Gorakhpur. In course of time, they became a scourge to almost the entire area. No individual chieftain was able to withstand their onslaught. These conditions came to an end with the cession of this territory to the domains of the British East India Company in 1801.

It seems that during the eighteenth century owing to these conditions the position of Bisin land-holding in this *sarkar* underwent complete change. Not only this, in the other four *parganas* of *sarkar* Bahraich, Khairabad and Lucknow, they are not even mentioned as the superior right holders of land. In the Gorakhpur *sarkar*, there were only a few Bisin estates with considerable land holdings. The prime family was of the Raja of Majhauli in 1900, held 152 villages, assessed at Rs 67,756. Their possessions were quite large, but in order to meet the threat posed by Anjara depredators, they abandoned a large portion of his estate to newly established estates of Tamkuhi and Padrauna. This created a powerful buffer zone between Majhauli and eastern portions of the *sarkar*, notorious for Banjara depredations.

The estates of Sarnet Rajputs may also be dealt with here. The great Sarnet house of Bansi Raj was established as a result of a dowry gift received from the Bisins of Majhauli.[88] In 1900 AD, the Bansi Raj was extensive enough to merit an assessment of Rs 1,21,685.

A precise comparison of the individual *parganas* held by Bisins in 1595, with their possessions in 1900 can not be attempted, but they seem on the whole to have declined. Muslim Pindari chiefs and Europeans also received estates during the British period, which reduced their relative position.

87. This information is from the *Gorakhpur Gazetteer*, pp. 180-2. There is no contemporary documentary confirmation of this. Qazi Khalilur Rahman was probably the '*amil* or revenue-collector.

88. *DG*, Vol. 31 & 32.

The *Ain* places most of the possessions of the Surajbansi and Sombansi Rajputs in *sarkar* Gorakhpur. Their share in the total *jama*' of the *sarkar* amounted to about 22.03 percent. The Sombansis held one *pargana* each in *sarkars* of Awadh and Khairabad. These two clans jointly controlled barely 3.49 percent of the total *jama*' of the *suba*. For the same reasons as far the Bisin, their position declined in *sarkar* Gorakhpur. However, in some adjacent areas, where they are not recorded as *zamindars* in the *Ain*, they came to possess large *ta'alluqadari* estates. In 1900 AD the Sombansi estates contained 80 villages and 8 *pattis* assessed at Rs 41,766, while the estates of Surajbansis consisted of 206 villages, 35 *pattis*, and accounted for Rs 1,84,282. In most of their *parganas* in Gorakhpur *sarkar* Europeans received large grants in the British period. However, in these areas as well as in many other places the Kalhans Rajputs are mentioned quite frequently with the Kalhans Rajputs. The Surajbansi as well as Sombansis had matrimonial ties.[89] In *pargana* Sandi *sarkar* Khairabad, the Sombansis held 55 villages out of 140 in 1900.[90]

In the *Ain*'s tables, the Ghelot Rajputs held jointly with Bachhili Rajputs the *parganas* of Sandila and Pachhimrath, while they held the exclusive *zamindari* of *parganas* of *sarkar* Lucknow. Their share in the total *jama*' of the *suba* amounted to 5.22 percent. Similarly the Bachhils, apart from the *parganas* where they were co-sharers with the Ghelots, had *zamindari* rights in four *parganas* of *sarkar* Khairabad. Their revenue obligations in the total *jama*' of the *suba* amounted to 5.11 percent. They appear to have lost their position subsequently and have been relegated to the position of under-proprietors. Their most conspicuous loss was in *pargana* Sandila, where Muslim *zamindars* were able to establish their large *ta'alluqadari* 'estates'. In modern times we get little or no information about the fortunes of either of the two clans in the localities where they were holding in 1595.

The Bandalghoti Rajputs are recorded in the *Ain* as co-sharers in *pargana* Garh Amethi (*sarkar* Lucknow) and accounted for barely 1.11 percent of the total *jama*' of the *suba*. They have however succeeded in maintaining their position in this area. The Bandalgoti *ta'alluqa* of Amethi and Shahgarh in the present district of Sultanpur have seen quite fluctuating fortunes, still in 1900, Bandalghoti possessions were consisted of 334 villages and 5 *pattis*, and the total assessment on them amounted to Rs 2,39,590.[91]

89. W. Crooke, '*The Tribes and Castes of the North Western India*', Calcutta, 1896. See S.V. Surajbasis and Sombansis in Vol. IV.

90. *DG*, Vol. 41, pp. 245-49.

91. *DG*, Vol. 46, pp. 95-7.

The other Rajput clans of Gaurs and Tomars are shown in the *Ain* as jointly holding two separate *parganas* in *sarkar* Khairabad and Bahraich respectively. Together they accounted for 2.33 percent of the *jama'* of *suba*. They are not prominent now.

Apart from the above major *zamindar* clans, there are many other castes recorded in the *Ain* with small shares in the total revenue of the *suba*. Such are the Chandels (1.5%), Amins or Ahmins (1.97%), Ahirs (1.77%), Kumbi (0.49%), Jats (0.08%) and the Kuhnas (0.23%). The presence of Jats in the province of Awadh seems quite curious. In the 19th century there were only some scattered Jats settlements in the districts of Gonda, Bahraich and Kheri, but by and large they were tenants or sub-proprietors.[92] Similar was the status of the Ahirs and the Kumbis.

'Unspecified' Rajput clans held the largest *zamindari* possessions in Awadh. Abul Fazl records them in almost every *sarkar*. In *sarkar* Awadh they were only next to the Bais Rajputs with a share of 23.43 percent in the total *jama'*, in *sarkar* Gorakhpur they followed the Bisin and had 16.87 percent of the total *jama'* as their share. In *sarkar* of Bahraich and Khairabad they formed the most dominant group of *zamindars* with 47.07 percent and 43.05 percent of the total assessment. In *sarkar* of Lucknow the position was different. Here they trailed behind the large *zamindaris* of the *Bais* Rajputs and the Muslims of various clans. In the total *jama'* of the *suba* their share amounted to a quarter (25.64 percent).

A study of the *zamindari* possessions in the modern sub-divisions of Awadh belonging to Rajputs other than the clans specifically recorded in the *Ain* presents some difficulties. In the *District Gazetteers* the *ta'alluqa* possessions are often recorded under ownership of a clan which does not appear in the *Ain*. It is quite possible that in the reign of Akbar their sub-divisions might not have acquired such importance as to merit separate mention. But even if some individual Rajput clans escaped Abul Fazl's notice, the large *zamindari* it assigns to unspecified Rajputs when combined with the *zamindari* possessions or named Rajput clans give us a very impressive size of the aggregate Rajputs possessions in Awadh. This position is largely confirmed by the *District Gazetteers*. Hence there is no reason to believe that Rajput *zamindari* possessions as a whole declined in the province, except perhaps for marginal decline affected by the post-Mutiny confiscations. Lalji in his *Mirat-ul Auza* (1850) tells us that, "among all the castes of the Hindu inhabitants (of the kingdom of Awadh) the Rajputs are most numerous and a large number of *zamindaris* and *ta'alluqadaris*

92. *DG*, Vol. 48, p. 159.

are possessed by them (the Rajputs). Next to them were the Muslim owners– this fact, says Lalji, "had made them so that they had grown quite contemptuous towards them (priestly class) of Brahmans".[93]

The Brahmans are recorded as co-sharers in two *parganas* of *sarkar* Awadh and they controlled 3.80 percent of the total *jama*' of that *sarkar*. In *sarkar* Khairabad their presence is recorded in four *parganas*, but they controlled as much as 17.73 percent of the total *jama*' of that *sarkar*. In *sarkar* Lucknow they are entered in 8 *parganas* and held 4.73 percent in *jama*'. Of the total revenue of the *suba*, the Brahmans as a whole paid 6.42 percent. Comparing this data with those of circa 1900, it appears that they made considerable inroads in other areas. While the *mahals* recorded in the *Ain'* continued to be held by them intact, they seem to have established their hold over an extensive area in *sarkar* Gorakhpur, where the *Ain* does not enter them at all. Ghulam Hazrat (c. 1810) informs us that "most of the villages (in *sarkar* Gorakhpur) were in the *zamindari* possessions of the Rajputs and Brahmans, while the Muslims and others (castes) had only a quarter share (in *zamindari*)".[94] Most of these changes, it appears, were affected during the period of 17th century, for, "since the introduction of British rule (1810 AD) there had been no great change in the relative position of the different castes in this respect (proprietory tenures), with the exception of the alterations affected by the confiscations of estates for rebellion during the Mutiny".[95] In the modern districts of Gorakhpur and Basti the Brahmans were the leading land-holding caste having 26 percent and 34 percent of the entire area respectively.[96] In *sarkar* of Bahraich, they are not recorded as *zamindars* in the *Ain* but by the close of 19th century, they had acquired quite considerable landed possessions. The *ta'alluqadars* of Singha Chanda[97] and the Raja of Ajodhya[98] owned large possessions in the district of Gonda, owing to favours from the Nawab Wazirs. The former held 325 villages and 78 *pattis*, assessed at Rs 2,09,760,[99] while the latter had 669 villages and 124 *pattis*, assessed at Rs 4,79,348 as in land revenue.[100]

93. Lalji, *op. cit.*, ff. 74b-76a.

94. Ghulam Hazrat, *Kwaif-i Gorakhpur* MS, (*Farsiya Akhbar*), Azad Library, AMU, ff. 6a-b.

95. *DG*, Vol. 32, pp. 87-8.

96. *DG*, Vol. 32, pp. 87-8 and Vol. 31, p. 108.

97. For the spectacular rise of this family see Derogha Haji Abbas Ali, *An Illustrated Historical Album of Rajas and ta'alluqadars of Oudh* (hereafter referred to as *Album*), Allahabad 1880, p. 22 and *DG*, Vol. 44, p. 102.

98. See *Album*, p. 4 and *DG*, Vol. 43, pp. 79-80.

99. *Album*, p. 22.

100. *Ibid.*, p. 4.

The estate of Sisandi falling under the limits of the modern districts of Unnao and Lucknow (and falling within *sarkar* Lucknow in Akbar's time) was actually obtained in *theka* or revenue farm in 1226 Fasli (= AD 1817) but was subsequently converted into a hereditary possession.[101] Since a comparison of their revenue paying capacity is not possible on the basis of the data provided for c. 1900, no exact impression can be formed of changes in their position between 1595 and 1900. But it can be observed from the total number of the Brahman *ta'alluqadars* and their vast possessions in various district by 1900, that they had become much more important an element among the landed proprietors of Awadh than they were in 1595.

The Muslim *zamindars* accounted for roughly 10.86 percent of the total revenue of the *suba* of Awadh about 1595. The Afghans are recorded as the exclusive *zamindars* of the *pargana* Utraula, *sarkar* Gorakhpur, while in *pargana* Sidhaur, *sarkar* Lucknow, they are recorded as co-sharers. Ansaris were in possession of the contiguous *parganas* of Ibrahimabad and Satrikh in *sarkar* Awadh and the *pargana* of Amethi in *sarkar* Lucknow. Sayyids only held the *pargana* Bilgiram and Unam, while the Shaikhzadas were co-sharers with them in the *pargana* Fatehpur and Haveli Lucknow in *sarkar* Lucknow. The *zamindars* of the *pargana* Inhauna and Satinpur in *sarkar* Awadh, were converted Rajputs of Chauhan and Bachgoti clans. It appears that by 1900 the position of Muslim land-holdings had undergone a drastic change. For one thing, deliberate attempts seem to have been made by the Government from time to time to create Muslim *zamindars* in the midst of recalcitrant Rajput chiefs. Sher Andaz Khan, the deputy *Faujdar* of Baiswara at the close of Aurangzeb's reign, specially recommend the creation of Muslim *zamindaris* in *pargana* Shapur and Hadha after the revolt of the Rajput *zamindars* of these *parganas*. The recommendations were made in favour of those officials who had led successful operations against the rebels.[102]

The Afghans had acquired large estates in many parts of the *suba* in addition to their continued hold over the *parganas* in which they are recorded as the *zamindars* in 1595. In *sarkar* Gorakhpur they held *pargana* Utraula and they retained it in their house till 1903 with a brief interruption caused due to seizure by the Janwar Rajputs of Balrampur in 1830. Soon afterwards

101. Album, p. 22.

102. *Insha-i Roshan Kalam* describes the rebellion of the Chauhan Rajputs of the village Khanjura, *pargana* Shahpur and its suppression by one Syed Muzaffar Mohani, who was recommended for the *zamindari* rights of these villages. While the creation of the *zamindari* right of the *pargana* Hadha for one Syed Ghulam Mohiuddin, who might prove useful in suppression of the revolt of the Rajputs. See ff. 3a and 7b.

they were restored to their lost possessions and by 1903 they held 73 villages and 5 *pattis* assessed at Rs 44,977.[103] The estate of Nanpara was a creation of later times. The founder of this house is said to have been appointed as *Qiledar* of *sarkar* Bahraich by Emperor Shahjahan. During *Nizamat* period Shujauddaulah bestowed upon this house the title of 'Raja' and granted the *jagir* comprising Sangha, Bahraich and Kaluapara. In 1903, the *ta'alluqa* had grown considerably and it included 333 villages and 9 *pattis*. The revenue paid by them amounted to Rs 2,48,500.[104]

In the district of Lucknow one Faqir Muhammad Khan, an Afridi Afghan, was granted a piece of land by Nawab Shujauddaulah. "In 1827 he obtained the land of the *pargana* (Malihabad) and held it till 1843, in the meantime acquiring several villages by default." He also obtained a lien on several other lands and thus founded an estate known as Tharri-Fatehnagar.[105] Later on the estate was divided between his two sons, becoming known as Sahlamau and Kasmandi Khurd. As a whole it consisted of 26 villages and 12 *pattis* assessed at Rs 39,342.[106] Another noticeable possession of the Afghans lay in the district of Hardoi, this being the estate of Basitnagar. It was bestowed upon Dildar Khan, the son of Diler Khan, (founder of Shahabad) as jagir by Emperor Aurangzeb. The grant was resumed by Nawab Sa'adat Ali Khan but the successors of Dildar Khan managed by means of purchase, mortgage, and other well-known means to acquire about 40 villages.[107] About 1903 the family possessions consisted of 29 villages and 6 *pattis*, and the total revenue demand was Rs 22,270.[108]

The Shaikhzadas (or Shaikhs) seem to have lost only their small possession of *pargana* Lucknow Haveli to Burhan-ul Mulk Sadat Khan in 1722 AD,[109] while their other possessions remained intact with many more additions during the subsequent period. The holders of the large *ta'alluqadari* estates of Mahmudabad, Bithara and Bhatwamau were actually the descendants of the Shaikhzadas of *pargana* Fatehpur. Their original possessions were enlarged as a result of the post-Mutiny confiscations of some Rajput estates; they obtained the large *ta'alluqa* of the Bisin Raja of

103. *DG*, Vol. 44, pp. 263-5.

104. *DG*, Vol. 45, pp. 75-76; see also *Album*, p. 15.

105. *Album*, pp. 59-60 and 65; see also *DG*, Vol. 37, pp. 92-3.

106. *Album*, pp. 59-60 and 65; see also *DG*, Vol. 37, pp. 92-3.

107. *DG*, Vol. 41, pp. 88-9; see also *Album*, p. 25.

108. *Ibid.*

109. Kamaluddin Haider, *Sawanihat-i Salatin-Awadh*, pp. 7-8, Lucknow, 1879.

Mithauli consisting of 68 villages and assessed at Rs 46,600. As a whole they now possessed 306 villages and 43 *pattis* for Rs 2,67,024 in 1903.[110] The estate of the Qudwai Shaikhs, Jahangirabad, dates back to the days of emperor Jahangir, in whose name it was founded. They purchased the Bisin estate of Simranwan, a portion of Usmanpur *ta'alluqa* and some other villages.[111] The more significant additions were made in this estate only during the last quarter of the ninteenth century. In 1873, they held just 65 villages and 30 *pattis*, while in 1903 this *ta'alluqa* comprised 94 villages and 67 *pattis*. The Government demand was fixed at Rs 1,32,547.[112] A branch of the Jahangirabad family was settled at Ambhapur in Bahraich district. Their possessions comprised a village and 25 *pattis*, all of them situated in the *pargana* Hisampur.[113] It was through matrimonial alliances that the Qidwais were able to acquire possession of this *ta'aluqa* from the *qanungos* of Hisampur. The Tipraha *ta'alluqa* of Khairati Shaikhs originated in quite a peculiar manner. It was established by a local *tahsildar* and flourished under his successors. But as a result of the post-Mutiny confiscations it dwindled to only 15 villages and 4 *pattis*, the total assessment being Rs 9,200.[114]

There were many Shaikh families possessing large estates in the districts of Barabanki and Hardoi. Their traditional account suggests that they had settled at an early date, but they came into prominence only during the 17th century and in the Nizamat period with their appointments as petty revenue officials. In the subsequent period they acquired superior rights over large tracts of land by using methods 'too well known' in Awadh. The ancestors of holders of the Bhilwal *ta'alluqa* are said to have been appointed *Chaudharis* by Shahjahan in 1616 in *pargana* Subeha. In course of time they enlarged their possessions to the extent that in 1903 they were the owners of 30 villages and 13 *pattis* assessed at Rs 32,569.[115] The *ta'alluqa* of Kakrauli owes its origin to Shaikh Firoz, who was appointed *Chaudhri* by Akbar. The family held this title during the *Nizamat* period, when their rights and privileges were assessed for Rs 10,000 with the absolute gift of certain villages as *Nankar*. In the later period, many members of this family worked as *chakledars* of the Awadh administration. About 1900, this estate

110. *DG*, Vol. 40, pp. 62-5; *Album*, pp. 8-10.

111. *DG*, Vol. 48, pp. 101-2; *Album*, pp. 14-5.

112. *Ibid.*, Appendix, pp. 39-41.

113. *DG*, Vol. 45, p. 85.

114. *DG*, Vol. 48, pp. 106-7.

115. *DG*, Vol. 48, pp. 106-7.

comprised 91 villages and 7 *pattis* assessed at Rs 89,140, including the confiscated property of the Unnao *zamindars*.[116] The Shaikhs of Gopamau are said to have been appointed Chaudharis by Humayun (1) and had retained the title till the Annexation. Subsequently, they acquired two rent-free villages and a cash *nankar* of Rs 1600. Many other villages were obtained by purchase. Around 1900 their possessions were large enough to be assessed at Rs 17,798.[117]

The Ansaris and Sayyids are recorded in the *Ain* as the *zamindars* of *pargana* Ibrahimabad and Satrikh in *sarkar* Awadh and *pargana* Amethi in sarkar Lucknow. They seem to have retained their possessions of Ibrahimabad and Satrikh intact for the succeeding three centuries. By 1900, 60 percent of the *pargana* was held by these proprietors in *ta'alluqadari* tenures.[118] In *pargana* Amethi, they seem to have continued their hold till 1900. The large estate of Salempur and Adampur Bhatpur, consisting of 30 villages and two *pattis* assessed at Rs 48,566, was held by scions of the old family.[119]

The Sayyids are recorded as the exclusive *zamindars* of the *parganas* of Bilgiram and Unam in *sarkar* Lucknow by Abul Fazl. During the period of the *nizamat* they had acquired landed possessions in other parts of *suba* Awadh as well. In district of Fyzabad, the *ta'alluqa* of Pirpur was established by one Mirza Muhammad Ali Beg during the reign of Shujauddaulah. Subsequently the neighbouring *ta'alluqa* of Saidanwan was also amalgamated in it. About 1900, it comprised 130 villages and 108 *pattis* assessed at Rs 1,26,898.[120] There was a spectacular rise similarly in the fortunes of the *ta'alluqa* of Samanpur. The family had originally three revenue-free villages, but between 1759-63, one Malik Nurullah rose to influence and obtained engagements for 50 villages. Subsequent additions were made in the *ta'alluqa* in course of time about 1900 the estate consisted of 65 villages and 34 *pattis*, the revenue standing at Rs 1,05,284.[121] The traditional account of the Bilgram Sayyids connects them with the celebrated house of the Barha Sayyids of Muzaffarnagar. During the Mughal period the place had attained a great name for the learning of its Sayyid inhabitants, a tradition which continued during the later period as well. Many persons of this place obtained

116. *DG*, Vol. 41, pp. 86-7.

117. *DG*, Vol. 41, p. 81.

118. *DG*, Vol. 48, p. 270.

119. *Ibid.*, p. 113.

120. *DG*, Vol. 43, pp. 97-100.

121. *Ibid.*, pp. 100-102.

high posts in Mughal service, a fact which might explain the continued ownership of land in *pargana* Bilgiram and its vicinity from the time of *Ain* to 1900. The old Sayyid families had two *ta'alluqas* namely, Bhogetapur and Asafpur, jointly consisting of 52 villages and three *pattis* and assessed at Rs 49,940.[122] In *pargana* Unnao the old Sayyid family retained their landed possessions, and about 1900, they were the chief *ta'alluqadars* of the *pargana* and held 9 out of a total 36 villages assessed at Rs 10,628 in addition to their position of *chaudhari* and *zamindar*.[123]

The holders of revenue-free grants also enlarged their possessions with full fledged proprietary rights in land, often with the connivance of the Government. There are instances when the old hereditary owners of land were dispossessed, on the pretext of rebellion coupled with the allegation of their refusal to pay land-revenue, in order to settle Muslim divines. On occasions these grants were made in hitherto barren land, expressly with the purpose of extension of cultivation and settlements. Such grants could have had but little effect on the overall position of land holdings of various clans. But some individual cases might be mentioned. The ancestors of the family of mystics established at Salon were granted 200 *bighas* of waste land by Aurangzeb in his 19th RY/1676 AD.[124] Subsequently a son of Shah Pir Muhammad was awarded the revenue-free grant of the village Ashrafnagar Singhol 1679 AD. Subsequent additions were made by later Mughal Emperors, such as Bahadur Shah I and Shah Alam II. During the *Nizamat* period a number of villages were added to the already existing grant. Asafuddaulah, is said to have paid a visit to the shrine at Salon and had granted 12 revenue-free villages in perpetuity by expelling the old clan of proprietors who were Kanhpuria Rajputs for their alleged 'contumacy or rebellion', these villages yielded annually Rs 25,000.[125]

Grants of a similar nature existed in Gorakhpur. The Sabzposh family received some *madad-e maash* grant from Babur, but in course of time their possessions were enlarged to such an extent that in the time of Asafuddaulah it consisted of about 49 villages and in 1900, the whole grant was assessed at Rs 14,778.[126] The house of Miyan Saheb Gorakhpur traces

122. *DG*, Vol. 41, pp. 90-92; 179-83.

123. *DG*, Vol. 38, pp. 247-8.

124. For the translation and a notation of the *farman* issued by Aurangzeb in 1676 and 1689 for revenue grants to the mystics of Salon. See my paper, '*Two Madad-e-Ma'ash farmans of Aurangzeb from Awadh*', *PIHC* (1979 session), pp. 302-14.

125. *DG*, Vol. 39, pp. 101-3.

126. W.H. Sleeman, '*A Journey through the Kingdom of Awadh*', Vol. I, pp. 234-5, London, 1858; see also Donald Buttler, *Topography Statistics of the Southern Districts of Awadh*, Calcutta, 1939, pp. 139-40.

its origins to the later days of Muhammad Shah. Their Shi'ite leanings brought them a revenue-free grant of 15 villages during the period of Asafuddaulah. Their loyal conduct during the Mutiny proved still more beneficial to them; they were rewarded with the grant of more villages. By 1900 the family possessions consisted of 61 villages at a light assessment of Rs 8,889.[127] Here it is not possible exactly to determine as to which clans of land-holders suffered due to these new allotments. Large Muslim Pindari estates were created in the present district of Gorakhpur by the officials of the East India Company in order to avert the possibility of further disturbances by setting some of the Pindari leaders in remote parts of the country. Their large possessions included the confiscated property of the Raja of Barhiapor in satisfaction of the arrears of revenue. It consisted of no less than 145 villages, but the revenue assessment was purposely fixed at the low figure of Rs 7,105.[128]

In the *Ain-i Akbari*, there is no entry under the *zamindari* column for the money-lending classes such as Banyas and Khatris, in *suba* Awadh. The extension of the landed possessions of these classes particularly in *kayasths* and the *khatris* in Awadh during the 19th century was not as substantial as in the Doab.[129] Awadh did not undergo the same turmoil in landed possession as the areas subject to the notorious *Mahalwari* system. During the time that this system was in operation at its highest pressure, Awadh (not annexed until 1856) remained immune from its inequities. Since fewer estates were put on sale there was smaller opportunity for the mercantile and bureaucratic inroads into land-ownership. The total landed possessions of Kayasth in Awadh (excluding Gorakhpur division) consisted of 156 villages and *pattis* 188 assessed at Rs 208,361, while the Khatri estates contained 103 villages and 72 *pattis* assessed at Rs 1,00,665.[130] In Gorakhpur division ceded to the British as early as 1801 the position of these classes was much better. The Agarwals and Kayasths district alone, while in Basti district the Kayasths possessed 7.1 percent of the total area.[131] It is possible that insecurity too had some role to play in the absence of land-purchases by financiers in pre-1856 Awadh. Lalji says that,

127. *DG*, Vol. 31, pp. 119-20.

128. *DG*, Vol. 31, pp. 119-20.

129. *DG*, Vol. 31, pp. 120-21.

130. The total of the *ta'alluqadari* possessions of these castes is obtained from the list given in the end of the volume of the *District Gazetteers* of Awadh. In the post-1856 Awadh districts, their most numerous possessions lay in Sitapur, Kheri, Rae-Bareili, Unao and Barabanki.

131. *DG*, Vols. 31 and 32.

"the bankers and the merchants of (the Awadh Kingdom) do not keep their capital at one place due to the fear of the depredations of the *ta'alluqadars* and *zamindars* — illegal revenue demands of the *'amils* and *tahsildars* — there are many who are the owners of the property worth two lacs of rupees and have purchased *zamindaris* and villages in British dominions."[132]

The establishment and the subsequent rise of the Sikh 'estates' in Awadh was also purely a post-Mutiny phenomenon. The large estate of Kapurthala came into existence by a deliberate act of Government in order to reward the 'loyalists' for their role in the Mutiny. As a result many old hereditary land owners were dispossessed of their *zamindaris*. The estate of Kapurthala consisted with 504 villages and 49 *pattis*, assessed at Rs 2,73,567.[133]

In Awadh, then, the superior land-holders appear to have maintained their composition broadly unchanged between the end of the sixteenth and nineteenth centuries. The *ta'alluqadari* tenure introduced some new elements, but even here the clans already possessing *zamindaris* seems to have dominated. The big *zamindars* appear to have had the earliest access to *ta'alluqa* engagements in the Awadh kingdom and this remained so under the British. On the other hand, some *zamindar* caste recorded in the *Ain-i Akbari* escapes notice in the *District Gazetteers*, this may well be due to their conversion into under-proprietors under the *ta'alluqadari* system. It may well be, as we have urged in the case of the money-lenders and bureaucrats, that the stability of composition of the *zamindar* class was due essentially to be the late date at which Awadh was annexed. Otherwise the story of its *zamindars* might have been the same as those of western Uttar Pradesh.

Table - V

***Zamindar* Castes in Awadh in c. 1595**

Zamindar Castes	*AWADH*		*KHAIRABAD*	
	Revenue	*Percentage*	*Revenue*	*Percentage*
(a) Rajputs: Bais	36,35,070	8.87	4,57,332	1.04
Gaur	-	-	36,93,053	8.29
Bachgoti	77,21,766	18.85	-	-
Surajbansi	-	-	-	-
Bisin	-	-	20,82,593	4.74
Sombansi	13,60,753	3.32	30,55,339	6.96

(*Contd...*)

132. Lalji, *op. cit.*, ff. 80b-81a.

133. *Album*, pp. 3-5 and also *DG*, Vol. Nos. 42, 45 and 48.

Gehlots	14,15,701	3.45	-	-
Janwars	-	-	4,15,587	0.9
Bachhils	14,15,701	3.45	39,77,894	9.07
Raikwars	-	-	-	-
Chandel	-	-	-	-
Chauhans	41,41,078	10.11	20,91,983	4.77
Rajwars	79,24,908	19.34	-	-
Tomars	-	-	-	-
Undifferentiated	96,98,537	23.68	1,03,09,841	23.51
Total Rajputs	3,73,13,514	91.07	2,60,83,622	59.28
(b) Other castes:				
Brahmans	15,57,763	3.80	76,33,331	17.4
Sayyids	-	-	-	-
Afghans	-	-	-	-
Ansari	15,71,712	3.83	-	-
Kumbis	10,04,183	2.45	-	-
Amins	-	-	39,67,684	9.04
Ahirs	-	-	35,66,055	8.13
Miscellaneous	3,08,788	0.75	12,21,733	2.78
Others	-	-	4,57,332	1.04
Total others	**44,42,446**	**9.93**	**1,68,46,135**	**38.39**

Source: Ain-i Akbari: The figures are the result of a comparison of the texts of the Texts of the following MSS, British Museum Add. 5645; Add. 6552.

Lucknow		***Bahraich***		***Gorakhpur***	
Revenue	***Percentage***	***Revenue***	***Percentage***	***Revenue***	***Percentage***
2,29,96,760	28.49	13,15,051	5.45	6,76,792	5.67
- -	-	-	-	-	
21,04,023	2.60	-	-	-	-
- -	-	-	10,67,385	8.94	
- -	15,82,345	6.56	51,61,321	43.27	
- -	-	-	15,60,294	13.08	
97,13,997	11.28	-	-	-	-
- -	12,11,843	5.01	-	-	
53,11,950	6.57	-	-	-	-
- -	47,40,221	19.65	-	-	
43,56,254	5.39	-	-	-	-
25,05,047	3.10	-	-	-	-
- -	-	-	-	-	
- -	9,66,539	4.00	-	-	
1,67,72,057	20.77	1,05,64,180	43.79	20,12,533	16.87
6,31,60,078	80.00	2,03,80,179	84.46	1,04,77,825	87.83
(c) Other castes:					
38,27,339	4.73	-	-	-	-
45,74,428	5.66	-	-	-	-

(*Contd...*)

8,46,240	1.04	-	-	13,97,367	11.7
52,39,457	6.48	-	-	-	-
-	-	-	-	-	-
-	-	-	-	-	-
-	-	-	-	-	-
-	-	21,40,858	8.87	-	-
-	-	16,19,480	6.71	51,100	0.42
1,44,87,464	19.91	37,60,338	15.58	14,48,467	12.13

(c) Armed Power of the *Zamindars*

It has been shown in the previous section of this chapter that the superior proprietary rights in land had an intimate connection with the domination of particular clan over an area. We have also seen that the major clans were able to maintain their hold broadly unchanged between 1595 to the annexation of Awadh. Although we have argued that such stability was essentially due to the late date at which Awadh was annexed by the British, one should not forget that such an uninterrupted possession of their rights also depended upon the capacity of that particular clan to maintain its hold with the help of armed power. "Armed force appears as the first historical pre-requisite for the establishment, as well as the retention, of *zamindari* rights."[134]

Use of armed power by various clans to keep their possessions intact and/or to acquire new possessions had been a continuous process in Awadh throughout the medieval period. The traditional account of the *Chakla* Gorakhpur bears testimony to this fact:

> "In ancient times the dominion and *raj* of the neighbourhood of this city belonged to the caste of Domes. Thus, remains of their forts at Batyalgarh, Ramgarh, Bhindiagarh, Domangarh etc. in the area adjoining the city are found to this day. And in the villages the caste of Tharus, i.e. the hillmen of the race of those who are now settled at the foot of the hills, had their settlements. The markets of Batwal for the sale of goods from the hills was held in Gorakhpur. From the time of the establishment of the rule of the Muslims, the markets and settlements of the *Tharus* gradually disappeared and exist now only in the *Terai*. Some Srinet Rajput natives of Srinagar having extirpated them, established their power and are uptill now known as Raja Gorakhpuri. Thus, their descendants hold the *zamindari* of some of the villages of Silhat and of the *pargana* of the environs of Gorakhpur and Silhat hold (their lands) in accordance with the deeds of the Gorakhpuri Raja.

134. Irfan Habib, *Agrarian System*, p. 163.

Afterwards in the time of Akbar, the ancestors of the *ta'alluqadar* of Kachhar, formerly residing in the *pargana* of Bhauwapora with their kinsmen seized the *zamindari* of the environs of Gorakhpur and Silhat which till now is in the hands of their descendants."[135]

Apart from such traditional accounts, Abul Fazl has given detailed statistical information in the account of the 'Twelve Subas' about the military resources of the *Buniyas* or *zamindars*, viz. Cavalry, infantry, number of elephants in each *pargana*. The *sarkar*-wise information is tabulated below:

Table - VI

	Sarkars	***Elephants***	***Cavalry***	***Infantry***
1.	*Sarkar* Awadh	23	1,340	30,400
2.	*Sarkar* Bahraich	-	1,170	14,300
3.	*Sarkar* Gorakhpur	-	1,010	22,000
4.	*Sarkar* Khairabad	-	1,160	27,800
5.	*Sarkar* Lucknow	36	2,680	77,050
	Total	**59**	**7,360**	**1,71,550**

Almost all the *parganas* of the *suba* possessed cavalry, and infantry. This makes it almost certain that every land holder of consequence maintained armed retainers. By the 17th century, they invariably had built mud forts (*garhis* or *qilacha*) in villages of their *zamindaris* to station these retainers. An interesting petition from *pargana* Hisampur, *sarkar* Bahraich, reports a night attack by certain malfactors on a village included in the *zamindari* possession of one Saiyied Muhammad 'Arif. He speaks of a *gilacha* he had built to protect his possessions.[136] In another document a reference is made to the razing of a *gilacha* by some usurpers and it was ordered that the same be rebuilt by those who had destroyed it.[137] In the *Insha-i-Roshan Kalam* a number of expeditions against such forts of recalcitrant *zamindars* are mentioned. R'ad Andaz Khan as well as his deputy Sher Andaz Khan boasted of their services in destroying and capturing various *garhis* of the *zamindar* of Bainswara.[138] In one '*arzdasht* it is said that the Chauhan *zamindars* of *pargana* Kanjura had refused to pay the land-revenue and with the help of 8 or 9,000 men had attacked *pargana* Shahpur. In retaliation, a number of their forts (*garhis*) were

135. Mufti Ghulam Hazrat, *Kwaif-e-Gorakhpur*, f. 7a-b. The translation of this passage is given in Irfan Habib, *Agrarian System*, p. 160.

136. *Allahabad-1225* (December 1689), New No. *RAA-1304*.

137. *Allahabad-786* (January 1684).

138. IInsha-i-Roshan Kalam, *ff. 2a-4a, 6a-8a.*

captured and many of the rebels were put to the sword. Finally they sued for peace and agreed to pay the land-revenue to the agents of the *jagirdars*.[139] In the similar manner rebellious *zamindars* of *pargana* Bijnore and Zaidpur were suppressed. A number of their forts were taken and handed over to the agents of the *Jagirdars* in lieu of arrears of land-revenue.[140]

Any *zamindar* of consequence always tried to keep his hold over his fortresses, and seize those of his weaker neighbours. The rebel *zamindar* of *pargana* Harha had captured the fort of Murtazanagar from its Saiyyid owners based in Unao. Later on its possession was restored to the owners with the help of the imperial forces.[141] Similarly, new forts were built by *zamindars* at places of strategic importance with the help of professional soldiers. Kharsen, the *zamindar* of *pargana* Jajmau, employed Salim Afghan and building a fort named it Salimgarh. But the Mughal forces stormed the fort, and a number of soldiers, including Salim Afghan, were killed.[142] Fortified houses situated alongside the highway were also used by the *zamindars* to block the passage of the imperial troops. The capture of such places and their control by the imperial officials was thought to be very necessary for establishing control.[143]

A number of the *mahzars* seeking redress against the wrongs suffered by the petitioners and imperial orders containing a recital to the same effect also provide important clues to the strength and the use of armed power by the local *zamindars*. It seems that established hereditary *zamindars* usually resented the induction of any new element, such as land grantees, within their territory. During the reign of Shah Jahan and Aurangzeb, the holders of the *madad-i-ma'ash* grants were therefore often faced with harashment from local *zamindars*, who enforced a non-payment of the land-revenue to the grantees or ensured a refusal of payment of the revenues by the peasants (*ri'aya*).[144]

Two *farmans* of Aurangzeb from *pargana* Sadarpur *sarkar* Khairabad direct the officials to investigate the allegation of the petitioners and report accordingly. It was contended that one Samar Singh *zamindar* of Mahsauti, *pargana* Fakharpur had a number of mounted and foot soldiers, and had became a freebooter. He raided and burnt the villages of the petitioners,

139. *Ibid.*, '*arzdasht* No. 1.

140. *Ibid.*, '*arzdasht* No. 2.

141. *Ibid.*

142. *Ibid.*

143. *Ibid.*, '*arzdasht* No. 3.

144. *Ibid.*

mosques, and tombs being razed to the ground. A number of inhabitants were killed; money amounting to Rs 8213 and 6376 heads of livestock had been taken away.[145] Similarly, the *madad-i-ma'ash* holders of a village in *pargana* Hisampur, *sarkar* Bahraich presented a *mahzar* in 1125 AH/1717 complaining that the residents (*zamindars*?) of the neighbouring villages had attacked their *a'imma* (grant) villages with the help of 500 persons. In the raid many inhabitants were killed, their property looted and destroyed, while the women had committed *jowhar*, even the corpses were not allowed to be buried. Moreover, the family graveyard of the petitioners was brought under the cultivation by the malefactors.[146] Similarly the *zamindars* of *pargana* Fatehpur Devi and of *pargana* Sahali in *sarkar* Lucknow had attacked and killed the representatives of what later came to be the house of Firangi Mahal, Mulla Qutubuddin. The incident occurred in the 35th RY of Aurangzeb.[147]

Often the *zamindars* defied the administration by refusing to acknowledge the authority of the local *qazis*. It seems that the holders of the religious offices and *a'imma*-holders were most vulnerable to the armed power of the *zamindars* since they had no force to back their claims, hence their existence in any area depended upon the help from the military officials of the area. A petition by the family of *qazis* posted in Baiswara especially mentions the tussle between their ancestors and the Bais (*zamindars*) of the area which was going on for the last 80 years. The *qazis* had all the 21 *pargana* of Baiswara under their jurisdiction, but due to the hostility shown by the inhabitants, they have been driven away from 15 *parganas* and now only six *parganas* actually remained within their judicial jurisdiction.[148]

During the first quarter of the 18th century, the local chieftains and the *zamindars* had acquired much power and were in possession of considerable resources. When Sa'adat Khan Burhan-ul-Mulk was appointed the *subedar* of the province, he had to fight a number of battles with these chiefs in various parts of the province. Prior to his appointment as the governor of the *suba*, these chiefs and the *zamindars* were strong enough to undermine the authority of the *nazims* and the agents of the Mughal *jagirdars* as to make the work of revenue collection nearly impossible. But Sa'adat Khan

145. *RAA-287 and 290* (4th RY of Aurangzeb).

146. *RAA-1315*.

147. *FM-185* (35th of Aurangzeb).

148. *NAI-2618* (4th RY of Aurangzeb). I owe this information to Mr Zakir Husain, Archivist, National Archives of India, New Delhi.

dealt these refractory elements with such firmness that in the very first year of his tenure, the total amount of collection increased from barely 70 lacs to 107 lacs of rupees. On realising his ability and competence these Mughal *jagirdars* too leased out their *jagirs* to him on *ijara* tenures. In the next two years, the total collection reached two crores rupees.[149]

The traditional account of the capture of Lucknow from the hands of the Shaikhzadas may well contain a considerable amount of exaggeration. However, from our point of view the importance of the episode lies in the fact that even the newly appointed governor had to resort to dubious methods to reach the provincial capital which happened to be in the hands of local *zamindars*.[150] Or one may think of the power gained by the Kanhpuria chief of Tiloin, Raja Mohan Singh, by plundering the Saiyyid owners of Mustafabad and the Bais chieftain of Khajurgaon. When Burhanul Mulk decided to end the growing pretensions of the chief a battle took place, in which Mohan Singh was killed and all his possessions which lay in the jurisdiction of *suba* Awadh were seized.[151]

Burhanul Mulk was able to keep the recalcitrant elements of the province in check, but with his death the local chieftains began to reassert their power. The successor's, Safdarjung's letters to Muhammad Shah are full of references to the rebellions of the *zamindars*. It was alleged that with the help of their strong forts and numerous armed retainers, they refuse to pay the land revenue and undertook depredations all round.[152] The *nawab-wazir* had to be throughout on the march; and the *nawab-wazir* offered this as an excuse for omitting to heed urgent summons from the imperial court.[153]

In Safdarjung's letters addressed to wazir Qamaruddin Khan, it is stated that due to the rebellious attitude of the chieftains, additional troops are to be maintained in order to carry on the work of revenue collection and keep the malefactors under the effective control. This had enhanced expenses while the actual income (from the *jagirs*?) had fallen, and the *nawab-wazir* had claims outstanding for which he had no *jagirs*. At another place he says that he had instructed his *wakil* (at the imperial court) to be present at the time when new *jagir* assignment orders were issued for the province of

149. Ghulam Husain Khan, *'Imadus-Sa'adat*, pp. 7-8.

150. Kamaluddin Haider, *Swanihat-e-Salatin-e-Awadh*, pp. 7-8; A.L. Srivastava, *FTNA*, pp. 33-5.

151. *'Imadus Saadat'*, pp. 7-8, *FTNA*, pp. 35-7.

152. *Mansur-ul-Maktubat*, pp. 6-7, p. 89.

153. *Ibid.*, pp. 4-6; pp. 38-40.

Awadh, so that he may invite the attention of the *wazir* towards the acute problem faced by the *nawab-wazir* in administering the turbulent province of Awadh.[154]

The *zamindars* and local potentiates were always prone to take to banditry. Roads and the highways were considered to be quite unsafe, and it was always considered necessary for heavy armed escort to accompany the treasures passing through the territorial limits of Awadh.[155]

Among the major rebellions by the *zamindars* during Safdarjung's reign, was a fresh one by the Kanhpuria chieftains of Tiloin. He had collected together a numerous body of armed retainers and possessed a very strong fort. It was surrounded by a deep ditch and the extensive belt of dense and thorny jungle. But the forces of *nawab-wazir* were strong enough to defeat the Rajput forces and to capture the fort in 1739.[156] Another important uprising was that of the Gaur *zamindars* of *sarkar* Khairabad. It appears that they had refused to pay the land-revenue and took to banditry. Safdar Jung, through forced marches reached their strongholds, the forts of Nabigarh and Katesar. These forts fell after a sieze of eleven days and with some difficulty the Rajputs were defeated and the area was brought under control.[157]

After the battle of Buxar Shuja-ud-daula was forced to reduce his regular army, and strong exception was taken by the Company officials at the reported attempts of the *nawab* to re-organise the army. As a result, the work of revenue collection could proceed only with the help of the British forces. Such help was always available to the local officials of the *nawab-wazir* as the Company was entitled to receive large sums of money out of these collections. Indeed, the English looked askance at the *zamindars*' refusal to pay revenue for the amounts so withheld were sure to be "expanded on those numerous forces which the *zamindars* raised and (?) up only to support them in their resistance to Government".[158]

The revenue contractors, had constantly to face armed resistance of the *zamindars* in their respective jurisdictions. Often they were ruthless in suppression of the uprisings. The atrocities committed by Almas Ali Khan

---

154. *Mansur-ul-Maktubat*, pp. 46-7.

155. *Ibid.*, pp. 7-8; pp. 14-16; pp. 17-18, 42,

156. *Ibid.*, pp. 30-31; In a letter addressed to Nawab Ishaq Khan (?) Safdarjung conveyed the news of his victory over the rebels of Tiloi. Their forts were captured and a number of Rajput chiefs were put to sword. *Ibid*, ff. 77-8. See also *FTNA*, pp. 92-4.

157. *Ibid.*, pp. 6-7.

158. *FDSC*, 12 January, 1778, *NAI*.

against the *zamindars* of Doab were reported to Middleton in 1778. However, in whatever he did he obtained the help of the British forces.[159] But it was thought that the destruction of the forts of the *zamindars* in Doab, "will have many ill consequences and accordingly the *nawab-wazir* was advised to adopt, "more conciliatory mode of proceeding" when using British forces against such elements."[160]

In the early years of Asaf-ud-daulah's reign, the *zamindars* of Gorakhpur went into rebellion. The intensity of these disturbances was such that *nawab-wazir* had to proceed in person to suppress the rebellion.[161] A group of bandits made a night attack on the royal treasury, when it was going to Lucknow from Baiswara. A good number of Company sepoys accompanying the treasury were killed. Obviously such an attack could have been made only with the help of local *zamindars*.[162]

The death of Asaf-ud-daulah in 1797 marks a watershed in the history of Awadh, it offered an opportunity to the Company to conclude new treaties with his successors first with Wazir Ali and then with Sa'adat Ali Khan (1798-1814). Now, the subordination of the kingdom of Awadh to the Company was complete in every respect. The army had to be disbanded and even the work of the revenue collection was to be done only with British help. The help had mixed results. It was alleged that the, "country was pillaged under the sanction of the British name and under the terror of sepoy bayonets" and also, "the more parties (of the sepoys) were sent out in support of the *amin*, the more were called for".[163] To remedy such a situation, it was suggested by the Resident that the 'crown dues' be leased out to the *zamindars* for a number of years instead of being collected by *amins*. Under this system 'proofs' were to be furnished by the king for the outstanding dues against the erring *zamindars* before military help was given by the British to coerce them into making payments.[164] Such a tedious process could only further encourage the *zamindars*. The king, accordingly remonstrated that, "his difficulties have arisen from his entire confidence in the friendship of the Company. That this induced him and his ancestors

159. *FDSC*, 8 January, 1778, NAI.

160. *FDSC*, 8th January 1778, NAI. For a later account of Almas Ali Khan, when he was around 80 years old, see J.V. Valentia, *Voyages and Travels in India Cyclone, the Red Sea, Abbysinia and Egypt 1802-6*, 3 Vols, London, 1809; See. Vol. I, pp. 136-7.

161. *FSC*, 26th February, 1777 © and 21st April 1777(D), NAI.

162. *Ausaf-al-Asaf*, ff. 69b-70a.

163. *Heber*, pp. 84-5.

164. *Ibid.*, p. 85.

to disband an excellent army and thus they have become unable, without help to enforce payment of their ancient revenues."[165] Under these circumstances the *zamindars* had acquired such power as to make the king plead for his own survival, "from the only enemies he has or is likely to have, his rebellious *zamindars*".[166] The 'judicious' care and 'scrutiny' of each and every case by the Resident, before the requisition of the king for sepoys was met, had adversely affected the fortunes of the kingdom. The king was unable to face the rebellious *zamindars*, as they had driven away many of his officials from their areas and in this process, "the chief actual sufferers at the present movement are the king, who gets little or nothing even of his undoubted dues, and the traveler, who unless he has such a guard as I have had better sleep in a safe kin on the other side of the Ganges".[167]

The *zamindars* were able to multiply their armed retainers, forts, cannons and guns after the death of Sa'adat Ali Khan (1814). This became possible as the king was unable to check their activities, and the British help too was not forthcoming to the king in his attempts if ever made to punish a rebellious *zamindar*. It should not be assumed that they were simply 'invincible' or Awadh government was in any way less competent to control the situation. Sleeman describes how the Kanhpuria Rajput chiefs of Nain were suppressed by Raja Durshan Singh and Bukhtawar Singh during their term of *nizamat* of the district Salon (in which lay the Nain estate). But when the affairs of this place were entrusted to a court favourite, Hamid Ali, the situation undergone a change. Thereafter, "the Kanhpuria have recovered all the lands they had lost, restored all the *jungal* that had been cut down, and they are now more powerful than ever. They have strengthened their forts, and built some new and added greatly to the number of their armed followers, so that the governor of the district dares not do any thing to coerce them into the payment of just demands of government or to check into their usurption and outrages."[168] The Gaur *zamindar* of Banthar in Bainswara named Kesri Singh paid Rs 1,50,000 annually in revenue, but thought it expedient to maintain 1000 matchlockmen. With these forces he defeated and slew a *chakledar* Sobha Ram and *faujdar*, Shaikh Karim Buksh.[169]

165. *Heber*, p. 86.

166. *Ibid.*, p. 87.

167. *Ibid.*, p. 88.

168. Sleeman, I, pp. 134-5.

169. Buttler, p. 100.

Such defence could have been broken very well, but the army employed to bring down these *zamindars* was never given adequate supplies as to carry any long siege of the *garhis*, most of which were situated in midst of thick bamboo jungle. On the other hand the supply line of the besieged rebels could not be successfully broken as the neighbouring *zamindar*, always entertained a strong sense of fellow-feeling for them. Although the total strength of Awadh forces was said to have been 54,000, it was, "an ill paid, disorderly multitude employed in coercing the *zamindar* under the orders of the *chakledar*.[170] It was thought of it to be, "useful only to the enemy, it is dangerous to the well-being of the state, utterly useless for war, most mischievous during peace".[171] The number of the retainers kept by the *zamindars* was computed at 100,000 men, and they were mostly drawn from the caste of the *zamindars*.[172]

The country was dotted with innumerable fortresses, surrounded with dense forests, carefully rendered inaccessible for state forces.[173] All the *zamindars* invariably kept cannons and big guns for the defence of their forts. A combination of all these factors always proved more than a match for the "royal forces". Sleeman estimated that some 250 mud forts and about 500 pieces of cannon were deployed in their service.[174]

It seems the British officials had no clear idea of the actual strength of the *zamindars*, and whatever they guessed was a gross under-estimate. The actual position came to light only after the Rebellion of 1857 was over, and the British officials started some sort of combing operations in the province. As a result 1575 forts were destroyed and 720 pieces of cannon were seized.[175] In addition to these general statements, we possess a statement showing the armed strength of 149 land-holders of southern portions of Awadh. It was prepared by the deputy commissioner of Salon (then a large administrative division of southern Awadh) in 1858. We find that every land-holder invariably had a *kacha* or *pacca* fort and a number of armed retainers. Even small land-holders having two villages, maintained a fort. The statement gives us the following statistics:[176]

170. Thornton, p. 36.

171. *CR-1845* (111), p. 388.

172. Thornton, p. 36.

173. *CR-1845*, (111), p. 421.

174. Sleeman, II, pp. 210-1.

175. *CR-1860* (XXXV), pp. 132-3 Cf. RD Reeves *Sleeman in Oudh*, Cambridge, 1971; see the introduction, p. 22.

176. Board of Revenue, Lucknow, File No. 395/1858 (Oudh General).

Table - VII

List of the Forts, Guns and Retainers Belonging to the Ta'alluqadars of Southern Awadh

Forts	*Infantry*	*Strength* *Cavalry*	*Total*	*Guns*
150	78,211	3,313	81,524	308

Although details regarding the other parts of the kingdom are not available, still one can have an idea as to what the actual strength of the land-holders was on the eve of annexation.[177]

As a necessary corollary, the British Government carried a systematic campaign to disband the retainers, confiscate the guns and destroy the forts of the land-holders after the fall of Lucknow. We have an interesting lease-deed (*patta*) executed in 1265 F/1858 in favour of a revenue grantee. It was stipulated that the leasee should have surrendered all pieces of cannon and guns to the government officials. All the forts situated in his area should have been destroyed, the forests cleared and the ditches filled. If any other land-holder in his area had concealed any guns or cannon, the matter be immediately brought to the notice of the government. In failing to discharge these duties, stern action would be taken including the forfeiture of the lease itself.[178] Other confirmatory *sanads* issued to recognise the previously existing allodial rights of the *ta'alluqadars*, the *zamindars* and the revenue-grantees invariably carried a recitation to this effect.

Lalji laments on the fact that, "among the Hindu inhabitants of the country (Awadh), the most numerous are the Rajputs. Most of the large *zamindari* and the *ta'alluqadari* of the kingdom belong to them. The fact that they possess large body of the (armed) retainers and forts, had made them arrogant and hence they had become disrespectful towards the others. Some of these idiots show no consideration towards the priestly class of the Brahmans ... and openly defy the religious customs."[179] Apart from this, the government annually incurred heavy loss to its income, as these land-holders tried to get the maximum concession by way of *nankar*.

177. The total number of the forts in Awadh belonging to the land-holders were said to be around 633 at the time of the annexation. Foreign consultation No. 136/53 dated 31st October 1856. *NAI-Delhi* (Letter No. 340 dated 18th August 1856 from Judicial Commissioner of Awadh to Secretary to the Chief Commissioner) Cf. A.A. Azmi, Position of *Ta'alluqadars in Awadh*, p. 18.

178. *Khairabad-10.*

179. Lalji, *Mirat-ul Auza*, ff. 74a-76b.

The actual mechanism as to how the *nankar* was increased has been discussed elsewhere.[180] The additional income so gained was again invested by the *zamindars* in raising the number of the retainers, forts and cannon.[181]

In many ways the increase in armed power of the *zamindar* was a direct consequence of the British interference in day-to-day affairs of the kingdom. No doubt the *zamindars* had always kept a number of the retainers maintained forts, rebelled or taken to banditry under Mughal rule. But by and large, they seem to have been kept in check till the reign of Shuja'ud-daulah. But after Buxar a sort of 'dyarchy' was introduced in Awadh and interference was attempted at all the levels without any recognised system of policy. The Awadh administration became a prey to changing policies of the British Governor-Generals. "Everything ... mere guess work and experiment. One Governor-General, or one Resident had adopted one plan; next had tried some thing wholly different."[182] On occasion, Company sepoys were deployed immediately to crush rebellions of *zamindars*, while on other such occasion, help was refused even on the requisition of the king himself. Such a situation could not but greatly encourage the *zamindars* to take up arms against the government as well as against their fellows.

180. See Section I of this Chapter.

181. Lalji, *op. cit.*, p. 91.

182. *CR-1845*, (111), p. 421.

Appendix

{The Baiswara region with 22 contiguous *mahals* forms a compact unit within the mughal *suba* of Awadh. It was dominated by the Bais clan of the Rajput as the rural overlords of the area since early 16th century. These zamindar had their reserve forest and in its midst the small fortress (*garhi, qilacha*), canons and other ammunition to protect themselves from any onslaught on their authority. It was during the 17th century that the region acquired considerable notoriety for the activities of the 'seditious people belonging to the *qaum* of bais.' The mughal administration tried to tackle the problem administratively. It created a separate *fauzdari* unit of Baiswara region and placed the unit under the command of a *fauzdar*. The incumbent of this office was invariably most of the time engage in suppressing the uprisings and lawlessness of these chieftains in the various parts of this region. On occasions these bais chieftains supported the uprising and revolts of the neighbouring Rajputs. The condition of the lawlessness in the Baiswara region finds a mention in the Mughal chronicles as well. However, we are fortunate in having a collection of letters and petitions drafted by Munshi Bhupat Rai on behalf of the *fauzdar* of the Baiswara region namely Ra'ad Andaz Khan as well as his deputy Sher Andaaz Khan during the last decade of the 17th century. These dispatches provided the description of the activities of the Bais Rajput in the locality and the efforts imperial forces took to suppress them. My teacher Lt. Professor Zahiruddin Malik perhaps was the only person to have used this source -the collection of letters available in the manuscript form known as *Insha –e Roshan Kalam*- so extensively. He has discussed the administrative problem faced by the *fauzdar* of this area to suppress the local zamindars and the measures he took in providing protection to the class of revenue grantees and 'new zamindars'. Professor Malik has also translated and summarized some of the petitions (*arzdasht*). Unfortunately, this paper of professor Malik was published without the appendix (where he has translated some of these letters) in the proceedings of Indian History Congress, Chandigarh Session, 1973. The full typed script of this paper is available at the library, Centre of advance study, Department of History, Aligarh Muslim University, Aligarh. I feel honoured to reproduce this important contribution of Professor Malik here as an Appendix. Therefore, this is a humble tribute to his memory and scholarship.}

Problems of *Faujdari* Jurisdiction in Baiswara

Dr. Zahiruddin Malik
Aligarh Muslim University

This paper attempts to discuss some problems of the *faujdari* jurisdiction in Baiswara in the last year of Aurangzeb's reign on the basis of petitions (*arzdashts*) and letters addressed by its *faujdar*, Ra'd Andaz Khan, to the imperial court and the *bakhshis* like Mukhlis Khan[1] and Ruhullah Khan[2]. It also attempts to translate and analyse some important petitions which mainly deal with the difficulties of the *faujdar* in the discharge of his duties, his relations with the local *zamindars* and *jagirdars* and the socio-economic conditions prevailing in that area. The contents of these records provide us with an important source-material for the study of sporadic out-breaks of agrarian unrest which were endemic among landholders of various categories and in areas under direct Mughal administration, and the working of the mansabdari system at the local level.

These petitions and letters numbering 14 and 54 respectively are contained in *Insha-i Roshan Kalam* compiled by Bhupat Rai, a *munshi* in the service of the *faujdar*. The author writes in his preface that after serving as diwan (*ba-khidmat-i-diwani*) under big nobles of his day he at last joined the service of Ra'd Andaz Khan who made him the head of *dar-ul-Insha*' (or office for drafting letters and documents).

He adds that in this work he has collected letters, written on his master's behalf, into four *fasals* heading) and gave it the title of *Insha-i Roshan-Kalam*.[3] On the fly-leaf of the India Office Manuscript W. Irvine, to whose collection it belongs, has remarked that "this work was used by C.A. Elliot in his Chronicles of Oonao."[4]

---

1. In the 36 regnal year Mukhlis Khan became the second *bakhshi*. He died on 3 January 1701. For details of his life, *Ma'asir-ul-Umara*, III, 641-644.
2. For details of his life, Ma'asir-ul Umara, II, 309-315.
3. Aligarh Muslim University Ms. 160/23.
4. India Office, No. 4011. This MS was transcribed on 15 May 1905 by Saiyid Muhammad Waliullah and was sent to Irvine in London by Abul Aziz of Bhitri in Ghazipur district. There is another work in his collection entitled *Guldastah-i Bahar*, sent by the same gentleman to Irvine who, it appears, worked as his agent for collecting Persian manuscripts on Indian History and sending them to him. *Guldastah-i-Bahar*, which Irvine has referred in his well-know work, *The Army of the Indian Mughals* (p. 53), is also a collection of *arzdashts* and letters written on behalf of Chhabilah Ram Nagar, *faujdar* of Kurrah Manikpur (in *Ma'asir-ul-Umarah*, II, 328-330 Kurrah-Jahanbad) to Zulfiqar Khan, *the mirbakhshi* of Bahadur Shah I. It was compiled by

Ra'd Andaz Khan was an officer with extensive military experience he had gained in the compaigns of the Deccan. His successful enterprises in the Deccan wars won him sufficient reputation to secure his promotion to a higher rank and appointment to the faujdari of Baiswara, an important and responsible charge fraught in the difficulties. He was raised to the mansab of 1,000/500.[5] According to *Akhbarat* he occupied the post of *faujdari* in the 45th regnal year of Aurangzeb's reign when he sent a congratulatory letter on the conquest of Panhala. He was transferred the same year to the *qala'adari* of Akbarabad; and in the same year again was appointed *faujdar* of Mewat, but before he could assume charge of his new office, he died in Agra.[6] The contents of his letters show that Ra'd Andaz Khan endeavoured hard to maintain the internal security of Baiswara and impart vigour and strength to the local administration by the example of his upright character and hard work. In one arzdasht he stated with a sense of pride that "whereas former *faujdars* incurred heavy expenditure and sacrificed the lives of a large number of soldier's but could not achieve their object, this obedient servant, without suffering any loss in man and money, thoroughly suppressed the disturbers of peace, sized large number of forts from the seditious *zamindars* and established imperial authority in the *mahals* under his jurisdiction."[7] To loyalty and integrity he added a soldier's sense of duty to his superiors. He always referred issues in dispute to the *bakhshi* under whose immediate direction he worked, and sought detailed guidance for carrying out the administration of Baiswara. Though distance from the imperial headquarters in the Deccan and peculiar character of people under his rule doubtless gave him wide latitude of action, but the *faujdar* did not abuse his powers and behave like a petty autocrate. His appointment to the

---

Bahari Ram in 1726-7 who calls himself the nephew of Chhabela Ram (d. 1719). Nearly all the *arzdashts* and letters contained in this work have been copied in verbatim from *Roshan Kalam*; only these congratulatory letters having references to the capture of Jinji (1698) and Panhala (1701) are missing. It is considerably smaller in size with only 23 *arzdashts* and letters; and the name of Ra'd Andaz Khan has been replaced by that of Chhabila Ram. It seems that because *Insha-i-Roshan Kalam* became popular as a treatise on epistolography, several copies were made out, some of which survived and are still available in the Oriental Libraries. It was used for long as a text for learning the art of letter-writing. In this process some one thought to give it the name of *Guldastah-i Bahar* for the purpose of sale as an independent work. India Office, Irvine Collection, MS. 4043.

5. Hadi Kamwar Khan, *Tazkirat-us-Salatin-i-Chghta*, I, f 287 b.
6. *Akhbarat-i Darbar Ma'ullah*, 45/232, 46/12, dated 27 Jamadi-ul Sani, 45 Regnal year, and 46th regnal year.
7. Insha-i Roshan Kalam.

qala'adari of Agra is an ample evidence not only of his administrative achievements but also of the trust in which he was held by the Emperor.

The *faujdari* juridiction of Baiswara extended to contigous areas in the provinces of Awadh and Allahabad, and it included *mahals* which formed parts of the *sarkars* of Lucknow, Awadh, Manikpur and Korra.[8] Most of the *mahals* of Baiswara, mentioned in *Roshan Kalam*, belonged to the *sarkar* of Lucknow. But the parganas of Lucknow, Bijnaur and Kakori lay outside the jurisdiction of the *faujdar* who could undertake military operations against the seditious *zamindars* (zortalab) of these places for non-payment of land revenue and other alleged acts of robbery only on the written petitions from the *karoris* of *jagirdars*. Ra'd Andaz Khan complained that he was not authorised to collect *rahdari* (toll-tax) from the *parganas* as the work had been entrusted to a different person. He in several of his dispatches pointed out and deplored the evils arising from the want of his controlling authority over that area. During the tenure of office he once launched campaign against the refractory zamindars of those places and after suppressing them he seized their cattle, property and forts and handed over to the agents of *jagirdars* who had made specific request for this punitive action, in lieu of the unpaid land revenue.[9]

In a letter addressed to the *mir bakhshi* he requested for his appointment to the *subedari* of Awadh in addition to the *faujdari* of Baiswara he already held.[10] The reason for the exclusion of the above-mentioned parganas from the faujdari jurisdiction of Baiswara was that in this particular area lay the *jagirs* of the Prince and big nobles like Aziz Khan Rohillah who wanted to direct their own affairs without the assistance of the *faujdar*. The Prince and the *mansabdars*, by using their political influence at the imperial court, had acquired the right to exercise executive functions usually vested in the *faujdar*. But as they governed their *jagirs* through their agents - *amils* and *karoris* - , who were by and large incompetent and corrupt, the administration of the area increasingly declined, giving rise to wide-spread unrest and lawlessness. Ra'd Andaz Khan emphasised that all the administrative defects

---

8. From a reference in *Badhshah Namah* it appears that during the reign of Shah Jahan the *Sarkar* of Lucknow and the district of Baiswara were placed under the charge of one *faujdar*. For instance, in 1047 Allahwardi Khan was replaced by Sar Andaz Khan as the *faujdar* of Lucknow and Baiswara. But later, in the same reign Daler Khan was appointed *faujzar* only of Lucknow, and he nominated Jamal Khan his deputy. Abdul Hamid Lahori, *Badshah Namah*, I, 243, 278; Muhammad Kazim, *Alamgir Namah*, 146-47, 450-51.

9. *Insha-i Roshan Kalam*, *Arzdasht*, 1, 4, 6, 11, 13.

10. *Insha-i Roshan Kalam*, *Arzdasht*, 32.

and lapses flowed from this concentration of power in the hands of *jagirdars* and he asserted that the evils could be remedied only by placing the area under his charge.[11] Thus, there arose a conflict on the issue of jurisdiction between the *faujdar* and *jagirdars*. The Mughal *faujdar* had established his headquarters in the *pargana* of Dalmau but in the rainy season he shifted to Lucknow where he stayed for few months.[12] Dalmau formerly belonged to the subah of Allahabad, but later, due to the turbulent character of the people had been added to the district of Baiswara. One letter informs us that at sometime the *parganas* of Dalmau and Bilgram were separated from his jurisdiction and put under the control of a new officer by the government. He bitterly complained against this policy and stressed the need of his continous hold on of the *parganas* without which he could not properly carry out the administration of Baiswara.[13] The names of other *mahals*, given in *Roshan Kalam*, which comprised the *faujdari* jurisdiction of Baiswara were: Kanjura, Harra, Kheri, Bilhaur, Rai Bareili, Unao, Radauli, Uncha Gaon, Amethi, Dewi Manohargadh, Shiupur and Sitapur, Bilgram, Sandila and Bilhar.[14]

The district of Baiswara and its adjoining areas occupied a central and strategic position in the northern part of the Mughal empire. This was populated by the warlike Rajput clans - Bais and Chauhans[15] - who hated the imposition of discipline and authority over them, and organised resistance

11. *Insha-i Roshan Kalam, Arzdasht*, 6, 11.
12. *Insha-i Roshan Kalam, Arzdasht*, 7, 28.
13. *Ibid., Arzdasht*, 27. The name of this officer was Dildar Khan, son of Diler Khan.
14. The names and areas of most of these *mahals* have been recorded in *A'in-i Akbari*, and they correspond closely with the *parganas* of the present day as given in different *District Gazetteers of Awadh and Allahabad*. Kakori in the west of Lucknow had a cultivated area of 30, 574 *bighas* and the revenue of 11, 34, 432 *dams*. Bijnaur in the *sarkar* of Lucknow was held by Chauhans; it had 80, 581 *bighas* of cultivation and the revenues of 25, 051, 047 *dams*. Bilgram is in *sarkar* Lucknow (now in the district of Hardoi) included the present *pargana* of Banger. Bhauli is in pargana Mahona in Malihabad. Amethi (in *pargana* and tehsil Mohan Lal ganj) had a brick fort and the revenue of 3, 0766, 480 *dams* on 117, 381 cultivated area. Unao (Unam in the sarkar of Lucknow) is at present a separate district, Dewi, Sandila Shipur were also in *sarkar* Lucknow. *A'in-i-Akbari*, 11, English tr. H.S. Jarrett, pp. 185-190. Dalmau and Rai Bareli were in *sarkar* Manikpur, and both were centres of Bais Rajputs, in the 18th century Nawal Rai, the famous minister of Safdar Jang, made Dalmau a *chakla* in the *Nizamat* of Baiswara. *District Gazetteer of Rai Bareli*, p. 169; *A'in-i Akbari* 11, p. 176. *District Gazetteers of Lucknow*, pp. 144, 145, 169, 175, 177, 223. The *District Gazetteer of Hardoi*, p. 183, *District Gazetteer of Unao*, p. 180.
15. For the history of these clans, vide, W.C. Benett. *A Report on the Family History of the Chief Clans of the Rai Bareli District*, Lucknow, 1870.

to the government was an outstanding feature of their political behaviour.[16] Resourceful and influential, the Rajput chieftains and *zamindars* had built small forts for defence and they were able to collect the impoverished but sturdy peasants from the surrounding villages in thousands. They withheld the payment of the land revenue and fought the armed forces of the government in the open battle-fields. They invaded and seized the lands, held in jagirs by the Mughal *mansabdars* in their villages, and frequently indulged in highway robbery.[17] Thus, the maintenance of law and order always constituted a major problem. The Mughal government tried to reduce the power of these refractory *zamindars* by using military force and by establishing the rights of new *zamindars*.[18] But the policy of force and counterpoise failed to solve the basic problem which was both economic and social, and the region remained the scene of turbulence, conflict and fighting throughout the period of the Mughal rule.

As the maintenance of law and order and military assistance to *jagirdars* and revenue-collectors was the principal responsibility of the *faujdar*, Ra'd Andaz Khan either marched in person or sent punitive expeditions against the *zamindars*, rebels and other unruly elements. For instance, when the Chauhans of Kanjura refused to pay the land revenue and revolted, he proceeded to put the menace to an end and restore order. The rebels oppressed the weak and respectable persons of the place and they managed to bring 8 to 9 thousand soldiers from the neighbouring villages to the battle-field. No former *faujdar*, he wrote, had been successful in crushing their power by defeating them and capturing their forts. In the fighting which continued for two days the imperial forces inflicted a severe defeat on the enemy; one thousand and four hundred soldiers were arrested and their twelve forts were occupied. The *zamindars* sued for peace and promised to pay the land revenue. Ra'd Andaz Khan received reports from the *karoris* of *jagirdars* that the malefactors of Bijnaur and seditious persons of Dewi had invaded and devastated villages and towns and oppressed the inhabitants and travellers of the area. He accordingly dispatched a military force which defeated the rebels, and seized their forts and property.[19] When he again

16. For details of mutual warfare, armed clashes with the government officers, and revolts, vide - *Alamgir Namah*, pp. 450-51, R.C. Elliot, *Chronicles of Oonao,* pp. 15, 22, 43, 74, Sleeman, *Tour in Oudh*, I, pp. 315-322.
17. Insha-i Roshan Kalam, Arzdasht, No. 3.
18. For instance, Ra'd Andaz Khan recommended the zamindari and mansab to Saiyid Muzaffar son of Anwar Muhani who had taken an active part in the campaign against the rebels of Baiswara. Arzdasht No. 3. Irfan Habib, The Agrarian System of Mughal India, p. 335.
19. Insha-i Roshan Kalam, Arzdasht, 3.

went to Baiswara his agent informed him that Khorsen, *zamindar* of Jajmau had employed Salim Afghan and on his instigation constructed a fort and named it as Salimgadh. The *faujdar*, therefore, sent an army against the *zamindar* and he himself marched to conduct the operations. But before he crossed the Ganges, the good news reached him that the rebels had been defeated and their large number, including Salim Afghan were killed in the battle.[20]

Not only the Rajput chiefs and *zamindars* defied imperial authority and fomented strife, but the warlike tribe of the *Mewatis*, the Shaikhs of Lucknow and Karori, and the Afghans of Rai Bareli raised disturbances, ravaged the country-side and raided the higways. Against each group of the mal-factors and miscreants Ra'd Andaz Khan launched operations and having thoroughly suppressed them, established tranquility in the troubled areas.[21] In one letter he informed the royal court that the Shaikhs had established their settlements but paid little or no dues to the government.[22] Even some *amils* of the *jagirdars* oppressed the peaceful peasants and laid waste their villages, while other protected the highway robbers and collected the forbidden cesses.[23] The reports of these horrifying event were sent by *sawanih-nigar* (a news writer) and the victims submitted petitions to the imperial court. Ra'd Andaz Khan received two *hasbul hukms* (royal orders) from the court. The first stated that the *jagirs* of Aziz Khan Rohillah in the *parganas* of Bhainder and Unao had been resumed and assigned to the Prince because his agent (*gumashta*) Khudadad Khan had invaded the above-mentioned places, and plundered the houses of the Saiyids and Shaikhs. Saiyid Arif, Saiyid Dost Muhammad and Ghulam Muhiyuddin had submitted petitions against the *jagirdars*. The royal order must be enforced and Khudadad Khan be sent to the court escorted by the mace-bearers. The second *hasbulhukm* stated that according to the waqa-i' (report) from Lucknow it was learnt that Aziz Khan again took possession of the jagirs and appointed Khudadad Khan the *mutasaddi* (manager) of the *mahals*, upon this the *jagir* had been resumed and placed under *khalisa* (or under direct administration of the government).[24]

Besides executing the policies of the government and assisting the *jagirdars* in the collection of dues, the *faujdar* of Baiswara performed other

20. *Insha-i Roshan Kalam, Arzdasht*, 6.
21. *Insha-i Roshan Kalam, Arzdasht*, 7, letter, 8.
22. *Insha-i Roshan Kalam, Arzdasht*, 11.
23. *Insha-i Roshan Kalam*, Letter, 15.
24. *Insha-i Roshan Kalam, Arzdasht*, 7.

duties assigned to him from time to time by the emperor. He once received a royal farman directing him to recruit six thousand matchlockmen in consultation with Muhammad Husain, the *mansabdar* on the payment of three months salary in advance and sending the recruits in parties, one after another, to the imperial headquarters. Ra'd Andaz Khan carried out the orders and accomplished the task. He reported that he had already recruited two thousand matchlockmen and having paid two thousand rupees in advance sent them under the command of Muhammad Mu'in. He also provided military escort consisting of 500 horsemen under the command of Wajih-ud-din for the dispatch of treasure of Gorakhpur across the border of his territory.[25]

The letters of Ra'd Andaz Khan show that the rules connected with the branding and verification (*dagh-o-tashiha*)[26] and feed of the cattle (*khurak-i-dawabb*)[27] were strictly followed at the local level in the last years of Aurangzeb's reign. The faujdar complained in a letter that the clerks in the department of *dagh-o-tashiha* had resumed his old jagir in Jajmau yielding an income of ten lakhs of *dams* because he had failed to produce certificate of branding and verification and he appealed for the restoration of his jagir which was the mainstay for his livelihood.[28] In another letter he requested for the exemption of *khurak-i-dawabb* as he was faced with acute financial difficulties. He wrote that for the term of one year he had been exempted from the payment of the tax, but he feared that after the expiry of the term, the officers would demand the payment of money and harrass him. He hoped that he should continue to enjoy the favour of exemption till his economic position was improved.[29]

ARZDASHTS

Arzdasht-I

Sher Andaz Khan,[30] after rendering homage to His Majesty, states that

25. *Insha-i-Roshan Kalam, Arzdasht*, 8.
26. For the rules and procedure of branding and verification, *A'in-i-Akbari*, I, A'in., 7, p. 265.
27. For details of this system, *The Army of the Indian Mughals*, pp. 19-22. "It was a deduction from a *mansabdar's* pay on account of certain number of horses and elephants belonging to the Emperor, with whose maintenance such an officer was saddled." p. 20.
28. *Insha-i Roshan Kalam*, letter 1.
29. *Insha-i Roshan Kalam, Arzdasht*, 8.
30. Sher Andaz Khan was the title of Ra'd Andaz Khan. But in one arzdasht it is given as the name of his son.

the Chauhans of Kanjura[31] attached to the *pargana* Shahpur, committed highway robbery and caused trouble and distress to the helpless and respectable people of the *ma'uza*. When the payment of dues (land revenue) was demanded they refused to pay it. At the time of fighting they managed to assemble 8 to 9 thousand seditious men from the neighbouring villages. Not a single *faujdar* in the past had been successful in his efforts of punishing them. When this obedient servant undertook to chastise these rebels and forcibly seize their fortresses, they submitted, and he was able to complete the settlement of land revenue (*mal*) of the *mahals* and *paibaqi* of the *jagirdars*. He invaded the above mentioned village, plundered it and put many rebels to sword; he also captured their fortresses and made arrangements for the collection of revenues. The rebels, having put reliance on the strenghth of their forts and the number of followers which they had collected from twelve villages, commenced fighting. The imperial forces fought bravely and inflicted a crushing defeat on them. Several persons on the opposite side were put to sword, while others took refuge in the fort. It was besieged and for two days fighting continued, till on the third day the vanquished foe sued for peace and came out of the fort. One thousand and four hundred men, women were arrested and twelve forts were captured. He handed over the prisoners and the cattle to the agent of the *jagirdars* as a part of the land revenue the rebellious *zamindars* had failed to deposit. He put the fort under the charge of Saiyed Muzaffar son of Anwar Muhani, the nephew of Mujhaid Khan, and *wala-shahi*, who with a strong contingent assisted the imperial army in the campaign and proposed *mansab* for him on the condition of the *zamindari* of this place because without conferring rank and authority on the officer the defence of the area could not be guaranteed.

Arzdasht - II

From Sher Andaz Khan to the Bakhshi

The provided military escort of 500 horsemen under the command of his son Wajih-ud-din Khan for the dispatch of the treasure of Gorakhpur (Mu'azzamabad) which had come from Lucknow up to the border of *mahals* under his jurisdiction. He then proceeded to Baiswara with an army of three thousand soldiers, on the written petition from the *karoris* of *jagirdars* against the mischievous persons of *mauza* Kali of *pargana* Bijnaur, and highway robbers of Unchagaon and Dewi in pargana Zaidpur who had

31. According to A'in-i Akbari, II, p. 189, the dominant race found in Kanjurah was Bais. It had 22,300 cultivated area and 818,472 dam as land revenue.

plundered and ravaged the towns and villages and oppressed the inhabitants and travellers and had refused to submit, he sent an army for their chastisement. After stiff contest and killing a large number of the rebels, the forts were captured and handed over to the *karoris*. The fortress of Murtazanagar which had been forcibly occupied by Jethi *zamindar* of pargana Harra from the Saiyids of Unao was recaptured and given to the gumashta (agent) of the jagirdar. After removing the sons of the seditious *zamindars* from the forts, he took possession of 17 fortresses and gave them to the agents of the *jagirdars* in lieu of the unpaid dues. He afterwards returned to Baiswara. He learnt from the report of his agent that Khorsen *zamindar* of *pargana* Jajmau had employed Salim Afghan and on his instigation the *zamindar* had constructed a fort and called it Salimgadh after the name of the Afghan. The fort was situated on a raised ground and there he established his residence. Having heard this news he stayed there and dispatched an army for his suppression. The fighting ensued between the imperial army and the force of the *zamindar*, and it raged day and night. He himself crossed the Ganges and moved towards the scene of fighting. The imperial army inflicted defeat on the foe, killing large number of soldiers including Salim Afghan and it recaptured the fort. Then he went to Dalmau for making other arrangements.

Arzdasht - III

The *faujdar* wrote that he controlled the *mahals*, the home of the seditious *zamindars* of Bais clan, the administration of which had been entrusted to him according to the royal *sanad*. He administered the district with vigour and efficiency and the zamindars of the area presented themselves to pay the land revenue. But the parganas of Lucknow, Bijnore and Sandila in which the jagirs of the Prince and *jagir mahals* of Aziz Khan Rohilla and other *mansabdars* lay, and where these assignees exercised the functions of the *jagirdars* had been excluded from his jurisdiction. On this account the *amils*, either due to avarice or want of strength, gave protection to the turbulent Mewatis who indulged in highway robbery and committed other acts of oppression by plundering towns and creating disorders. For example, Nahali,[32] a *zamindar* of *pargana* Bijnaur, created disturbances and was engaged in robbery. If he punished the miscreant, the *karori* would lodge a complaint against him, but in case he refrained from taking any action out of fear for the protest, every one would criticise him for interferring in affairs not directly connected whatever orders were issued

32. In *Guldasta-i Bahar*, the name of the *zamindar* is given as Shahbaz, f 7a.

would be enforced. Moreover, Jhanni and Raja, *zamindars* of *ma'uza* Thatar[33] in *pargana* Harra have fortified their houses and made them strong forts, rendering the passage to the few *mahals* lying on the road difficult and unsafe. It is hoped that orders from the royal court would be issued for the *zamindars* suppression. He also recommended that Saiyid Ghulan Ali Bilgrami, the *mansabdar*, should be appointed *zamindar* of the area on the condition that he in addition to the payment of the stipulated amount of land revenue should deposit 10 to 15 thousand rupees as *peshkash* in the royal treasury.

Arzdasht - IV

A royal *farman* directing the *faujdar* to employ 6 thousand matchlockmen from Lucknow in consultation with Abul Hasan, *diwan*, Muhammad Amin *mansabdar* and Narutam, a servant in the department of artillery, and to send them in parties to the imperial headquarters after making the payment of six months' salary in advance to them was received Ra'd Andaz Khan in reply wrote that before the receipt of the *farman*, Muhammad Amin Khan had recruited the matchlockmen and having paid Rs. 32 thousands sent them to the court. The *yaddasht* (a memorandum) under the seal of Muhammad Amin Khan had also been sent to the court. The remaining number of soldiers would be recruited and sent to the court in due course of time. It was suspected that Muhammad Amin Khan in league with Narutam *hazari* was causing delay in this work of the government. Moreover, it was feared that the party of soldiers, already dispatched to the court, might have been prevented from their destination.

If Saiyid Muhiyuddin, a *mansabdar* appointed in the times of Tarbiyat Khan, and an experienced person in the collection of revenues, was assigned with this duty, the work of employing the soldiers would be completed quickly and properly. He further requested that he should be exampted from the charge of *khurak-i-dawabb* as his financial position was not satisfactory. His expenditure exceeded the income.

Arzdasht - V

He received the *hasb-ul hukm* regarding the eviction and suppression of a group of Afghans of Rai Bareli in *sarkar* Manikpur *subah* Allahabad who had taken possession of the village and the lands of the people. The orders under the seal of Bakhshiul Mumalik Mukhlis Khan were also issued

33. In *Guldasta-i Bahar*, it is Sandila, f 7a.

to the governor and *faujdar* in this matter, and he was directed to take measures in agreement with the governor for taking back the *mahals* from the central of the refractory Afghans. The letter was brought by the two mace-bearers, namely, Muhammad Taqi and Muhammad Zahid. According to the instructions contained in the letter he waited to join the governor and the *faujdar* (of Manikpur) when they both started to march against the rebels and perform the duty assigned to them. But as the governor was in attendance to the Prince, and because he had not been entrusted with the task, he (Ra'd Andaz Khan) could not undertake operations.

Arzdasht - VI

He received a *hasb-ul-hukm* directing to march against the turbulent elements of *ma'uza* Bati Mau attached to pargana Lucknow and *ma'uza* Kanjura and settle the affairs of the area in such a fashion as he had administered his own *mahals*. The disturbers of peace had invaded the villages and plundered the money and effects of the people. At present he was engaged with six thousand horsemen and two thousand footman in the chastisement of the rebels of Baiswara and seizing their forts. After accomplishing this work he would march in that direction and would act in accordance with the instructions issued to him.

Arzdasht - VII

By the royal *sanad* he was appointed to administer the *mahals* of Baiswara. But the parganas of Lucknow and Bijnaur were in the *jagirs* of the Prince and had been excluded from the jurisdiction of his *faujdari*. Laxity in administration and the avarice of the *amils* of these *mahals* encouraged the seditious highway men to oppress the travellers. Inspite of this the service of *rahdari* of this place had not been assigned to him, but a different officer performed this duty. But on every occasion these events and occurances were recorded in the *waqa'i* and *sawanih* pertaining to the district of Baiswara, and reported to the Emperor. The chronic weakness and various defects found in the administration of the *pargana* of Lucknow and Bijnaur were attributed to his inefficiency and therefore orders were frequently issued to him to improve the administration of the area. He hoped that his patron will explain the whole situation to his Majesty and point out that the above-mentioned *parganas* were not included in the *sanad* of his *faujdari*. In the meantime Mu'azzam Ali Bilgrami prepared a statement of recommendation (*tajweez-namah*) to secure the *zamindari* for himself and continued to make the document apparently valid by placing on it the seal of this obedient servant. He keeps this document (*dastawez*) with himself. He (the *faujdar*) in fact did not put his seal on the above document which, it was hoped, would not be considered as genuine, and he should not be appointed the *zamindar*. In spite of a very meagre income from the conditional *jagirs* and the maintenance of a large number of people, he had devoted himself to the performance of duties assigned to him. The clerks of the department of *dagh-o-tassiha* had resumed his old *jagirs* in Jajmau yielding the revenues of ten lakhs of *dams* for his failure in producing the certificate of branding and verification. They assigned the jagir which was held by the obedient servant (*fidvi*) Sher Andaz Khan and others, to different persons whose names had not been previously recorded in the *sanad* of grant. Now he was sending Khwaja Khandi Rai, his old servant, with the relevant certificate to the court. It was hoped that his *jagir* would be restored to him.

Arzdasht - VIII

Mirza Sahib,

very kind and affectionate, a place of hope to his (people) may God preserve him.

........It is to say that the service of *Rahdari* from Lucknow to the bank of the Ganges and the *mahals* of *faujdari* of the writer have been assigned to Sheikh Jar-ullah, *faujdar* of Khairabad. The above mentioned officer could not discharge his duty of administrating the area properly owing to long distance, and had appointed another person to perform the responsibility of *rahdari*, who has started encroachment in the affairs of the *faujdari* and collecting from the travellers of the area. He did not respond to his appeal for abandoning the illegal practices. He, on the other hand, continued to harass the travellers and interferred in the affairs of the *faujdari* giving to attention. Since the writer had considerable force in the *thanas* of the above mentioned *mahals*, he is maintaining law and order in the area. Establishment of a dual rule in one *mahal* can not be helpful by any means for the maintenance of law and order, and the security of the roads and highway. It is hoped that the matter will be reported to the His Majesty by your gracious-self and the service of above mentioned *rahdari* from the said Sheikh may be removed and assigned to the writer without the increase of 100 horses .....; and the complaint of the Sheikh against this servant to the His Majesty should not be given any consideration. Since the applicant considers you as a benefactor, this is written with the confidence that you will kindly pay proper attention to this request.

Arzdasht - IX

Your kind letter informing about the petition lodged by the vakil of Mangal complaining against the cruelty of Abdus Samad and Muhammad Taqi etc the Shaikhzadas who had killed two brothers of the petitioner and five others and plundered their money and effects, was received. A report regarding the results of the investigation and judgement for the punishment of the seditious people has already been sent. Whatever was investigated was already reported. In fact the petition is correct and a section of the mischievous persons are proud and naughty and they seldom appear before the court of law. Therefore, one officer (*vasawal*) is despatched with a *parwanah* summoning Abdus Samad and Mohammad Taqi etc and this letter is sent to the kind one that they should be directed alongwith the officer to your presence so that the case may be decided in accordance with the law of Devine (*shara*). In case they refused to present themselves in the court of the *subedar* with the officer sent to summon them military separations would be launched against them; and they would be terrified by severe punishment.

Arzdasht - X

The *faujdar* received a *hasb-ul hukm* under the seal of *Bakhashi-ul-Mumalik* Mukhlis Khan. It stated that a complaint regarding the highway robbery and sufferings of the people due to the mismanagement and inefficient administration of this obedient servant had been lodged. Moreover, in the city of Lucknow the intoxicants and other forbidden things were practised unchecked. Accordingly royal orders had been issued to improve the administration in the above-mentioned *mahals*, expell the turbulent persons and eliminate the unlawful practices in the city. It is to be submitted that the city of Lucknow was outside his jurisdiction, and even the service of *rahdari* had been assigned to a different person. This complaint had been made by the interested persons against him, and its facts had no foundation. The *mahals* of Baiswara were under his jurisdiction, and in that area the *zamindars* had always paid the revenue and its administration had been properly conducted.

Chapter - 7

Jagirs in Awadh

(a) Seventeenth Century

Most of the civil and military officials holding a *mansab* in the Mughal empire were paid their salaries by assigning them the revenues of well-defined tracts (in terms of *parganas* or villages therein). The total pay claim (*talab*) of an official had to be exactly equal of the *jama*' of the area assigned in his *jagir*. Some of these *mansabdars* were also paid their salaries in cash (*naqdi*) by the emperor out of his income from unassigned areas (*khalisa*). The mode of payment was always decided by the emperor himself, at least in theory. The *jagirdars* were supposed to make their own arrangements to collect the land-revenue and to administer their *jagirs*. Often the small *jagirdars* or those posted in far-off areas used to farm-out their *jagirs* to people known as *ijaradars* for a fixed sums after allowing the deduction on account of the local claims and the cost of collections.[1]

The earliest form of the term *jagir* appears to have been *jai-gir*, (*jai* meaning 'place' and *gir* meaning 'holder') as is indicated by a document of 1559/ from Awadh.[2] Subsequently, through a linguistic corruption such assignments were called *jagirs*, though the earlier spelling also recurs rarely.[3] *Iqta* and *tuyul* were also used as synonyms for *jagir* and *tuyuldars*

1. For discussion of *jagir* system in the Mughal empire see, Irfan Habib, *Agrarian System*, Chapter VII and Athar Ali, *The Mughal Nobility under Aurangzeb*, Bombay, 1966, Chapter III.

2. *FM-1 (967/1559)* one among the earliest known *farmans* of Akbar confirming a *madad-e-ma'ash* grant of 2600 *bigha* in *pargana* Sahali, *sarkar* Lucknow to the ancestors of latter Firangi Mahal family.

3. *Abdul Qadir Collection-4 (1026 'amii/1617) in UPSAL*. This *chaknamah* stipulated of demarcating 480 *bigha* as *madad-e-ma'ash* to one Shaikh Abul Qasim from *pargana* Nasirabad *sarkar* Manikpur. The assigned way made out of the *jai-gir* of one Jam 'Ali Beg.

as a synonym for *jagirdar*.[4] The assignments held by the princes of blood were put under the formula, *tuyul-e-wuklae' padshahzada-i-walatabar*.[5]

About the extent of the *jagirs* in Awadh prior to 1780 AD we have no statistical information. Awadh was one of those provinces in which all *jagirs* were resumed to the *khalisa* (imperial lands) in 1574-75 by Akbar. Presumably, the *jagirs* began to be given here from 1581 onwards, after Shahbaz Khan Kambo's unauthorised concessions to the nobility in that year.[6] In the 31st R.Y. of Akbar (1586-7), the emperor remitted one-sixth of the revenues of the *khalisa* in the *subas* of Allahabad, Awadh and Delhi, on account of low prices, and the remissions totalled 4,05,60,596 *dams*.[7] This suggests that in these *subas*, the *khalisa* had a *jama*' of 24,33,63,576 *dams* as against the total *jama*' of the subas of Allahabad, Awadh and Delhi as 1,01,58,01,546 *dams* recorded in the *Ain*. Though the size of the *khalisa* in the *suba* of Awadh cannot still be separately determined, it is probable that it could not have been much less than 8,11,21,192 *dams* of the total revenue yielding area, the mean of all the three *subas*. The reminder must have been assigned in *jagirs*.

There is little specific information about the relative sizes of the *khalisa* and *jagir* lands in Awadh during the seventeenth century. But the *Dasturul 'amal-i Shahjahani*, belonging to Aurangzeb's later years, shows that the vast bulk of the revenues in Awadh had been assigned in *jagirs* and little remained in the *khalisa*. Unluckily, the *sarkar*-wise figures do not accord with the *suba* totals, but the general picture is clear enough:

---

4. See 'Abdul Hameed Lahori, *Badshahnamah*, Bib. Ind., Calcutta, 1867-68, I (ii), p. 216 for the *iqta* of one Fidai Khan at Gorakhpur; about the *iqta* of Madha Singh at Khairabad, *Ibid*., I (ii), p. 222; about the *iqta* of *suba* Awadh to Islam Khan, *Ibid*., II, p. 164, also in Muhammad Saleh Kambo, '*Amal-e-Saleh*, Bib. Ind., Calcutta, 1912-46, II, p. 310; Mutaqid Khan son of Najabat Khan was assigned the *faujdari* as well as the *tuyuldari* of *sarkar* Bahraich during 31st R.Y. of Shahjahan at the *mansab* of 2000 z/2000 s (800 1-3H). *Ibid*., II, p. 272.

5. See *Insha-e-Roshan Kalam*, f. 7 about the complaint of Sher Andaz Khan that the bandits, highway robbers and Mewatis carried on their activities in *pargana* Lucknow, Bijnore and Sandilah unchecked as their areas of operations in which lay the *jagirs* of the princes (*tuyul-e-wuklae*' *padshahzada-i-walatabar*) and the big nobles like Aziz Khan and others and these areas were outside the *faujdari* jurisdiction of Sher Andaz Khan.

6. Abul Fazl, *Akbarnama*, III, p. 494.

7. *Ibid*.

Table - I[8]

	Suba/Sarkar Total	*Total jama'*	*Jama' of the Khalisa*
	SUBA AWADH	27,95,79,419 *dams*	67,74,800 *dams*
1.	*Sarkar* Awadh	5,20,31,300 *dams*	———
2.	*Sarkar* Lucknow	10,85,56,025 *dams*	62,00,000 *dams*
3.	*Sarkar* Bahraich	44,16,306 *dams*	———
4.	*Sarkar* Khairabad	7,02,33,000 *dams*	48,00,000 *dams*
5.	*Sarkar* Muazzamabad Gorakhpur	2,43,250 *dams*	4,32,210 *dams*

(b) Administration of *Jagirs*

If we examine the surviving documents from Awadh during the seventeeth century, we would find that those relating to the *jagir* administration are very rare, while papers relating to the *madad-i ma'ash* grants and even *zamindari* rights are quite numerous. This is obviously because the families that have preserved the documents have been more concerned for maintaining their claims on the *ma'afi* and *zamindari* titles, while the *jagir* papers were of no interest from such motives, unless, of course, they related to *in'am* or *altamgha jagir*. Nevertheless, explorations at the Regional Records Office (Allahabad), Research Library of the Department of History (AMU) and the National Archives of India (New Delhi), resulted in the discovery of a certain number of papers, which, studied together, help to give some picture of the *jagir* administration as it functioned in Awadh during the seventeenth century.

A *jagirdar* receiving his assignment in an area would invariably be an outsider. The documents show that a *jagirdar* would either appoint his own agents to collect the taxes on his behalf or farm out the taxes of his *jagir* with a view to assuring stable revenue-receipts. When the *jagirdars* made their own arrangements by appointing some agents, they used to take from the latter a *qubuliyat* (agreement) to collect certain amounts. Such deeds were executed, keeping in view the *hasil* (previous revenue collection) figures of the *jagir*. The cost of the collection and other obligations of the *jagirdar* were always deducted from the amounts agreed to be paid by these agents. We possess an actual specimen in the form of a *qubuliyat* deed executed in 1116 F/1708 by one Dilawar for a *jagir* in *pargana* Sandila,

8. *Add 6588*, ff. 36b-37a. However, the total *jama'* of the *khalisa* for the entire *suba* according to the *sarkar* total was 1,14,32,210 *dams*, a much higher figure than has been actually shown. Similarly, there is an apparent error of transcription for *sarkar* Moazzamabad, Gorakhpur.

having a *jama*' of 41 lakh *dams*. In all, excluding the cost of maintaining the *sehbandi* troops and *peshkash* to *faujdar*, Rs 22,001 were to be paid to the *jagirdar* in two instalments.[9]

The '*amils* generally belonged to the *jagirdar*'s own staff, and were, like their masters, usually outsiders. One recalls that Charles Elliott on the basis of his own reading of documents relating to the Unao district, gained the impression that the '*amils* "were hardly ever natives of the *pargana*, and did not necessarily hold the office for more than a year".[10] The '*amil* had to maintain an armed contingent for quelling any minor resistance to his authority, and in case he met stiffer opposition, he could call the *faujdar* to his help.[11] Very often the big *jagirdars* were also entrusted with the *faujdari* jurisdictions in their respective *jagirs*. The payment to the '*amil* was done either by allowing him a certain percentage of the revenue-collection or a fixed salary.[12]

The assistance of hereditary village officials such as the *qanungos* and the *chaudharis* was indispensable for the '*amils* of the *jagirdars*. They used to present the previous year's assessments, which were accepted in toto, but in case the '*amil* asked for a higher assessment, the revision of the previous figures was also done by these officials. Similarly, they helped the '*amils* in collecting the outstanding balances from the peasants as per their records, against which there were no appeals.[13]

From an early document (c. 1619) from *sarkar* Bahraich, it appears that some *jagirdars* used to assign a village of their *tankhwah jagir* to their troopers directly. If in such a village some areas had been already granted to the *madad-i-ma'ash* holders, the troopers were directed not to interfere with such possessions.[14]

The small *jagirdars*, or those having their postings in a far-off area, always tried to farm out their *jagirs*. Certain conditions were imposed

9. See *NAI 1487-(1116 F/1708)*. This *qubuliyat* was executed in the presence of village official including Jangash Das, *amin*, *shiqdar* and *mehta*, Kishan Das, *waqai nigar*, Tilak Chandra, *Karkun* and *mutasaddis* of the Government. The instalments were not equal. Rs 13,200/- were to be paid in *kharif* and Rs 8,800/- in *rabi* seasons.

10. Elliott, C.A., *The Chronicles of Oonao*, Allahabad, 1862.

11. *Ibid.*, p. 109.

12. *Ibid.*, pp. 106-7.

13. *Ibid.*, pp. 112-3.

14. *Allahabad-789*. The village Kapana was in *tankhwah jagir* of one Mirza 'Isa, and he had assigned this village to four of his troopers. A *madad-i ma'ash* grant made over to a lady by imperial *farman* was to be exempted from their collections.

upon these revenue contractors or *ijaradars*. There are actual instances where they were asked to treat the *ri'aya* gently so that they might remain settled and carry on cultivation. It was thought to be the duty of the *ijaradar* to see that even "one *biswa* of cultivable land should not be left uncultivated".[15] It appears from the claim by a *patwari* (village accountant) that hereditary officials serving in the *ijara* villages were paid their salaries by the revenue-farmers.[16] The system of *ijara* had become so popular during this period that even the *a'immadars* or holders of *madad-i ma'ash* grants started this system of the revenue realisation in their villages.[17] The *ijaradars* had no salary or land grant in view of the services performed by him; but, as Buttler put it, "the difference between the sum, which he has for the year engaged to pay into the public treasury" constituted his official income.[18] In case of natural calamities, the *ijaradars* could be provided some relief by being allowed a deduction, and by the *jagirdar* not insisting upon the full amount for which the contract was held.[19]

The terms on which *ijara* of a *jagir* was given are set out in a document of 1081 F, (1673 A.D.):[20]

> "Agreement (*Qaul-o-qarar*): I, Mir Abu Turab, *mansabdar*, affirm that (tract carrying a *jama*' '*dami* of) 2,10,000 *dams* from *pargana* Hisampur, *sarkar* Bahraich has been assigned in our *jagir* with effect

15. *NAI-1574* (37th *RY of Aurangzeb*). This *qaul-o-qarar* relates to village Somb in *pargana* Sandilah *suba* Awadh in the *jagir* of prince 'Azimuddin ('Azimushshan) at a total *jama*' of Rs 445/- for the year 1101 F/1693. The *qubuliyat* was given by Muhammad Qa'im, *the* Gumashta. *The total* arazi *(area) of the village was 445* bighas.

16. *NAI-1287 (1254/1838)*. This *parwana* was issued to the *chakledar* of Sandila to enquire into the complaint of a village *patwari* regarding his pay claims against the *mustajir*.

17. *Firangi Mahal-84 (4*th *RY of Farrukhsiyar)*. The village in question belonged to Mulla Nizamuddin and was situated in *sarkar* Bahraich, while the grantee's residence happened to be at Lucknow. (This collection of *Firangi Mahal* documents is preserved in the Department of History, AMU, Aligarh).

18. Donald Buttler, *Topography and Statistics of the Southern Districts of Awadh and Sultanpur*, Calcutta, 1839, p. 99.

19. A *jagir* having a total *jama*' of 4,40,000 *dams* belonged to Durvesh Beg *mansabdar* and others. It was situated in *pargana* Husampur and 'Arif held it on a *ijara* tenure. He had agreed to pay Rs 7,332/- in two instalments. (See *Allahabad 8 885* (1080 '*amali*). But the perusal of the receipt issued by the *jagirdars* to 'Arif for the same year shows that he paid only Rs 4,000/- (1,60,000 *dams*). He was also exempted from any further obligation of any subsequent payment for the year (1080 '*amali*) (See *Allahabad-889).*

20. *Allahabad-884* (1081 F/1675).

from the beginning of the kharif, Udi II, 1081 '*amali*. Therefore, at my own will, I have given the said (territorial assignment of) *dams* in *ijara* (farm) to Mir Sayyid Muhammad 'Arif in fixed payment of Rs 2,850, to continue so long as the *jagir* is retained by me, so that he may pay the said amount to me annually according to the following particulars. Should, God forbid, a natural calamity happen, then according to the (official) rate (of remission) for the said *pargana*, I will allow a deduction in the said amount. But if by God's grace, more is realised in excess of the said amount, that is left to the said Sayyid." The following figures follow:

Table - II

(Jama'	2,10,000 *dams*
Comprising original	2,00,000 *dams*
Enhancement	10,000 *dams*
Equivalent, for the year at 7 months, 7 days	Rs 3,162
Deduct on account of *nankar*	
(salary of officials), *muqaddami*	
(*muqaddams*' pay) (illegible)	Rs 312
(Balance)	Rs 2,850

From this document, it is clear that the *ijaradar* pledged himself to pay a certain amount annually to the *jagirdar* – in this case, a fixed proportion of the *jama' dami* (7 months, 7 days in the month-scale). From this he was allowed a fixed deduction for payment to local officials, etc. This explains the claim of the *patwari* on the *ijaradar* we have just mentioned. The *jagirdar* allowed him the profits of the enterprise, as Buttler defines them; but the *ijaradar* could claim a reduction on account of officially sanctioned tax-remissions for the locality.

While the *jagirdar* had to make arrangements locally to collect the revenue either directly or through contractors, he had to meet certain obligations to the government. For this purpose the more substantial *jagirdar*, at any rate, used to keep a *wakil* permanently at the imperial court to safeguard his interests and to receive the orders on his behalf. Two very interesting papers concerning a dispute between a *jagirdar* and his *wakil* have survived, which shed light on this part of the functioning of the *jagirdar*'s establishment. The two documents are translated in Appendix to this Chapter.

One major obligation on the part of the *jagirdar* was the maintenance of a number of animals of standard breed for the imperial stables, providing the cost of feeding them as per schedules and a number of other supplies under the general name of *khwurak-i dawabb*.[21] It appears that the amount required for the purpose was sent by the *jagirdar* to his *wakil*. The *wakil*, in turn, paid the required money to the *ijaradars* (farmers) of the *Khwurak-i Dawabb*, who met the expenses for maintaining the animals (horses as well as elephants) and, when the time of maintaining the animals was over, handed them over to the officials of the Imperial stables.

In addition to these duties, the *wakil* was called upon to look after the interests of his master at the Court such as getting him a better *jagir*. In the present case the *wakil* was allowed the sum of Rs 300 by the *jagirdar* to be spent on the business (*muhimsazi*) of getting a new *jagir* assigned in *pargana* Amethi.

The accounts submitted by the *wakil* in connection with these expenses were subjected to rigorous scrutiny. He had to present all the original receipts under the seals of the *ijaradar* of *khwurak-i-dawabb* and the *mutasaddis* of *dawabb*, at the time of the audit by the *jagirdar*'s officials.

In case of any dispute between the *wakil* and the *jagirdar* regarding the settlement of these accounts, the matter was apparently placed before some Imperial officials. Unfortunately, the exact designation of this official is not given in our documents; he might well have been the *diwan* or *faujdar*.

The work of revenue assessment and collection in the *jagirs* was greatly facilitated by the *qanungo* and the *chaudhary* at the local level. Elliott says that they were appointed by a *sanad* from the Emperor from amongst the leading families of the locality. Elliott who used documentary material from the Unao district and other areas of Awadh, believed that there was little material difference in the nature of the work performed by these officials. Normally a *zamindar* of the area was always appointed as the *chaudhary*. While a member of an accountant caste (notably Kaisths) was appointed to the post of *qanungo*. Very often they acted in a manner antagonistic to each other i.e. the *chaudhari* tried to protect the interests of the land owning classes, while *qanungo* acted in a manner to serve the imperial cause well.[22] In ordinary article of property freely

21. For a discussion of these obligations see Irfan Habib, *The Agrarian System of Mughal India*, Bombay, 1963, p. 269 and M. Athar Ali, *The Mughal Nobility under Aurangzeb*, Bombay, 1966, pp. 50-53.

22. Elliott, *op. cit.*, p. 112. W.C. Benett holds for 'Ray Bareilly district that the office of *chaudhari* was held by the respectable but thoroughly second rate families and the great houses never took any appointment as local officials under the Mughal government. (W.C. Benett, *A Report on the Family History of the Chief clans of the Ray Bareilly District*, Lucknow, 1870, p. 58).

saleable.[23] The *qanungo* were always consulted by the '*amils* before the revenue demand was fixed upon a particular village or upon any landholder. Generally their recommendations were accepted by the authorities, but in case the demand was to be raised, it was left to the *qanungo* to distribute the additional tax burden keeping an eye over the actual conditions.[24] In the *raiyati* villages as well, he was held primarily responsible for the payment of the revenue by collecting it from the peasants. The presence of these revenue officials with more or less well defined tracts of country was conspicuous enough in the 'Ray Bareilly district to merit Benett's remark that "the *pargana* boundaries generally corresponded with the limits of the chieftains authority and the distribution of his clan and each was already furnished with a body of hereditary revenue officials".[25] The tenures, so created, were somehow considered 'sacrpsamct as the holders of these offices were seldom 'turned out and replaced by the new families' though it happened that different branch of the same family was installed in these posts.[26]

Apart from Elliott's description of these officials in Onao district and Benett's remarks pertaining to the *qanungo* of 'Ray Bareilly' district, we have a series of Persian documents belonging to a family of *qanungo* in *pargana* Laharpur, *sarkar* Khairabad, beginning from the seventeenth century. The information of these documents, apart from confirming the features already noticed by Elliott, brings out a number of other interesting features.

It is almost certain that these *pargana* officials acted in a manner as to exercise some check upon each others jurisdiction, thus precluding the possibilities of fraud. A *parwana* of 25th R.Y. of Aurangzeb recalls a representation by the *wakil* of a *qanungo* to the effect that the 'Hindu *chaudharies* and *qanungo* of the area always put their signatures over the *tumār-i Lama*'. Now these Hindu officials were refusing to do on account of the *qanungo* being a Muslim. The earlier practice was ordered to be restored.[27]

The *qanungo* might make recommendations for the imperial favours and subsistence grant to the needy and poor. A *parwana* of 1074/1663 records that Sheikh Muhammad Amin, the *qanungo* had brought to the

23. Irfan Habib, *Agrarian System*, pp. 129-30.
24. Elliott, *op. cit.*, p. 113.
25. Benett, *op. cit.*, p. 59.
26. Elliott, *op. cit.*, p. 111.
27. Tagore Library, Lucknow University – 46885.

notice of the court the poverty of Sheikh Nazar Muhammad and recommended a subsistence grant for him, as a result, 155 *bigha* of land was assigned to Sheikh Nazar Mohammad as *madad-e ma'ash*.[28]

An interesting *mahzar* recites the services rendered by the predecessors of the petitioner, the present *qanungo* and their dealings with the imperial officials of the area. Most of these services related to religious and social welfare. The preceding *qanungo* (ancestors of the present) are said to have helped the inhabitation of the *qasba*, building, mosques, *madarsa, khanqahs* and *sarai* (inn). Due to their efforts the tenets and practice of Islam had been established, *juma*' and '*Id* prayers were held in congregation and food was distributed among the poor. Similarly, arrangements were made for the instruction of the students. They maintained good relations with the *jagirdar*, by securing payment of the revenue dues in time and treating their *gumashta* (agents) in a befitting manner. In the 40th R.Y. of Aurangzeb, one Lal, a Bais Rajput of *haveli* Laharpur had raised the banner of rebellion, and to suppress this uprising, *naib-faujdar* of Khairabad came to Laharpur and stayed with the petitioner, who, in turn, entertained him in a befitting manner. But the petitioner was arrested and was forced to pay Rs 5,680 to the *naib-faujdar*. He was released as a result of the intervention of the influential persons of the locality.[29] A number of respectable persons of the locality signed in their endorsement of the statement. The possibility of the involvement of the *qanungo* in the said rebellion can not be ruled out.

In remuneration of these services, the *qanungo* were entitled to get either 2½ percent of the total revenue collected or held 2½ percent of the assessed land on revenue free tenures.[30] This gave him a direct interest in raising the amount of assessment and collection. His counterpart, the *chaudhari* was always rewarded by grants of rent free land or a money grant. In addition to their sanctioned perquisites, they seems to have usurped a number of fiscal rights during the 18th century.[31] Another *mahzar* from the family of *qanungo* at Laharpur records that the *qanungo* felt entitled to extort *bhent, nankar* and other gifts within his jurisdiction.[32] Similarly, a *parwana* of 1048/1638 records that Shaikh Hamid *qanungo* held responsibilities of *kotwali* in *pargana* Laharpur and was also collecting the

28. Tagore Library, Lucknow University – 46887.
29. LUL – 46905.
30. Irfan Habib, *Agrarian System*, p. 131.
31. Elliott, *op. cit.*, p. 112.
32. LUL – 46904.

sair taxes from *haveli* Laharpur. But these rights were being usurped by one Lakman *chaudhari*. The *parwana* sets aside the latter's claim.[33]

The *qanungos* in collusion with the '*amil* often managed to become land holders themselves, thus doing away with the difference that had existed between them and the *chaudharis*. At the same time the position of the latter receded into the background and, according to Elliott, their interest in the work of revenue-collection declined, leaving the *qanungo* in the undisputed authority. As a matter of fact there was only one among fourteen *pargana* in the district of Unao, where the *chaudhari* could manage to maintain his position unmolested before the Annexation.[34] In The Ray Bareilly district, Benett points out that there was a strong tendency among the *qanungos* to enter into *ta'alluqadari* settlements. However such attempts were mostly thwarted by their powerful neighbours, still they were able to acquire the "small estates of Hardaspur and Binohra".[35]

In case of the Laharpur family it is not clear whether the *zamindari* rights were acquired by the *qanungos* subsequent to their gaining the office. But a *parwana* of 1122/1711 recognises these two as separate rights held by a member of the family, possessed from earlier times within the particular village of Laharpur. The village headmen (*muqqadam*), cultivators (*muzariau*) etc. being the *ri'aya* of that place were called upon to recognise these two separate rights of the said *qanungo*, and hence he alone was entitled to get all the perquisites attached to the *zamindari* and *qanungoi* rights.[36]

But while the *qanungo* might have scored off against the *chaudharis* within the machinery of revenue administration, they were themselves becoming subservient to the *zamindar*. As the *zamindars* grew stronger, the *qanungo* tended to collect the land revenue on behalf of the land-holders instead of the government. Their other fiscal rights simply depended upon their proximity to the respective land holders, while in the ordinary villages their services were dispensed with altogether. This at least was what happened in Rae Bareilly district.[37] It may well be that, with the collapse of the transferable *jagir* system in the 18th century, the basis of the twin offices of *qanungo* and *chaudhari* in the old form had already been removed.

---

33. LUL – 46883.
34. Elliott, *op. cit.*, p. 112.
35. Benett, *op. cit.*, p. 49.
36. LUL – 46890.
37. Benett, *op. cit.*, p. 67.

(c) Collapse of the *Jagir* System

The *jagir* system underwent considerable transformation in Awadh during the 18th century. As Mughal authority declined, officials assigned *jagirs* in Awadh found it more and more difficult to collect revenue. They thus began to lease out their *jagir* to the Governor Burhanul Mulk Sa'adat Khan on *ijara*.[38] His successors as *nawab-wazirs* began to insist that no new *jagirs* be assigned in the province effectively.[39]

After the battle of Buxar in 1764, Shujauddaulah was obliged to pay Rs 50 lacs as the war indemnity. Similarly, a number of subsequent treaties between the English on the one had and Shujauddaulah and Asafuddaulah on the other side stipulated for the maintenance of a large sepoy army at the *nawab*'s cost. The amount to be paid by the *nawab* on this account kept on fluctuating. This ultimately created serious dislocations in the finances of the Awadh kingdom. The *nawab* delayed the payment on one pretext or the other, while Company insisted for full and early payment of the amount under the subsidiary alliance. It became increasingly necessary for the Company officials to know all the financial resources of *nawab-wazir*'s government. Hence the revenue documents were obtained by the Residency officials and this now forms an important source of knowing the exact extent of the *khalisa* land, and the area held under the *jagir* tenures, in Awadh at this time.[40]

These account papers pertains to 1187 F/1780. The total *jama*' of the *khalisa* land in Awadh kingdom was Rs 2,13,10,790/14. The entire amount was the area granted in *jagirs* was only Rs 28,58,55/10/6, and more than half of this amount or Rs 14,80,000 was assigned by the *nawab* to the Company. Thus, Rs 13,78,555/10/6 now represented the income of the *jagirs*. But even the holders of these *jagirs* were none else but the blood relations, mother of Shujauddaulah, some close relations and a few petty officials of the *nawab*. There was no noteworthy *tankhwah jagir* held by any high military or civil official of the state. Such situation clearly portrayed, "the reduced level of state service and the aristocratic status after the decay of the Mughal Empire".[41]

---

38. Ghulam Husain Khan, *Imad-us-Sa'adat*, pp. 7-8.

39. *Mansur-ul Maktubat*, ff. 46b-47a.

40. Charles Purling to Culcutta Council, 30th April and 22nd June 1780, *Foreign Department Suret Consultations*, 1780, *NAI*. For an analysis of these documents and a subordinate position of the aristocracy in *nawab regime see Richard B. Barnett, North India Between Empires*, pp. 173-181.

41. *Ibid.*, p. 174.

(d) *In'am Al-tamgha*

One form of *jagir* instituted by Jahangir was *al-tamgha*. It was non-transferable and supposedly for life or hereditary. Quite naturally, it was very sparingly granted. But as the Mughal Empire decayed, the *al-tamgha* grants not only became common but began to be converted into hereditary properties. In Awadh, we can trace the fortunes of one particular *al-tamgha* grant in special detail owing to the richness of surviving documentary material.

The original documents and oral traditions preserved in an Urdu work, the *Nama-i-Muzaffari* relate to the *inam-al-tamgha* grant held by Diler Khan Afghan and his successors during the 17th and the 18th centuries.[42] The assignment was situated in what was originally the *tappa* of Shahabad in *pargana* Pali *sarkar* Khairabad, *suba* Awadh. Since here we have an authentic account of a *jagir*-holding family, setting its roots in the soil from the above documents and the history of the family they expose, are of great interest.

Diler Khan Baqarzai Afghan, son of the rebel Afghan noble Darya Khan, had a chequered military and political career. He rose to prominence under Emperor Shahjahan and he reached the zenith of his career under Aurangzeb. He held a number of important administrative and military assignments. In the 21st R.Y. of Shahjahan he received the *mansab* of 1000 *zat*/1000 *sawar* along with *faujdari* jurisdiction over the *sarkars* of Kalpi and Kannuj. The title of Diler Khan was also conferred to him this year. In 23rd R.Y. he was asked to accompany prince Aurangzeb in Qandhar campaign. He was instrumental in capturing the famous fort of Bust along with Raja Rajroop from the *qizilbash* forces. As a reward of these notable deeds his *mansab* was raised to 2000 zat/2000 *sawar*. Similarly in Bijapur campaign he fought under the command of prince Aurangzeb and got admiration for his heroic deeds. In 32nd R.Y. he was sent to chase prince Shuja from Benaras along with prince Sulaiman Shikoh and as he performed the job successfully, his *mansab* was raised to 4000/4000 and after the defeat of Dara Shikoh at Samugarh, he switched over his allegiance to Aurangzeb and received the revised *mansab* of 5000/5000 with the *faujdari* jurisdiction as well as *'a mil*ship of *sarkar* Lucknow.

His son Jamal Khan was made his deputy and was granted the *mansab* of 1000/1000. In the battle of Deorai, it was he who broke the

---

42. Muzzaffar Husain Khan, *Nama-e-Muzzaffari*, 2 Volumes, Mujtabai Press, Kanpur, 1917. See Vol. I, pages 165-72 for the text as well as the photographic reproduction of the original *farman* and pages 7-42 of the same volume for the biographical details.

strong defence built by Shah Nawaz Khan for which Emperor awarded him a cash *inam* of Rs 50,000 and his 1000 *sawars* were made *du-aspa seh-aspa* (2-3 H).[43] Emperor sent him to expell prince Shuja from Eastern India, where he was firmly established. He fought a number of closely contested battles with the Assamese under the command of Mir Muhammad Saeed Mir Jumla. There were a number of occasions when the imperial forces were at the verge of defeat but the personal courage and valour displayed by Diler Khan had saved the moments of crisis. Indeed the chronicles of the Mughal court allude in a high tone the victories of Diler Khan. In 7th R.Y. he was called back to the capital and was asked to accompany Mirza Raja Jai Singh to check the Maratha advances. The expedition was quite prestigious for the emperor as it was being sent at a time when *Amir-ul-Umara* Shaista Khan and Maharaja Jaswant Singh had failed to achieve the desired results. Diler Khan was able to capture a number of strong Maratha forts. Now 2000 of his *sawars* were made 2-3 H. He turned his attention towards the chieftains of Deogarh and Chanda, who had not paid the tribute as per agreement. Raja Chanda submitted and presented a *nazar* of 20,000 rupees and 1000 *asharfis* to Diler Khan, while Rs 5 lacs and 7000 *asharfis* were paid for the imperial treasury. As a settlement for future was arrived at, Diler Khan left for Delhi where his *mansab* was further raised to 5000/5000 (3000 2-3 H).

In the beginning of Aurangzeb's reign he held much of *pargana* Pali in *jagir*. He possessed the text of the *farman* issued by Emperor Aurangzeb in 1072/1661 granting *inam-al-tamgha* to this assignment. It transpires that he already held a *tankhwah jagir* of a total *jama'* of 26 lac *dams* in *pargana* Pali *sarkar* Khairabad. According to his requests the total amount of *jama'* was increased by 6 lac *dams*, but the enhancement was to be adjusted against *inam al-tamgha* which was granted to him and was to contain 37 villages of *tappa* Shahabad alias Angai. The territory assigned in *inam* assignment was to be deemed Diler Khan's *watan*. This grant was to be held in perpetuity.[44]

A subsequent representation by Diler Khan's son and successor to the title, Kamal-ud-din Khan claimed that in the area of *inam* against the 6 lac *dams* of *al-tamgha*, which is now said to have comprised 26 villages, which

43. Regarding his exploits at Deorai it is said, "In that contest – which was a testing ground of bravery – Diler performed such feats as obliterated the memory of Rustam and Isfandyar", *Mathir-ul-Umara*, Vol. I, pp. 497.

44. The text as well as the *zimn* of this *farman* has been carefully preserved by the author of *Nama-e-Muzzaffari*, Vol. I, pp. 174-79, along with its photographic reproduction (obverse portion).

originally contained little cultivation, Diler Khan had extended cultivation, settled people and laid out mosques, tombs and gardens. No further documents illumine the actual state of affairs under Diler Khan. However, according to local tradition a place known as Angai' or Angai' Khera in *pargana* Pali was in the *zamindari* possession of the Pandey Brahmans. Most of the time these *zamindars* were engaged in highway robbery and other acts of depredations. It is alleged that once they plundered the imperial treasury. Consequently a punitive expedition was sent by the emperor to punish them under the command of Diler Khan. It was in reward of his success in this expedition that Angai Khera and the adjacent township of Maheshpur were granted to him in *jagir*.[45]

Diler Khan had five sons, namely Kamal-ud-din Khan, Chand Khan, Jamal Khan and Fateh Mamur Khan. It appears that in respect of *inam jagir* the law of primogeniture was followed as it was not inherited by the other members of the family as an ordinary article of property. However, the other sons also obtained substantial means to maintain themselves either out of the other landed possessions of Diler Khan other than the *al-tamgha* grant, or they themselves had purchased *zamindaris* of villages from the other proprietors. The history of these minor branches will be touched upon at the end of this section.

After Diler Khan's death in 27th R.Y./1683, the *inam al-tamgha* passed on to his son Kamal-ud-din Khan. He petitioned to the court in 29th R.Y. 1686 that one Muhammad Tahir *mutassadi* of the *tuyul* of prince Muazzam (Shah Alam) had been harassing people within his *al-tamgha* assignment by exacting forbidden taxes; he had also levied some cesses on the artisans. It was thereupon ordered that the *al-tamgha* villages were to be exempted from all interference whatsoever from the revenue officials of the princes' *jagir*.[46] Again in 31st R.Y./1688, Kamaluddin Khan protested that the deputy *faujdar* of *sarkar* Khairabad was making illegal exactions on account of *peshkash, sair* and *tankhwah* within his al-tamgha *of six lakh* dams. *In response, it was ordered by a farman* that the *jagir* was to remain in perpetuity with Kamaluddin Khan, and his descendants and no forbidden exactions were to be imposed therein by the *faujdars*.[47]

---

45. *Ibid.*, Vol. I, pp. 165-173.

46. The text as well as the *zimn* of this *farman* has been carefully preserved by the author of *Nama-e-Muzzaffari*, Vol. I, pp. 174-79, along with its photographic reproduction (obverse portion).

47. *Ibid.*, Vol. I, pp. 284-6.

Kamaluddin Khan, too, had a very celebrated military and administrative career. Apart from his hereditary *al-tamgha jagir* of Shahabad, he held a *tankhwah jagir* assessed at 7 lac 7 thousand *dams* in *sarkar* Kalinjar, *suba* Allahabad. Another *jagir* comprised of seven *parganas* in Hindon Biyana, *suba* Akbarabad. He held *faujdari* jurisdiction of various *sarkar* at different period. Even the *subedari* of the province of Awadh was entrusted to him for sometimes. In the 15th R.Y. he was asked to lead the imperial forces to crush the *satnami* rebellion in the townships adjacent to Narnaul. Though the group of these mendicants lacked any war-material and other ammunitions, still they gave much trouble to the imperial forces as we hear about the extensive deployment of cannons and other fire-arms. It was with great difficulty that the *satnami* rebellion was crushed. The historians of Aurangzeb's reign tells us with a degree of sorrow that they had repeated the scenes of great Hindu epic Mahabharat.[48] Kamaluddin Khan was greatly helped by one Sarmast Khan in his drive against the rebells. A contemporary Hindi poem tells us that "these two generals had beaten back the group of *satnamis* consisting of one crore *janwars*."[49]

Similarly, in 35th R.Y. an imperial *farman* was issued to Kamaluddin Khan to meet out the threat caused due to the *Jat* depredations. A perusal of the *farman* suggests that in early stages prince Bedar Bakht was sent at the head of an imperial army to crush the rebellion in *pargana* Hindon and Biyana. The prince succeeded in reducing the *Jat* stronghold of the fort of Sasni. The prince left the place, leaving behind him one Raja Bishen Singh Sisodia as his deputy. Raja was provided with the necessary ammunition including the cannon. He tried his best efforts to achieve the desired results, but he could capture only the fort of *sarkar*. Meanwhile the *jats* had extended their activities to the *parganas* of Roopban, Bhasawar etc. The '*amils* and the *jagirdars* of these *parganas* were unable to face their onslaught and hence they fled to the capital. Thereupon Kamaluddin Khan was appointed the *jagirdar* as well as the *faujdar* of *pargana* Hindon, Biyana and its *mahals* to deal the malefactors firmly. So as to enable the '*amils* and their *gumashtas* to realise the revenue without any hindrance.[50] Kamaluddin Khan proved his worth and crushed the *jat* rebellion fully. In the 40th R.Y., a *farman* was issued to him to accompany prince Muazzam at Lahore and to take any assignment from him in connection with Baluch disturbances at Multan. He was asked to act in place of Sher Afghan Khan.[51]

---

48. Saqi Musta'id Khan, *Mathir-i-Alamgiri*.
49. *Nama-i-Muzzaffari*, Vol. I, p. 252.
50. *Ibid.*, pp. 255-7.
51. *Ibid.*, Vol. I, p. 260.

After a very severe engagement and a closely contested battle, the imperial forces emerged victorious.

The period of Kamaluddin Khan marks the watershed in the history of Diler Khan's family. He had enormous resources at his disposal in the form of *al-tamgha* and *tankhwah jagirs*. A number of additions were made to the landed possessions of the family by purchasing the *zamindari* villages from the hereditary land-holders. Only in the vicinity of Shahabad, there were as many as 1450 villages possessed by Kamaluddin Khan. We are told that most of these villages were purchased by him. These villages were spread over in the *parganas* of Pali, Sandi, Sandilah, Malihabad, Sirsa, Banan, Barwar. Kamaluddin had made out to each of his five brothers a share from the ancestral property, consisting of 12 villages, one *bazar* and one *mohalla* to each. Even after affecting a distribution of the shares among his brothers, Kamaluddin Khan possessed, "an estate so extensive that hundred of the people were employed to work over there".[52]

With the death of Kamaluddin Khan in 1125/1713, the family fortunes came to an end. As none among his descendants was able to perform any remarkable act of military skill or to attain such laurels. His eldest son Muhammad Sardar Khan was confirmed with the possessions of *inam-al-tamgha* grant of his father. The imperial *farman* was issued under the seal of one Saiyed Ubaid Khan, 'Abdullah Khan (Barha) Qutubul Mulk in the first R.Y. of (Farrukh Siyar). By this time the *jama* of the *al-tamgha* was increased to 7 lac *dams*, but whether this was done by increasing the number of villages or by a paper enhancement of the *jama* of the existing grant is not clear. It was now ordered that the entire *parganas* of Shahabad *sarkar* Khairabad, having a total *jama* of seven lakh *dams* be confirmed to Muhammad Sardar, and the *zamindars* of the area were directed to pay the *mal-o-wajib* to his '*amils*.[53] The total absence of the words like *inam al-tamgha* from this imperial order is noteworthy. He too had purchased a number of *zamindari* shares in various villages, like his ancestors. In 1728 a group of hereditary *zamindars* of Rajput Gaur clan had sold a number of shares in *tappa* Rasulabad, *pargana* Sirrah *sarkar* Khairabad. The total amount paid by Muhammad Sardar for these considerations was Rs 1744/11 annas.[54] It appears that still the family had large revenue resources at its

52. *Nama-e Muzzaffari*, Vol. I, p.

53. For the actual text of the *farman* issued under the seal of Abdullah Khan Qutubul Mulk in the Ist R.Y. of Emperor Jahandar Shah, see *Nama-e-Muzzaffari*, Vol. I, p. 317.

54. *Allahabad-228, 229*, The earlier sale-deed was executed for the sale of 19 *biswasI in five different villages in* tappa *Rasulabad and tappa* Haveli for Rs 1124/12 annas

disposal, to enter upon such costly adventures. Muhammad Sardar is said to have died in 1150/1737. Afterwards we have no documentary evidence to reconstruct the fortunes of the family, still the account in the *Nama-e-Muzzaffari* is worth reproducing.

Sardar Khan's eldest son Sher Andaz Khan succeeded him in his *jagirs*. He continued to manage the same till his death in 1172/1758. He was succeeded by his son Muhammad Aijaz Khan, who died in 1211/1796, leaving no male issue. However his wife had adopted her nephew Muhammad Khan as successor to the *jagir* of her husband. He held the possession of the property till his death in 1255/1838. Ghulam Ghaus, alias Rad Andaz Khan, his son and successor to the title actively participated in the mutiny of 1857, but afterwards he was executed and his estate was confiscated. This, more or less brought the main line to a close. The fortunes of the other branches of Diler Khan's family are discussed elsewhere.

The superior land-rights of the family had originated as a result of *al-tamgha* grant and apart from this grant Diler Khan and thereafter Kamaluddin Khan had quite high position in the civil and military hierarchy of the Mughal empire. They held many *jagirs* in *tankhwah,* had *faujdari* jurisdiction and *amilship* in a number of *sarkars*, got cash rewards on a number of occasion. Their resources were quite substantial to enable them purchase a large number of *zamindaris* in the *parganas* adjacent to Shahabad. The hold of the family over the estate continued for quite sometimes. In a judicial decree of British period it was remarked in some court of *pargana* Daryabad that, these *nawabs* (the descendants of Diler Khan) had acquired such a large estate either by mortgage or by fraud or by the use of their armed power. The estate was kept intact for a considerable period, till it was divided into small fractions. In most of the cases the old hereditary *zamindars* had purchased a number of such shares.[55]

We find that a large number of sub-assignment were made by Diler Khan and afterwards by his successors to the various individuals out of the *inam-al-tamgha* grant. Some such allienations were even ractified through imperial *farmans*, but in most of the cases, the *sanads* were issued by Diler Khan and his successors directly. In 25th R.Y/1682, a *farman* was issued by the Emperor to confirm the grant of 100 *bigha* of cultivated land in *pargana* Pali as *madad-e-ma'ash* and 20 *bigha* in *tappa* Shahabad for

while another 16 *biswas* in three different villages of *tappa* Rasulabad were sold for Rs 560. Both these deeds were executed in the year 1141/1728 by the same proprietors in favour of Muhammad Sardar Khan.

55. *NM (i)*, p. 167.

setting an orchard upon one *diwan* Azmatullah, on the basis of an earlier *sanad* issued by Diler Khan.[56] In 1666, fifty *bighas* of barren land were assigned by Diler Khan to one Maiku, who was working as the *chaudhari* of the markets in Shahabad. This *inam* land was in *pargana* Pali. The incumbent was expected to treat the peasants and other inhabitants with kindness.[57] In 1676, Diler Khan allotted five *bigha* land to some Muslim *chobdars* for setting their separate quarters and settlement in *qasba* Shahabad.[58] In 1679, he assigned to his son Fatehamur Khan the village Khanpur Khas out of his own various villages held in *al-tamgha*'. The assignee was to take special interest in the extension of cultivation and the settlements, erecting of the new buildings etc.[59] A *parwana* from Diler Khan next year clarified the limits of this grant. It included the garden of Wali Niamat and ferry as well.

In 1685, Kamaluddin Khan allotted 21 *bighas* of barren land in the vicinity of the township of Shahabad to one Malik Ismail Khan Amanzai, an Afghan, with his sons, in order that he might settle peasants there.[60] By another deed Kamaluddin Khan rectified the settlements made by Taj Khan Afghan Mehmood and his brothers in the township and reconfirmed his possessions over forty *bighas* of (cultivated) land.[61] Perhaps in this way as many as fifty-two *mohallas* were established by the members of various Afghan tribes in Shahabad.[62]

Within his *al-tamgha jagir* Kamaluddin Khan seems to have dealt with the *chaudharis* and the *qanungos* as he pleased. He dismissed some incumbents of these offices on grounds such as incompetence and inability to perform their assigned duties, their ill-treatment of the *riaya* and acts of high handedness. New persons were appointed at their place. They were instructed to treat the *raiyat* gently and to carry out their duties honestly.[63] Again in 32nd R.Y./1688, the office of the *chaudhari* of Dilergunj and its ferries was assigned to a new incumbent dismissing the old one. The person so appointed was asked to look at the welfare of the general population,

56. *Ibid.*, I, pp. 182-5.
57. *Ibid.*, I, p. 191.
58. *Ibid.*, I, p. 191.
59. *Ibid.*, I, p. 188.
60. *Ibid.*, I, p. 266.
61. *Ibid.*, I, p. 267.
62. Each *mohallah* was named after the chief of the tribe which resided there, see the compiled list of these *mohallas* in *Nama-e-Muzaffari*, I, p. 181.
63. *Ibid.*, I, pp. 269-70.

bankers and the traders.[64] Similarly, Sher Andaz Khan in 1162 A.H./1748 appointed one Muhammad Qadirdad as the *chaudhari* in his *jagir*.[65]

Quite often the holders of rights have acted like the *jagirdars* in their respective jurisdictions, for they used to bestow the *zamindari* rights of the villages to their loyal servants. A *sanad* issued by Muhammad Sardar Khan in 1145/1732 to one Muhammad Jafar sets out assigning the *zamindari* rights of the village Bhadsi by way of a free gift (*bakhshish*). It stipulates that the superior fiscal rights of the village in question were purchased by the ancestors of Sardar Khan. The present and the future *mutassadis* of the estate were asked for allowing Muhammad J'afar to appropriate all the dues by way of the *rusmat-e-zamindari* of the village in entirety. The new incumbents were to pray for the well-being of grant-holder.[66] Similarly, Sher Andaz Khan in 1162/1748 appointed one Muhammad Qadirdad as the *chaudhari* of some area in his *al-tamgha* grant.[67]

A number of *madad-i ma'ash* grants were also made by Diler Khan and his successors to the various individuals from their *jagirs*. The sons of Shaikh Muhammad Mehdi Qadri established themselves at Shahabad and their successors in interest were granted the revenues of the village Kanharpur and Jogipur. We find a very interesting *sanad* issued by Diler Khan confirming the grant. It states specifically that the grantees should have concern only with the *hasilat* (revenues) and should not interfere with those who held their dwellings or land under the cultivation in the said villages. The *sanad* was issued in 1087/1676.[68] An imperial *farman* then confirmed the grant to one of the sons (Shaikh Hidayatullah in 20th R.Y./ 1677) who claimed to be holding the villages for, "meeting his needs, setting-up his residence, setting (the place) with people and laying out a *sarai*,

---

64. *Ibid.*, I, p. 268.

65. *Ibid.*, I, pp. 317-8.

66. For the text of *sanad* see *Nama-e-Muzzaffari*, Vol. I, pp. 315-6. We know that Muhammad J'afar was one of the grandsons of Muhammad Mubarak, who happened to be an important functionary in Kamaluddin Khan's establishment and had worked in the capacity of *diwan* and *mutassadi*. For some time, he held the office of the *chaudhari* as well. In view of these services he too had received a number of favours and land as well as the cash grants.

67. *Ibid.*, I, pp. 317-8.

68. *Ibid.*, II, pp. 151-2. A perusal of the *zimn* suggests that the total realisation amounted to Rs 380/4 annas (*asl* Rs 339/-; *izafa* Rs 41/4 *annas*); the *jama* opf Jagipur was Rs 78/4 annas (*asl* Rs 64/-; *izafa* Rs 14/4 *annas*); while the *jama* of Kanharpur was Rs 302/- (*asl* Rs 275/-, *izafa* Rs 27/-). Of course the ratio between *asl* and *izafa* figures is quite interesting.

garden, tanks, well and a *Khanqah*.[69] The possession of these villages continued under the uninterrupted control of the successors of Shaikh Muhammad Mehdi, as we come across a number of confirmatory *sanads* and *farman* in the subsequent period. A *parwana*, issued in the 19th R.Y. of Emperor Muhammad Shah clearly speaks that these villages, out of the *watan* and *zamindari* of Sardar Khan, bestowed earlier upon the predecessors in interest of Shaikh Inayatullah. The same villages are now confirmed to them from 1144 F/1736.[70] The family seems to have acquired a large number of villages by way of *madad-i ma'ash* and *zamindari* rights. In 1129 A.H./ 1716, Shaikh Hidayatullah by executing a *taqsimnamah* had distributed all his possessions among his five sons. In all there were 17 *madad-e-ma'ash* villages, 8 ¼ *zamindari* villages and a number of *chaks*.[71] Although we get papers regarding the title and disputes till 1200 A.H., but for the moment we are not concerned with these details of the fortunes of the family.[72]

Nawab Sardar Khan had also made certain alienations in respect of his property by the way of *madad-i ma'ash* and *zamindari* grants. In 1125/ 1713 AD he assigned five *bighas* of land by way of *madad-i ma'ash* to the wife of one Jamaluddin Khassakhel from the village Khanpur, *pargana* Shahabad.[73] In 1145/1732 AD *zamindari* rights of the village Bhadrori in entirety were bestowed by free gift upon one Muhammad Jafar, a grand son of Muhammad Mubarak, who had been an important functionary of the *jagir* under Kamaluddin Khan makes it clear that the said village had been purchased by his ancestors so that here the *al-tamgha* holders had also become *jagirdars*.[74]

The five sons of Diler Khan established their houses in the various quarters at Shahabad. Kamaluddin Khan had *bari deorhi*, Fateh Mamur Khan at *chauk deorhi*, Chand Khan at *Kheradeorhi*, Ilahdad Khan at Nala *deorhi* and Diler Khan at *chetideorhi*.

Fateh Mamur Khan, a younger son of Diler Khan was a rank holder under Aurangzeb and is said to have died in action during the seize of Bijapur in 1096/1684 AD We know that in 1679 Diler Khan himself had given him the village Khanpur out of his *inam* grant. Apart from this, he

---

69. *Ibid.*, II, pp. 153-5.
70. *Ibid.*, II, p. 165.
71. *Ibid.*
72. *Ibid.*
73. *NM-I*, p. 314.
74. *NM-I*, pp. 315-6.

inherited 12 villages (presumably of *zamindari* possessions) out of ancestral property and had himself purchased the *zamindari* rights over a number of villages. His sons Murtaza Khan and Mustafa Khan held *mansabs* and the titles and were in possession of a large number of the villages. Saleh Muhammad Khan his grandson received the title of Diler Khan in 1171/1757 from emperor Shah Alam II. Afterwards the branch disappears from our records.[75]

Very little about the family of Chand Khan is known to us. His son Pardil Khan is reported to have received the title of Daud Khan and a *mansab* of 4000 z/4000s by emperor Farrukhsiyar. In 1129/1716 he granted a *sanad* of *ma'afi* to one Shah Muhammad Faqir for the upkeeping of a tomb and the performance of the ceremonies of '*urs* of the departed mystics. Pardil Khan seems to have been in possession of 12 villages in the ancestral property, presumably as *zamindar*.[76]

Ilahdad Khan inherited and acquired a considerable property, but he died issueless. Consequently, his wife transferred this property to her nephew in 1137/1724. This comprised *zamindari* rights over the villages Suhagpur, Naurozpur and a number of other urban possessions such as markets and ponds.[77]

The descendants of Dildar Khan, the fifth son of Diler Khan survive in records till quite recent times. In 1246/1830 the *ta'alluqadari* rights of Basit Nagar (in Shahabad) were reconfirmed by the king of Awadh on this family. It includes 45 villages along with a recognised *nankar* of Rs 5000. The incumbent was allowed to retain the necessary number of the troops to ensure the smooth administration and security for the peasants. Sa'adat Khan, a member of this branch was a *tehsildar* in Awadh administration so that he was able to ensure the continued possession of this *ta'alluqa* in his family. It is said that the descendants of Diler Khan who held as many as 200 villages till the days of Sa'adat Ali Khan who is said to have resumed their grants.

75. *NM-I*, pp. 322-28.

76. *NM-I*, pp. 337-8.

77. *NM-I*, p. 338.

Appendix

(i) Allahabad – 896

I, Buland Khan, *mansabdar* in the *biradari* (clan) of His Highness Diwan Khudadad Khan Jiv affirm as follows: Sayyid Muhammad 'Arif held the office of *wakil* at the Imperial Court on behalf of the said Khan. After the termination of his appointment as *wakil,* the said Sayyid handed over the *tashihanamas* (certificates of contingents) and other documents and papers of *jama'-kharch* (income-expenditure) of the *khwurak-i dawabb* to Miyan Muhammad Yusuf, son of the said Khan. As a dispute ensued, the matter was taken before Faulad Khan. On this account Sayyid 'Arif presented the receipt (*qabz*) of the farmer (*ijaradar*) of *Khwurak-i dawabb* and *dastaks* (certificates) under the seals of the officials (*mutasaddis*) of the imperial horse stables and elephant stables and other papers, to the agent of Faulad Khan and Ghasi Ram, the new *wakil* of Khudadad Khan. However, the case before Faulad Khan not having yet been settled, Diwan Khudadad Khan Jiv and Miyan Muhammad Yusuf maintained their dispute with the said Sayyid. Now that Miyan Muhammad Yusuf came to the town of Biswa, I took Sayyid 'Arif along to the town of Biswa. Muhammad Yusuf told Sayyid Muhammad 'Arif; "Previous to this you had given in writing a *tamassuk* (bond) for Rs 3000 for the expenses of *badr navisi* (audit) from the beginning of your term as *wakil* to termination of appointment: Sayyid Muhammad 'Arif replied that *badarnavisi* (audit) has not been in accordance with proper norms (*be-hisab*). Miyan Muhammad Yusuf told Sayyid Muhammad 'Arif: "The *Jama'-khurch* of *khwurak-i dawabb* etc. of the period of your wakilship have been lost". Now he should submit copies afresh so that the accounts of his period as *wakil* might be settled. Sayyid Muhammad 'Arif produced copies of the *jama'-kharch* of *khwurak-i dawabb* etc. together with receipt (*qubuliyat*) of the farmer of *khwurak-i dawabb* before Miyan Muhammad Yusuf, Ghasi Ram, Diwan of Khudadad Khan, Shaikh Habib Ullah, the *darogha* of the Court of justice. Miyan Muhammad Yusuf allowed deductions (*mujra*) of Rs 200 which the said Sayyid had paid to Miyan Muhammad Yusuf in *rawal-bandi,** and also Rs 556 that Shyam Das *shiqqdar* of *pargana* Hisampur had forcibly realised from the village Bedaura of the property and *zamindari* possessions of the said Sayyid in excess of the *jama'* and had recorded under receipts (*wusul*). Finally, after disallowing (*bazyafi*) the (expenditure of) Rs 200 on account of Muhammad Khan, *mansabdar*, and not writing off the expenditure of Rs 300 on account of expenses for assignment of *pargana* Amethi, in all Rs 1,480 annas 5 came out as the balance due to the said Khan, (itemised) as follows:

1. The sum the said Sayyid asked Udai Singh banker (*sahu*) of Shahjahanabad to pay to Muhammad Khan *mansabdar*, and entered as deduction in his accounts of *jama'-kharch*, not allowed by Muhammad Yusuf, and required to be refunded. Rs 200

2. The sum Diwan Khudadad Khan Jiv had got paid to the said Sayyid for arranging the assignment of *pargana* Amethi, and the said Sayyid truthfully admitted that without spending the sum, he had drawn

* The meaning of this term could not be traced.

the amount from the *jagir* and entered in the *jama'* and *kharch* register; he sought condonation, but Miyan Muhammad Yusuf refused to condone it.

Rs 300

The balance (*tattima*) in the accounts of the

Jama' and *kharch* Rs 980 annas 5

(ii) Allahabad – 1232

MEMORANDUM

List of receipts of the *ijaradars* of *khwurak-i dawabb* and other papers which were given by Sayyid Muhammad 'Arif to the undersigned Ghasi Ram 38 sheets received by the signatory, Ghasi Ram (seal).

Receipts (*qubuz-ul-wusul*) for Rs 3128, 11 annas under the seal and signature of Shaikh Firoz *ijaradar* of *khwurak-i dawabb* of the imperial establishment (*khassa-i sharifa'*) Rs 3128, 11 annas; 28 sheets.

Dastaks under the seal of officials of the *dawabb*, 6 sheets:

(i) For handling over 10 horses under the seal of Darab Khan etc., one sheet.

(ii) For handling over one imperial elephant under the seal of Abdul Rahim Khan, one sheet.

(iii) For medicines for imperial elephants, one sheet.

(iv) For medicines for horses, one sheet.

(v) For the straw shed for the stable of horses, one sheet.

(vi) Repairs of the tiled roof for horses, one sheet.

The certificates for monthly payments to Shaikh Firoz, (*ijaradar* ?), one sheet.

Qubuzul wusul for Rs 227 received by the signatory, Ghasi Ram, according to accounts, one sheet.

Qabzul wusul for *8* asharfis under the seal of officials of the office for fines on account of absence, one sheet.

Certificate (for receipt) of interest under the seal of the security (*malzamin*) of Miyan Khudadad Khan Jiv, Rs 1900, one sheet.

Chapter - 8

Origin and Growth of *Talluqadari* Tenures in Awadh

The *ta'alluqadars* of Awadh came into focus during and after the great uprising of 1857. As after the suppression of the rebellion and the restoration of law and order, the British policy-makers reshaped their agrarian policies formulated during the summary settlement immediately after annexation of the kingdom of Awadh in Feb. 1856. They thought that recognition of the peasant proprietorship would reduce the power of the landed aristocracy, but the events proved otherwise. The peasantry joined anti-British struggle mainly on the caste lines, they whole-heartedly supported leaders of their clan. This social reality forced British to change their pre-1857 policy by making peace with the class of the *ta'alluqadars*.

A change in British agrarian policy was affected after 1859, and recognition of the allodial rights of the *ta'alluqadars* made them abandon their anti-British attitude and in course of time they became natural allies of the Raj also. The cultural landscape of Lucknow came to be dominated by the *ta'alluqadars* and the British officials, their collaborative efforts brought forward associations like *Avadh Ta'alluqadar's Association, British India Association, Avadh Bar Association*; institution like *Colvin Ta'alluqadar's College, Jalsa-e Tahzib Library, Refah-e aam Club* and a large number of the buildings and hostels in *Canning College* and *Lucknow University*. The same process was replicated at the other district headquarters where a number of schools and colleges were established and cultural associations were formed by the *ta'alluqadars* in close association with the British District officials, some of these schools where named after district collectors with suffix of Islamia like Neblet Islamia Inter College Bara Banki and other institutions at various district headquarters. Such interaction and an almost dependence of the landed elite on the pleasure of

British officials by and large prevented them from joining national movement; when they did join, some of them become the leading lights of Muslim League, thus isolating themselves completely from the leadership of Indian National Congress.

The whole range of questions was taken up afresh for a public debate, a second time when the aspects related to the very existence and continuance of the institution of *Zamindari* and *Ta'alluqadari* were taken up. It was in August 1946 when the legislative assembly of United Provinces passed the resolution agreeing in principle *'to accept the abolition of Zamindari involving the removal of intermediaries between the cultivators and state.'* It was also resolved that such "*rights of the intermediaries should also be acquired by the state on payment of equitable compensation.*" Thus, the question acquired altogether new dimensions. Most acrimonious debates took place in press and at other forums[1] between the *zamindars* and those who advocated abolition of the system; in pursuance of the assembly resolution a committee was also formed.[2]

The committee met seven times between Nov. 1946 to June 1948 and submitted its final report recommending the abolition of *zamindari* from UP and the manner in which the compensation was to be paid. The Report of the Committee was compiled quite meticulously, but the historical portion does not go beyond Baden Powell and Holt Mackenzie. It has not cared to examine the data from the pre-British times as it was considered view of the committee that institution of *zamindari* was the British creation, hence there was no need, felt the members of the committee, to examine the evidences from Mughal and Nawabi period, which could have provided them some clinching data for the historical questions they were looking for.

1. Mainly the faculty of the Lucknow University and the leaders of the Congress party in the newspapers, inside and outside the assembly, carried the debate. A selection of few such pieces including the lead editorial of Daily *Hindustan* was compiled and published as *Abolition of Zamindari*, with a foreword by Gopi Nath Srivastava, the then editor of *Hindustan*, Oudh Publishing House, Lucknow, 1946.
2. A high powered committee of 15 members was constituted to prepare the necessary schemes for *zamindari* abolition under the Chairmanship of Mr Govind Ballabh Pant, the then Premier of U.P. It included besides ministers and Government Secretaries, members of the legislative assembly and council. The recommendations of the committee were not unanimous. There were three notes of dissent. Two of them were quite detailed and forcefully argued the point of view of the *zamindars*. These were by Mr Z. H. Lari and Begum Aizaz Rasul, *Report of the United Provinces Abolition Committee*, Vol. I, Govt. Press Allahabad, 1948, see especially pp. 585-610 (for the notes of dissent).

Contrary to the perceptions of the UP Zamindari Abolition Committee, enough data exist on the historicity of the institutions of *zamindari* and *ta'alluqadari* tenures. Some evidence was examined by me earlier[3], alongwith that I offer below some fresh evidence on the question.

I

Considerable controversy exists about the rise of the *ta'alluqadari* tenures in Awadh. It has been assumed that it was a part of the well-defined policy of the British after the tragedy of 1857 to "preserve this class (of *ta'alluqadars*) for useful purpose, and to prevent its impoverishment by idleness."[4] Although Lord Canning did not have a favourable opinion about the growth of these tenures, he yet thought the continuance of such tenures necessary for "Obtain(ing) a hold over the country which shall be beneficial to all the classes of its people."[5] But his view of their origin was that it lay in a delegation or usurpation of government claims to revenue, and not in any previous existing allodial property. A relevant extract from Lord Canning's letter is worth reproduction :

> "When we assumed the government of Oude in 1858, the greater part of the province was held by the *talluqadars*, who represented it. They have been called 'Barons of Oude'. But this term applied to them as a class is misleading. Some had received titles from the kings of Oude, for services rendered or by court favours, some few are the representatives of ancient families; but the majority are men distinguished neither by birth, good service or connection with the soil, who having held office under the native government as *nazims* or *chakledars*, or having formed the revenues of extensive tracts, had taken advantage of the weakness of the 'native' government and its indifference to all considerations of justice, so long as it received revenues, had abused the authority confided to them by that government, and by means of deeds of sale, sometimes extorted by violence, sometimes obtained by fraud, had become the nominal proprietors and the actual possessors of the village, or the majority of the villages which formed what they called their *taalluqa* or estate."[6]

---

3. See, "The Origin and Growth of *ta'alluqadari* tenures in Awadh", *PIHC*, 1984 (Annamalai Session), pp. 410-18; reprinted subsequently in my book Studies *in the Anatomy of a Transformation: Awadh from Mughal to Colonial Rule*, Delhi, 1998, pp. 73-81.
4. *Report of the UP Zamindari Abolition Committee*, Vol. I, p.111.
5. *Ibid.*
6. *Ibid.*, p.110.

Indeed such an impression about the origin of the holders of superior rights in land was popular enough to receive the attention of Karl Marx as well. He discussed the issue of the ownership of land at some length in his despatches to *New York Times* and *Daily Tribune*. Although he made certain untenable assumptions, the one like, "the property of the land was in the village corporation, in which resided the power of allotting it out to individuals for cultivation", he asserted explicity, "the *zamindars* and *taalluqadars* were nothing in their origin, but officers of the government appointed to look after, to collect and to pay over to the prince the assessment due from the village."[7] Marx was led to the conclusion that the proprietary rights claimed by the *taalluqadars* and the *zamindars* originated, "in usurpation at once against the government and the cultivators." The period between the annexation of Awadh in February 1856 and mutiny i.e. mid-1857, was to prove a testing ground for the future survival of *taalluqadars*. For, the government made every effort, "to get rid of them, as an incubus on the real cultivator of the soil and the general improvement of the country." Still the fact remains that under the feeble reign of the *nawabs,* they were able to establish, somehow, there legal claims over the land, and it was but natural for the settlement officers to be engulfed in an, "acrimonious controversy with them as to the extent of their rights." Ultimately this resulted in a state of discontent and, "led them (the *taalluqadars*) to make common cause with the revolted sepoys."[8]

This view of the position of the *taalluqadars* even preceded the annexation of Awadh in Feb, 1856. As in 1849 it was contended that the *taalluqadars* enjoyed their rights as a result of the delegation of the rights by the government officials in respect of revenue-collection. The *taalluqadar* was a "person previously unconnected with the spot, and (were) permitted to realise on his own account the share of the produce otherwise due to the state."[9]

On the other hand it was argued that the class of the *taalluqadars* did not solely consist of the people elevated to their position by the rulers, but a good number of them were the representatives of the hereditary chiefs, in

7. Karl Marx, 'Lord Canning's Proclamation and Land Tenure in India' *New York Daily Tribune* No. 5344 of 7th June 1858; included in *The First Indian War of Independence* published by the Progresive Publishers Moscow (English Version) 1952, pp. 140-2
8. *Ibid.*, pp. 141-2.
9. C.A. Elliott, *Chronicles of Oonao*, Allahabad 1862, pp. 155-56. The passage has been quoted by Elliott from an article published in *Calcutta Review* (Dec. 1849) p. 422.

possession of large estates in their own rights. Recognisation was accorded to their superior proprietary rights by successive governments. This school took the view that the *taalluqadars* could not just have been favoured outsiders.[10] Charles Elliott in *Chronicle of Oonao*, examined the issue at some length and concluded that a number of the big *taalluqadari* houses in the district of Oonao, Fyzabad and Sultanpur were the descendents of old hereditary chieftains. But at the same time, he too admitted that on occasions, it so happened that the revenue-officials seized the opportunity of acquiring superior proprietory rights by way of *taalluqa* arrangements.[11] It would be unhistorical, argues Elliott, to regard Raja Daya Shankar Dikshit of Purenda, or Gulab Singh, the Purihar of Surosee, or Dost Ali, the Saiyed of Oonao, as persons having acquired their possessions without any previous background of their own.

On the Indian side Lalji, a well-informed critic of the Awadh regime prior to annexation, analysed the question in details under a separate chapter in his *Mirat-ul-Auza* entitled, "Reasons for the ability of the *taalluqadars* to increase the *malguzari*."[12] Besides, broadly confirming the impressions of the English officials he describes the actual mechanism through which a *taalluqadar* applied fraudulent or forcible means to enlarge his landed possessions at the cost of the government and weak neighbours. He says that most of the villages included in the estates of the *taalluqadars* actually belonged to those *zamindars*, who had little means of defending their villages. They even did not bother to get any sort of deed executed in their favour. Similarly some *zamindars*, in order to escape the high handedness of the *amils*, sought the help of the *taalluqadars* by putting their possessions under their 'farm'. But this often subverted the *zamindars* own position. For, after a year or two, the *taalluqadars* used to take *tamassuk* from the *zamindar* under the pretext that so much amount had been paid to the *amil* on his account. Ultimately such fictitious amounts would grow too heavy for the *zamindars* to pay it and then the *taalluqadars* would get them to transfer their lands to him by a fictitious sale. If the aggrieved *zamindar* ever thought of approaching the court, he would receive no remedy. It was through the use of such methods, comments Lalji, that Beni Madho Buksh *taalluqadar* of Shankarpur, Raghunath Singh of Khajurgaon (in Baisnara distt.); Harpal

10. Elliott, p.156.

11. *Ibid.*

12. Lalji, *Mirat-ul-Auza* Ms. In Maulana Azad Library, A.M.U., Collection (supplementary) *Farsi Tarikh* – 60 see ff. 74b – 75b; see also Shaikh Abdul Rasheed, 'Mirat ul Auza', *Proceedings of Indian Historical Records Commission,* 1954.

Singh of Sapehi in Sultanpur, and Ram Dutt Pandey of Gonda had been able to seize innumerable villages yielding them lakhs of rupees.

The *nazims* and the *chakladars* too, did not lag behind in making out fortunes by such methods. Lalji, especially points out the case of Raja Darshan Singh and his family. They had seized the villages of the defaulting *zamindars*. In return for large sums of pretended balances of the revenues, the *zamindars* were forced to execute sale deeds. Any scrutiny of the titles of the family would reveal, says Lalji, that only they held a negligible portion of the entire state, as hereditary. The rest was acquired in the above-described manner. However, a few exceptions to the generally prevailing chaotic conditions have also been recorded. Lalji informs us that the *ta'alluqadars* of Tulsipur and Balrampur; Debi Buksh, the *ta'alluqadar* of Gonda had already held hereditary *zamindaris* worth lakhs of rupees.

Thus, two categories of the *taalluqadars* one of hereditary *zamindars*, the other outsiders, came to be firmly established by the close of the kingdom of Awadh. It is necessary to enquire about their origin, and privileges during the seventeenth and eighteenth centuries, as to understand the degree of power which they attained subsequently.

Etymologically the word, '*ta'alluqa*' means connection but technically it was, "used in the sense of land or area over which any kind of right was claimed".[13] Nothing can be said with certainty as to when this term came into ordinary use. The *Ain-i- Akbari* does not use the word at all. But from the 17th century, it begins to appear in documents. The testimony of Patrick Carnegy, "who have seen them (the terms) mentioned in a deed of the year 1642, under the seal of emperor Shahjahan[14] is difficult to prove or disprove. In Awadh, the earliest reference where the word *ta'alluqa* has been used in a proper context, as we understand it now, comes from a *mahzar* petition presented by one Qazi Maudud from Baiswara in AD 1662, from the large number of the documents I had the occasion to examine.[15] Generally, such

13. Irfan Habib, *Agrarian System of Mughal India*, Bombay, 1963, p.171 and notes.
14. Patrick Carnegy, *Notes on the land revenue assessment of upper India*, London, 1874, pp. 69-70. However, a petition seeking redress against the high handedness of the *chaudharies* of *Pargana* Bilgram of course refers the word, *taalluqa* as early as in 1668, but in a different context. See *Bilgram Documents* (in the department of History, AMU, No. 4).
15. See collection of acquired Persian documents in the National Archives of India No. 2618/6; while Prof. Irfan Habib refers to a *qaul o-qarar* document executed in *sarkar* Bahraich in 1685 where the assessee has been described as *malik wa ta'llaquadar* of certain villages and he considers it as the earliest reference to the institution on the basis of *Allahabad Document* no. 897; I also subscribed to the same view unless I came across to the rich collection of the above referred series of the documents from National Archives of India (acquired after 1970's).

arrangements were made by the *amils* and later on by the *nazims* or the *chakladars* owing to the convenience of revenue collection through big *ta'alluqadars*, instead of making the same with a number of intermediaries, or small *zamindars*.

The *ta'alluqadars* might have the *zamindari* rights over a few villages of his *ta'alluqa* as well; but in case of the remaining villages, in which he was only an intermediary, *zamindari* rights would be vested with other persons. Thus, to be a *zamindar* was something more substantial than to become simply a *ta'alluqadar* of the same area.[16]

Similarly Mufti Ghulam Hazrat in his *Kawaif-i-zila-i -Gorakhpur* [local history of the area] describes three types of *zamindari* tenures and says that the *ta'alluqadar*, or the owners of the *ta'alluqa* are like *rajas*. Theoretically, they were recognised as the owners of the villages included in their jurisdiction. In most of such villages the *birtiyas* also existed, and they always claimed *jalkar* [rights on the forest ponds] and *bankar* [rights on the water produce], while they paid only the land revenue to the *taalluqadars*, and at the time of assessment, these (*birtiyas*) were entitled to *do-biswi* rights, or 10 percent of the revenue.[17] It seems that *taalluqa* arrangements in *sarkar* Gorakhpur were made on an extensive scale during the 18th century. A letter in the *Mansur-ul-Maktubat* explicitly mentions that Nawab Badr-ud-din Khan, son of Nawab Wazir-ul-Mumalik, (?) had became a wondering ascetic, and his exact whereabout was unknown. He was heard last, when he went to, "*pargana* Hansi and Gorakhpur in the *ta'alluqa*[18] of the Banjaras. We know for certain that, it was during the 18th century that the *Banjaras* emerged at the political horizon of the eastern part of Awadh Kindgom. The origin of their landed possessions lay exclusively in their numerical strength and the use of violence against the hereditary chiefs.[19]

---

16. A reference in *Fathiya Ibriyah* lends support to this assumption. The claimant to the throne of Arkan joined the mughal banners during Shaista Khan's Chittagong campaign in the hope that atleast, "if they could not become *rajas*, they might become *zamindars*, if not *zamindar*, then *ta'alluqadar*". ff.155b-156a, Cf. Irfan Habib, *op cit*, p.172.
17. Mufti Ghulam Hazrat, *Kawaif-i-zila-i-Gorakhpur*, A.D. 1810, Aligarh, Subhanullah collection 954/12 ff.14a-b.
18. Awadhi Lal, *Insha-i-Mansur* or *Mansur-ul Maktubat*. It consists of the letters drafted by Santokh Rai, *munshi* of Safdar Jung. These letters were addressed to Emperor Muhammad Shah and his Wazir Nawab Abul Mansur Qamaruddin Khan. The only known copy of this important manuscript is available at Tagore Library, Lucknow University, Lucknow.
19. Banjara depredators had acquired considerable notoriety and in course of time they, not only carved out a territory for themselves, but became a scourge for almost the entire region. No individual chieftain was able to withstand their onslaught. To meet

...(Contd.)

One is struck by the fact that barring a few stray and often insignificant references, there is little information about the growth of the *ta'alluqadari* tenures and the actual position of *ta'alluqadars* in the Awadh kingdom during the 18th century. Persian texts and the documents have used the word *ta'alluqa* often in connotation different from those in which it was used during the first half of the 19th century.[20] Certainly, *ta'alluqadars*, begin to be heard of by the close of the 18th century.[21]

As such the *taalluqadari* tenures grew in Awadh at a massive scale as a result of the slackness which creeped into the administrative machinery of the kingdom after the death of Nawab Sa'adat Ali Khan in 1814. Elliott points out that as a result of the *ijardari* system of the revenue collection, things had became quite favourable for the growth of *ta'alluqa* tenures. As long as the *amani* system was practiced, "the collector of the revenue had no need to be over bearing...... if the harvest failed or sickness broke-out, he had but to state impossibility of the collection and the amount was remitted." But under the contract system, the revenue contractor was bound to pay the entire stipulated amount irrespective of natural calamities or difficulties of collections. Often it happened that some new speculator without having an accurate knowledge of the revenue paying capacity of the area might enter upon an agreement with the government. On such occasions he was forced in self-preservation to extort more than what was due from the payers. The native government was not to be blamed for all the malice, as it placed, on the other hand, unlimited powers in their hands by, "shut(ting) its eyes to the way in which they re-imbursed themselves". Under such circumstances it was thought to be more useful for the collectors of the revenue to avoid dealing with small *zamindars* and to convert big *zamindaris* into *ta'alluqa* or intermediaries between the smaller *zamindars* and government. As such the cost of collection too was minimized "beside making the receipt of the revenue much safer."[22]

---

the threat posed by these *Banjaras*, the Bisin Raja of Majhauli had abandoned a large portion of his estate to the newly established estates of Tamkhulli and Padrauna. Thus, created a powerful buffer between his domain and that of the Banjaras. These conditions came to an end with the cession of this territory to the East India Company *District Gazeetteers*, Vols. 44 and 45.

20. *'Imad-us-Sa'adat* uses the words *raja* for Mohan Singh of Tiloin, who had his skirmishes with Sa'adat Khan Burhanul Mulk, while *Mirat-ul-Auza* explicitly calls him the *taalluqadar* of Tiloin (f.76a). It is quite possible that the local chieftains who enjoyed considerable power and were by now reduced to the mere status of the *taalluqadar*.

21. See *Akhbarat* in Central Records Office Hyderabad-AR *No.5746* (dated 20th Rajab 1213 AH/28th Dec. 1798). Some of these have been published alongwith English translations by Yousuf Husain Khan, *News letters; 1767-1799*, Hyderabad, 1955, p. 66.

22. Elliott, pp. 133-4.

As a necessary collorally of such arrangements, there was always a possibility that the power and the influence of the respective *ta'alluqadar* might grow to great proportions, and in case of their going in to rebellion, "large amount of the revenue would be imperiled." In case of any such eventuality, the *Chakladars* and other government officers were often compelled to accommodate their ambitions. Even underhand methods were applied to keep 'peace' with the *ta'alluqadars* to reduce the risk to the minimum, "by throwing him a sop of an extra village or two at judicious movements" while, the *ta'alluqadars* "were nothing Loth to accept these sops." As a result of such state of affairs, the, "old *ta'alluqa* waxed fat, and new ones sprang up on all sides under this vivifying influence."[23] Such a policy in the long run had the result of continuously enlarging the *ta'alluqas*. In the *pargana* of Fyzabad in 1814, there was no *ta'alluqa* which could pay a revenue of Rs 10,000; but by 1856, one estate was capable of paying an amount of Rs 2 lacs to the treasury, while two estates paid Rs 70,000 each, one had Rs 50,000 as its rent roll, while there were several estates yielding Rs 30,000 annually to the state treasury.[24]

Broadly speaking, all the *ta'alluqadars* in Awadh during the 19th century could be divided into two major categories. The first belonged to the hereditary chiefs who has been in the possession of their estates since long and took advantage of their prime position to enlarge their 'estates' by the use of 'force, fraud and violence.' A comparison of the *Ain's* data with that of 19th century information suggest that the clans which has been recorded by Abul Fazl as *zamindars* of certain *pargana*, had the main access to the *ta'alluqa* arrangements made in 18th and 19th centuries. But it should not be assumed at the same time that all the *ta'alluqadars* or even most of them had a hereditary basis for possessing the large estates under these tenures.

(i) The *Zamindars*

In the category of the hereditary chiefs turned *ta'alluqadars* mention may be made of the Tiloin estate. The Kanhpuria Rajputs held the sway over the area since the Mughal times. Although Abul Fazl has recorded the *pargana Jais* (where the possessions of the Raja Tiloin lay) under the *zamindari* possession of the 'various castes.'[25] In all probability the

23. Elliott, p.134.
24. *Ibid*, note.
25. Abul Fazl, *Ain-i Akbari*, edited Blochmann, Bib., Indi. Calcutta, 1867-77, p. 429.

dominant position was occupied by the members of Kanhpuria Rajputs, a fact testified by the latter accounts.[26]

Little information is available about the fortunes of the family during the 17th century. It is almost certain that they enjoyed considerable power and position. With the appointment of Sa'adat Khan Burhanul Mulk as the *subedar* of Awadh, they made an appearance at the political horizon of the province. The battle between Burhanul Mulk and Raja Mohan Singh, Tiloin Chief, is too well known to mention. The Raja was killed in the pitch battle, and all his possessions which lay in the province of Awadh were captured.[27] Next, we hear about the Tiloin Chief when he raised the banners of rebellion against Safdar Jung. But again he was defeated and killed.[28] However, because of the internal disorder and the financial difficulties, the *nawab* invited the "fugitive Raja to Lucknow and was invested with the government of the estates, which were subsequently divided among, and are still held by, seven of his descendents."[29] The senior most Shankar Singh was styled as Raja and he, on behalf of the entire estate paid an amount of Rs 7,50,000 to the *chakladar* annually as the land-revenue.

Although highly critical of the administrative arrangements of the *nawab-wazirs*, Buttler praises the good and judicious administration of the Tiloin estate. He thought it as a 'pleasing oasis' 'amid wide-spread social waste.' All the brothers of Raja too were called Raja, while his nephews were called Thakurs. All share-holders paid their share of revenue to the head of the family, who in turn paid it to the *chakladar*. He had the jurisdiction over the civil and criminal disputes as well as boundary disputes among the sub-proprietors.

Apart from these share-holders there were a number of the *zamindars* in all parts of the Tiloin estate, whose share of the revenue was also realised by the Rajas of the respective regions accompanied by the *chakladar*. In case the *zamindars* showed any obstinacy they were, "left to be dealt with by the *chakladars*" but at the same time, the presence of the Raja with *chakladar* ensured that the latter could not, "make any undue demand from the *zamindars*."[30]

---

26. Donald Buttler, *An Outline of the Topography and Statistics of the Southern Districts of Dudh, and Cantonment of Sultanpur*, Calcutta, 1839, pp. 109-110.
27. Ghulam Husain Khan, *Imad us-Saadat*, Nawal Kishore, Lucknow, pp. 7-8.
28. *Mansur ul Maktbut*, pp. 30-81.
29. Buttler, *op.cit.*, p.110.
30. Buttler, *op.cit.*, p.113.

Similarly, the Shaikhzada *zamindars* of *pargana* Fatehpur, *sarkar* Lucknow were able to maintain the uninterrupted hold since the days of Akbar[31] to the 19th century. Indeed they had enlarged their landed possessions by this period. The *ta'alluqadar* of Mehmudabad was the most important member of the family, while the minor branches were established at Bilhora and Bhatwamau. The *ta'alluqa* of Mehmudabad under the efficient management of Nawab Ali achieved its farthest limits, while originally they were merely the *zamindars* during the course of time they have augmented their territory greatly, absorbing into it the estates and villages of their weaker neighbours.[32] We are told specifically about his sources which lay in, "money at command to purchase influence and a brave and well armed force to aid the *nazim* in crushing a refractory land holder. Any way by using such methods, he was able to enlarge his possessions to the extent of being able to pay Rs 1,50,000 to the government in 1849."[33]

The second category of the *ta'alluqadars* consisted of those belonging mainly to the bankers and traders possessing large capitals who came to enjoy a significant position in the official establishment of the revenue department. They often stood as sureties for *zamindars* and the *ta'alluqadars*, before the *chakladar* or the *nazims* for the payment of the revenue-debts. On occasions it so happened that the amount of 'debt' and interest became too heavy for the land holders to repay; sales of rights therefore followed, by which the creditors obtained the *ta'alluqas* of the debtors. Some of the bankers enlarged their estates by way of genuine purchases as well. But generally the cases of bankers turning *ta'alluqadars* in Awadh were few. Lalji says that the bankers and the merchants of Awadh did not keep their capital at one place due to the fear of the rebellious *ta'alluqadars* and other depredators. Similarly, they were afraid of the machinations of the '*amils*' and the *tehsildars*, who might held them responsible for the sureties, which they took on behalf of the defaulting land holders. Hence, they build their houses at different places to keep their business alive, and there were several such merchants who owned property worth Rs 2 lakh and had purchased the *zamindari* rights in the English dominions. They used to put their valuables and cash in houses built in the Company's jurisdiction as to cross over with their families in case of danger.[34]

---

31. *Ain-i-Akbari*, p. 440.
32. W.H. Sleeman, *A Journey Through the kingdom of Oudh,* London, 1858, Vol. II, pp. 270-1.
33. *Ibid.*
34. Lalji, *op.cit.*, ff-80b-81a.

(ii) *Ta'alluqa* tenures held by the Bankers and the Officials

This class consisted of bankers, merchants, and the agricultural capitalists on the one hand and the *ijaradars*, *nazims*, *chakladars* and other officials on the other. As compared to their counterparts, the hereditary claimants of the superior rights, they had grown more numerous as well as powerful at the close of the Awadh kingdom.

The details of the *ta'alluqadari* possessions held by Raja Gauri Shankar of Mauranwan and Chandan Lal offers us an opportunity to study how the bankers had spread their net throughout the kingdom. The ancestors of these *ta'alluqadars*, one Seth Ghuran Mal was actually a resident of Agra and was brought to Awadh by Burhanul Mulk. After some time, he was relieved from the services of the *nawab* and Rao Murdan of Dundiyakhera persuaded him to settle there and to act as the family banker and as the chief accountant of the estate. But their successors could not pull-up together for longer, as having developed a bitter quarrel over the issue of the rate of interest and the accounts of the estate. The family bankers used to pay the government demand of land-revenue, in case of the *ta'alluqadars* inability. Such advances were always debited against the 'estate' to be paid with interest. The Rao wanted that the rate of interest should be reduced to 12 percent from 24 percent, while the banker insisted on this rate, his plea being that since he advanced loans to other land-holders at the rate of 36 percent, he would incur heavy losses in case he yielded to the Rao's pressure. As the dispute went on the banker alongwith his establishment thought it expedient to leave Dundiyakhera secretly and settle down at Daya Ram's Katra, near Murarmau. Gradually he increased his land holdings, and utimately became one among the big *ta'alluqadars* of Unnao district. This rapid growth might be judged by the fact that in the year 1800, Raja Gauri Shankar was not a land owner at all but in the mid of 19th century his *ta'alluqa* had become prosperous enough to pay Rs 1,16,900 annually to the government as the land-revenue.[35]

In a similar manner Chandan Lal made good fortunes in the *nizamat* of Baiswara; in 1810 AD he possessed only 3 villages, but in 1825, his estate had paid Rs 2½ lakhs to the government. His un-interrupted possession continued till 1850, when Ghulam Ali, the *naib-nazim* tried to raise the revenue demand by Rs 50,000 and this led to a conflict between the parties. As a result, Chandan Lal was thrown out of his possessions, but his influential friends at the court sought the king's intervention and ultimately the possessions were restored to Chandan Lal.[36]

35. Elliott, *op.cit.*, pp.134-5.

36. *Ibid.*

Another important *ta'alluqa* of this class was held by one Ramdut Pandey in the *nizamat* of Gonda-Bahraich. He was, "one of the most substantial and respectable of the agricultural capitalists of Oude, and highest of his rank and class."[37] His wealth and position can be judged from the fact that he used to stand surety for the punctual payments of the revenue dues of the principal land-holders to the extent of Rs 6 lakhs for a year. On such loans, a certain percentage of interest was charged varying with the character and capability of the land-holders. He enlarged his own landed possessions occasionally by taking advantage of the necessities of his clients and his influence over the local authorities of the government."[38] His *ta'alluqa* could pay Rs 1,66,744 to the *nazim*. But some differences arose between him and the *nazim*, Muhammad Husain over the amount of loan and interest. Consequently the 'estate' was attached, he was killed and the property worth Rs 12 lakh plundered. However, the influential friends of the banker at the court succeeded in restoring the possessions of the family though on the condition that the demand be increased by Rs 40,000. About 1850, the rent-roll of his *ta'alluqa* was Rs 2,06,744 per annum.[39]

Another segment of this category of the *ta'alluqadars* comprised of the government officials such as the *chakladars* and *nazims*. After the death of Nawab Saadat Ali Khan the states control over the activities of the officials greatly slackened. Hence, these officials had immense latitude in exercise of their powers and in collecting and depositing taxes, thus enriching themselves at the cost of both the government and the land holders. As a result they were able to carve out some territory for themselves in hereditary tenures. There were cases of actual and forcible sales, usurpations and seizures. In case any small land-holder, refused the payment of government claims an invasion of his 'estate' was sanctioned, and his estate was given over to some other *ta'alluqadar*.

Among the officials who became *ta'alluqadar* with substantial landed possession and thus attained a prominent position in the agrarian society, mention may be made of the families of Bukhtawar Singh and his younger brother Darshan Singh. Their father had migrated from Buxar in Bihar to settle at Faizabad, in Awadh. Bakhtawar Singh was the first to enter the service of Saadat Ali Khan as one of his "favourite orderlies and rose to the command of a regiment of Nujeebs in 1814." It was in the reign of nawab Ghaziuddin Haider, that the fortunes of the family began to grow to the

37. W.H. Sleeman, *op.cit.*, Vol. I, p. 82.
38. *Ibid.*
39. *Ibid*

astonishing dimensions. For the first time in 1817, Darshan Singh was entrusted with the contract of Bhadarsa and five of its adjacent villages for an annual amount of Rs 60,000. With this beginning and his sustained effort for a name, he hold the contract for Rs 59 Lacs during the years 1827-30, and between 1830-36, for Rs 58 Lacs per annum; while in 1837 the annual amount payable by him in *ijara* stood to 47 Lacs. Most of his *ijara* estates were situated in Sultanpur-Fyzabad *nizamat*.[40] With such enormous resources and his high official status, it was quite easy for him to raise the stipulated demand from the *zamindaris*. In case of their inability to meet out their new-revenue obligation, he could force the defaulting proprietor's to sell their villages. Thus, during his own life time, Darshan Singh was able to carve-out a large *ta'alluqa* for himself; the process was continued by his son with the active support of still influential uncle, Bukhtawar Singh. W.H. Sleeman estimated that the rent-roll of Darshan Singh's family amounted to Rs 2,54,000 over with Rs 68,000 was admitted as *nankar*. Hence the total amount payable to the exchequer was only Rs 1,86,000.[41] Similarly, Bukhtawar Singh had also came to possess an 'estate' having the rent-roll of Rs 2,52,000 annually.

Hakim Mehdi was the prime minister of Awadh during the reign of Amjad Ali Shah; his heir and nephew Munawwar-ud-Daulah was able to acquire the possession over 300 villages in Khairabad *nizamat* under the *ta'alluqadari* tenures. The revenue obligation of his estate amounted to Rs 40,000 per annum.[42]

The *taalluqa* arrangements had became so popular and common by the close of Awadh dynasty, that every district contained a number of *taalluqas*, and many *ta'alluqadars* wielded considerable power and influence through being the important officials of the state. They maintained large numbers of armed retainers and had built a number of mud-forts (*garhis*). The use of fire-arms and deployment of large cannons for the defence of *garhis* was also a common phenomena.

Fortunately, we possess a detailed break-up of the total number of the villages held under the *ta'alluqadari* tenures at the time of the summary settlement in 1856. Keeping in view the methods adopted by the *ta'alluqadars* to enlarge their possessions, one need not be astonished to find that out of 35,174 villages, 23,522 or 67% were settled with the

40. Sleeman, *op.cit.*, Vol. II, p. 153.
41. *Ibid.* Vol. I, p.154.
42. Sleeman, Vol. II, p.126.

ta'alluqadars, while only 11,652 or 33% of the total villages were under the possession of the village proprietors; viz. *zamindars and paatidars.*[43]

Table - I

Sl. No.	*A District*	*B Villages*	*C Ta'alluqa Tenures*	*D Other Tenures*	*% of C to B*	*% of D to B*
1.	Bahraich	3,949	3,761	188	95	5
2.	Gonda	4,129	3,484	646	84	16
3.	Partapgarh	3,633	3,032	601	84	16
4.	Faizabad	4,215	3,116	1,099	74	26
5.	Rae Bareili	1,591	1,052	499	68	32
6.	Sultanpur	3,351	2,132	1,218	64	36
7.	Sitapur	4,421	2,692	1,730	61	39
8.	Mohammadi	3,131	1,754	1,372	56	44
9.	Daryabad	2,560	1,087	1,473	42	58
10.	Lucknow	1,570	575	995	37	67
11.	Onao	1,236	368	868	30	70

It is necessary to point out that the British presence in Awadh and English Resident's interference in day-to-day affairs of the kingdom, indirectly helped the growth of the *ta'alluqadari* tenures. To begin with, the treaty of Buxar had stipulated a drastic reduction of the native army and a strong exception was taken on every reported move of the *nawab-wazir* if ever made, to reorganise his forces. Consequently, the *nawab* had to look for the British authorities to carry on the work of revenue collection. As a result, the forces maintained by the then *nawab* for the purpose known as *muta'aeyanah* and *seh-bandi* were always thought to be inadequate in quelling rebellion of the land-holders, in case the later refused the payment of the land-revenue. Although the revenue-officials, atleast in theory, were fully entitled to ask the commandant of the English forces for, "sending him the aid of one or two battalions and heavy artillery."[44] Yet the English officials were directed to exercise the utmost caution before they "comply with the requisition of the *aumil*."[45] In 1808, Lord Baillie, the Resident at Lucknow informed the Governor General that, "he sanctioned it (use of British troops) after a careful and minute investigation of each and every case."[46]

43. Major Borrow's *Memorandum* relative to the Summary Settlement of the province of Oudh Foreign Secret Consultation, No. 844-50 dated 8th *Dec., 1859 National Archives of India Delhi* CF. Arshad Ali Azmi, "Position of the *ta'alluqadars* in Oudh – 1814-1856", read at the Session of Indian History Congress (Allahabad Session 1965), see cyclostyled volume of *Aligarh Papers* for the Session, Library of Centre of Advanced Study in History, Aligarh Muslim University, Aligarh

44. *Foreign Secret Consultations (iii)* 8th *Jan., 1778, NAI*, Delhi.

45. *Ibid.*

46. Jagdish Raj, 'The Revenue System of the Nawabs of Oudh' *Journal of Economic and Social History of the Orient*, 1958, p.101.

It was thought by the English officials that the help extended by English forces to the revenue-officials was so thoroughly misused and it had such devastating affects at the countryside that in 1833 Colonel Paton suggested that such assistance to be discontinued.[47]

Thus, the genesis of the *ta'alluqa* tenures essentially lay in the growth of the power of elements from the *zamindar* class during the weakening of Mughal power as represented in Awadh by the *Nawab wazirs*, in the 18th century. Although, some of the *ta'alluqadars* had a hereditary basis for their allodial rights, but they too had applied force, fraud and violence to enlarge their landed possessions in the form of *ta'alluqa* tenures. However, the British presence and interference in day-to-day affairs of the kingdom also aided the extension of *ta'alluqadari* tenures. The Awadh government had to look for British help even for the purpose of the revenue collection and the maintenance of law and order. Such conditions helped the local magnets and other speculators to usurp more at the cost of the weaker neighbours, the state exchequer and the very system which had sustained them so far.

47. *Ibid.*

Chapter - 9

Revenue Grants and the Grantees

(a) Revenue Grants

Our information on revenue grants tends to be exceptionally rich owing to the survival of a large number of *farmans, parwanas, nishans* and other Persian documents, such as sale-deeds, *taqsim-namahs, mahzars*, judicial decisions and other papers relating to the grantees. Many of these documents belonging to particular families whose fortunes can be traced through these records for a hundred years or more.[1]

During the Mughal period and later under the *nawab-wazirs*, there was a well established system through which the Emperor or the *nawab-wazirs* granted the right to appropriate the land revenue and other specified fiscal perquisites from a given area of land or village in entirety (*dar-o-bist*) or in part for the life time of the grantee or (at a later stage) in perpetuity. The grants provided that the grantees themselves would be exempt from payment of these taxes to government. The grants were known by the designations of *suyurghal*,[2] *madad-i-ma'ash*,[3] *aimma*[4] and *imlak*.[5] Along with land-grants some cash grants were also made in order to support certain individuals or institutions, and these were known as *rozina*[6] and *saliana*.[7]

---

1. For example, there are large sets of documents belonging to a family of Bahraich and another of Sandila at the Regional Archives, Allahabad and of families of Khairabad, Firangi Mahal, Jais, Bilgiram and Shamsabad at Research Library, Department of History, AMU, of Laharpur at the Tagore Library, Lucknow University and the papers relating to the family of mystics established at Salon (private custody at Khanqah-e-Karimia, Salon).
2. Irfan Habib is of the view that the term was brought by the Mughals from Central Asia, *Agrarian System*, p. 298 and note.
3. Literally, subsistence allowance.
4. Literally, plural of *imam*, but technically meaning the grantees and later on the land grants. *Ibid.*
5. Plural of *milk* (property) was also used to identify the lands assigned in grants. *Ibid.*

The '*amils* and the *fotadars* were asked to pay the specified amounts to the grantees out of the revenue collections of particular *parganas*. During the later half of the 18th century and the first half of the 19th century in the kingdom of Awadh, cash allowances were sanctioned for benevolent purposes, out of the interest on loans advanced by the *nawab-wazirs* to the East India Company.[6] At the provincial level, the affairs of the grantees were looked after by the *sadr-i-juzv*,[7] while at the *pargana* level, matters relating to the grantees were supervised by *mutawallis*.[8]

Classes of Grantees – Most of the grants were made for the benefit and maintenance of the individual grantees. The basic consideration for such an act of charity was the maintenance of religious and pious classes. They were thought to stand in need of such support because, not taking to service, they kept themselves engaged either in pursuing or imparting religious education or offering in prayers. While most grants were made with the specific purposes as well, such as maintenance of mystic institutions (*Khanqahs*), payments to their servants or other expenses.[9]

Another class of the grantees comprised those persons who had been entrusted with some religious office. In lieu of remuneration for the service, they were granted *madad-i-ma'ash* lands. These offices were generally of *muhtasib* (censor of morals), *qazi* (judge), *imam* (prayer-leader), *khatib* (sermon-reader), *mutawalli* and *nirkh-navis* (price-reporter).[10]

The widows of the divines and their sons or the descendants, were also entitled to receive the imperial favours by way of land as well as cash-grants.[11] Others could lay claim to grants on the basis of their being 'scholars' (*talib-i Ilm*).

The grants made for the purpose of the maintenance of the particular institution or for some other specified purpose were fairly numerous in

6. *Jais documents* CAS, Aligarh Muslim University, Aligarh– 11 (29th R.Y. of Aurangzeb/1688).
7. *Jais documents* – 12 (49th R.Y. of Aurangzeb/1704).
8. For such grants see, C.U. Aitchinson, *A Collection of Treaties, Engagements and Sunnuds*, Vol. II, especially the treaty nos. XLVI, XLVIII, XLIX and I.
9. Ibn Hasan, *Central Structure of the Mughal Empire*, Delhi, reprint 1970.
10. The *mutawalli* had an important role in managing the affairs of the grantees at *pargana* level. *Allahabad-1* (1063/1653) 5, (1060/1650); C.A. Elliott, *Chronicles of Onnao*, p. 111.
11. In some *farmans*, it is stated that since the expenses of such and such divines have been enhanced due to the fact that the poor and students flock to them in large numbers, See *Jais-1* (1124/1716), *Jais-12* (1704); 7 (1144/1738) etc.
12. *NAI-1434* (1680 AD), *1273* (1673 AD).

Awadh. The same policy seems to have continued in the days of the *nawab-wazirs*. These grants were made for the upkeep and other expenses of a mosque, a *khanqah*, *imambara*, temple and other places of worship.[13] Some grants were made on promise of providing works of public utility like digging of wells, upkeep of *sarai* and planting of the trees on the roadside for the benefit of the travellers.[14]

The holders of the cash-grant, and those who received some customary grants on specific occasions generally felt rather insecure in respect of the rights conferred on them. In the Jais documents we come across a number of instances, where these grantees represent to the governor of the province for the transfer of their grants from one *pargana* to another. Probably the '*amil* refused the payments on the pretext of the non-realisation of the revenues. We find that when such a request for transfer to another *pargana* is conceded, it is usually with the reduction of the amount of the original grant.[15] On the other hand, when the *qazi* of *pargana* Sandila who received an annual amount of Rs 60 and a shawl on account of *resum-e Idain* (payments on the occasion of two 'Ids); got a fresh *parwana* issued for the grant from the same treasury, this was without any loss whatsoever.

There appear to have existed no hard rules as regards the classes of the grantees entitled to receive *madad-i-ma'ash* grants. Everything depended upon the will of those in authority to exercise their full discretion in this respect.

It seems that local elements often resisted the induction of grantees from outside. Even after the grantees took possession of the land, they faced great difficulty in realising their dues. In some cases the grantees would seek to have their area of grant transferred from the disorderly (*zortalab*) area to a 'tax-paying' (*raiyati*) locality. Sometimes the hostility of the *zamindars* derived from a curtailment of their rights. In Shah Jahan's times we find that the refusal of the peasants of the area to pay revenue to the grantee forced the latter to get his grant transferred from one *pargana* to another with the usual reduction of the original grant.[16] In a unique *chaknama* executed in 1056/1664, we are informed that 40 *bighas* of land earlier measured in certain

---

13. *NAI-2166* (1128-1715, *1249* (9th R.Y. ?).

14. Francis Buchanan in Montgomery Martin's *Eastern India*, Vol. II, pp. 347-9. Also in Buttler, *op. cit.*, pp. 138-9.

15. *NAI-1341* (1670 AD), *1343* (1679 AD); Also *Nama-i Muzzaffari*, Vol. II, pp. 153-5 especially for the words like:

16. *Jais-7 (1144/1736), 11 (29th R.Y./1688).*

17. *NAI-1285* (1189/1775), *1425* (This is an undated letter, but it relates to the same *qazi* who has been mentioned in the earlier document).

pargana are now transferred to another *pargana* as the cultivators (*karindas*) had not paid the due revenue (*mal-o wajib*) to the *a'immadaran*.[18] The grant was an imperial one, though the transfer was affected by agents of the *jagirdar*. In yet another *parwana* (1095/1686) we are informed that the *qazis* of Sandila had been given 10 *bighas* of cultivated land in a village to establish an orchard with a well; but the *malikan* (proprietors) having shown their unwillingness to relinquish the cultivated fields, that land from which the *qazi* was apparently taking revenue was brought back under *jama*; and 17 *bighas* elsewhere were given to the *qazis* "to establish a mosque, religious house, orchard, well and habitation."[19]

Apart from these direct references, we have a number of *mahzars* (statements of facts), prepared by an affected person seeking attestation from those who knew the facts, to be submitted to an appropriate authority (for the redressal of the grievances) presented by various revenue-grantees. They allege in most of the cases that the local *zamindars* in collaboration of other officials had raided the villages held by the grantees and destroyed their property. They frequently demand enquiry and punishments.[20] Often enough of the recalcitrant *zamindars* were Rajputs.[21]

SUCCESSION, OBLIGATIONS AND PERQUISITES

The *madad-i ma'ash* grants did not theoretically affect the status of the hereditary proprietors of the land. What was transferred to the grantees were essentially the taxation rights; the proprietors continued to enjoy possession or claims to the produce as before, and the two rights on the same land remained distinct.[22] The grantees derived their rights from the documents (*farman, parwana*) assigning them the grant, and the revenue officers were entitled to demand a scrutiny of the papers (*sanads*); but they were usually asked not to require the grantees to have the *sanads* renewed every year.[23] With every fresh administrative change (new emperor for

---

18. *NAI-1474*.
19. *NAI-1651*, *1389*.
20. *UPSA-278* (1627), *1546* (1636).
21. *AQ Collection-4* (1026/1617); *LUL-46905* (40 R.Y. of Aurangzeb); *RAA-1315* (1125/1717), *1304* (1101/1693), *950* (17 R.Y./1676), *287* (4th R.Y./1663), *FM-23* (50th R.Y./1706), *185* (38th R.Y. of Aurangzeb).
22. For a distinction between these two claims see *Allahabad 457* (1177/1763); Irfan Habib, *op. cit.*, p. 301.
23. This clause was always appended in every *farman* and *parwana*, irrespective of the fact whether the grant was old or new one.

imperial grant; and new *jagirdar* for the grants from nobles) the grantees had to prove their credentials and get renewal orders.[24]

Before Aurangzeb, the grants used to be normally curtailed at the death of the grantee, and its distribution among the heirs did not necessarily follow the *shari'at* prescriptions. Aurangzeb's *farman* of 1690 deserves particular mention in this regard.[25] He calls the *madad-i ma'ash* as something held on '*sariyat* (loan) by the grantee; it was not therefore, the grantee's property in legal terms. As such the *farman* gives the following rules:

(a) If a grantee dies leaving a grandson whose father had predeceased the grandfather, the grandson would get the share which his father would have got, had he been alive.

(b) A daughter who is married and expects to receive land from the property of her husband is not to get her share in her father's grant since she has an alternative means of subsistence.

(c) The daughter of a deceased grantee is to get his land in spite of the presence of other relatives.

(d) The wife is to enjoy the land of her deceased husband, but after her death it would go to the husband's heirs - and failing them – to her own.

(e) If a grantee dying left the offspring of his brother or sister as legal heirs, the grant land was to be distributed among them keeping in view their legal claims.

(f) If a grantee leaves no heirs his land be resumed and entered into land reserved for *Baitul mal* (charity department).

These rules of succession were different from those prescribed by the *shari'at* (Muslim law) for personal possessions.

Another feature of these grants was that even the natural heirs and the legal representatives of the deceased grantee could succeed only after obtaining the confirmatory orders from the authorities. Generally such orders were issued as a matter of course, but there were quite few cases when the area of the grant was either reduced or curtailed. Moreover, continued actual control over the land was an essential condition; every confirmatory order carried a recitation to the effect that "if the land was still under the possession and control (of the heirs) and (the same) has not been resumed.

---

24. *Ibid.*

25. *RAA-1880* (34th R.Y. of Aurangzeb).

It appears that during the 16th and 17th centuries, these grants could neither be sold, nor transferred to others by the grantees. The earliest instance of a sale of such grant reported to us from Awadh belongs to 1136/1723. One Saiyed Mohammad Panah is reported to have sold 46 *bighas* of *madad-i ma'ash* land in village Akhtiyarpur, *pargana* Bilgiram along with the *muqqadami* rights of the same village.[26] It is quite curious to see that a person was in possession of these two rights at the same time and was selling them together without making any distinction.[27] In the following decades of the 18th century, a full-fledged market of such lands seems to have been established throughout the province; and no official restrictions appear to have been enforced. In effect the grantees came to possess full proprietory rights, for their land could be sold, mortgaged and inherited in the ordinary manner.

The *farmans* and *parwanas* conferring these grants normally carried a set passage listing all the taxes and cesses from the payment of which, the grantee was exempted and the perquisites to which he could lay claim. Broadly speaking the taxes from which exemption was granted were *mal-o ijhat, akhrajat, awarizat takalifate-diwani* and *matalibat-e sultani*. But in addition to these privileges, the grantee have acquired some other fiscal rights which were the exclusive claims of the *zamindars* and the village headmen. A *parwana* issued in the 7th R.Y. of Jahangir/1612 stipulates that the grantee of village Mahsona, *pargana* Sandila was to enjoy all the fishing rights in the ponds of the village. The fishermen were prohibited from making use of the ponds without paying the *malikana* (proprietory due) to the grantee.[28] In the course of time the grantees came to possess a number of perquisites in the village. In 1858, one Aminuddin, the *mutawalli* of village Panwaria, *pargana* Khairabad presented a statement of the facts duly endorsed and certified by thirty persons, about the perquisites alleged to have been enjoyed by him as well as by his ancestors. These included, "the realisation of one *tanka* and sweetmeats as *bhent* from every person laying the foundation of his house, and the rate of one *ser* (of produce) per *bigha* from every one setting up a *nova* (water-raising scoop) to water their

26. *Bilgiram-60* (1136/1723).

27. Theoretically *madad-i ma'ash* grants were made as an act of charity and hence could not be held by those who had other means of livelihood or were in service. See Irfan Habib, *Agrarian System*, p. 307 and note.

28. *NAI-1596*. In fact this *parwana* was issued on the basis of the alleged complaint of the grantee that Sita *Mehtar* and his kinsmen were in the habit of fishing in the pond of the petitioner without paying the *malikana* dues. By virtue of this *parwana*, the fishermen were to be restrained from fishing without the grantee's permission.

fields from the tank of the village."[29] We know for certain that Shaikh Diam, the predecessor in the interest of Aminuddin, was originally granted five *bighas* of *khud-kashta* land in village Panwaria in 1068/1658 with the specific purpose of establishing a mosque and *Khanqah* and maintaining a graveyard.[30] There exist in the earlier document not a single word about the perquisites which were now claimed by the petitioner. It seems that either the grantees in course of time tended to add to their fiscal claims as *madad-i ma'ash* holders, or they purchased or otherwise acquired or usurped other rights, viz., of the *maliks, zamindars* or *muqaddams*. The progressive combination of these rights can be illustrated from the histories of the families of certain grantees which are reconstructed in a separate section of this chapter.

In the 16th century, *madad-i ma'ash* grants used to have some real or nominal conditions attached to them. We are fortunate in possessing an original *farman* of Sher Shah relating to *pargana* Sandila. It grants 60 *bigha* of land (half mazrua and half *uftadah*) to some Shaikh (?). It laid down a number of obligations to be fulfilled by the grantee. He was expected to offer the five daily prayers in congregation and to practice archery after midday prayers by discharging ten arrows. In addition, he was also to assist the '*amil* and *shiqdar* in the revenue realisation and to fight against malefactors whenever called upon to do so by the officials for the purpose.'[31] But, the *farmans* of the Mughal emperors normally drop any such conditions from the grant. Instead we find Jahangir calling the *madad-i ma'ash* holders as 'Army of prayers' to him this was as important as the real army of the state.[32] As now the only duty which was expected from the grantees was one of mere lip service; to pray for the perpetuity and long life of the everlasting empire.

EXTENT

The *Ain-i Akbari* provides us rich statistical information regarding the revenue-alienated through *suyurghal* in the different *parganas* of the *suba* of Awadh. An analysis of these data leads us to some interesting conclusions. In the five *pargana* of the various *sarkar* of *suba* Awadh, where the caste of the *zamindar* is recorded as Muslim, the percentage of total *naqdi* alienated

29. *Khairabad-9*; see also Iqbal Husain, 'A Calendar of Khairabad Documents: 16th-19th Centuries', *Islamic Culture*, Hyderabad (1979), ii, pp.
30. *Khairabad-3*; see also Iqbal Husain, *op. cit.*
31. *RAA-318* (1541 A.D.).
32. *Tuzk-i-Jahangiri*, p. 5, Cf. Irfan Habib, *Agrarian System*, p. 310 & n.

by way of *suyurghal* ranged from 0.49 percent to 12.60 percent. The *pargana* of Ibrahimabad in *sarkar* Awadh records a high percentage i.e. 23.30 percent of the total *naqdi*, but this seems to be an exception. In another six *pargana* where the Muslims along with the Hindus appear as *zamindars*, the *jama*' alienated ranges from 1.78 percent to 18.49 percent. In 72 *parganas* of various *sarkars* where the *zamindars* happened to be Hindus only mostly Rajputs, these grants constituted between 0.03 percent to 18.74 percent of the total *naqdi*. The remaining 47 *pargana*, recorded no *suyurghal* grants at all. This included the *pargana* Anona, *sarkar* Awadh, where the *zamindars* were *chauhan* Rajputs, newly converted to Islam.[33] An Awadh at least, the grantees appear to have been indifferent to the community of *zamindars* while seeking grants.

In absolute terms, the total amount of the *jama*', alienated through such grants in c. 1595 was only 4.5 percent, apparently not a very large amount. But the *madad-i ma'ash* grants as a rule, were made out of the cultivable waste with the implicit purpose of making it cultivable (under the formula, *zamin-i uftada laiq-i zira'at, kharij-az jama'*) or at the most one-third of the total and at later stages half of the total grant was made out of the cultivated land (*mazrua*).[34] It is to be remembered that the *Ain*'s *suyurghal* figures represent only the loss of revenue to the state through such alienations, and not the actual income from the *madad-i ma'ash* land. It might, on the other hand, have included the amount distributed through the cash allowances, but this is not clear.

With the coming of the *nawab-wazirs* at the helm of affairs, a few changes appear to have occurred in the state policy towards the *madad-i ma'ash* holders. Owing to their *Shi'ite* leanings *Imambara* and the *Shia*' divines came to be patronised quite liberally by the *nawab-wazirs* and their 'royal' successors. Correspondingly, in the beginning at least there was some containment or restriction of *madad-i ma'ash* grants given to other scholars and beneficiaries.

Ghulam Ali Azad Bilgrami indeed criticizes Burhanul Mulk Sa'adat Ali Khan and Safdarjung for resuming the cash and land-grants (*waza'if-o-*

---

33. See Table at the end of the Chapter.

34. Sher Shah divided *mazrua* and *uftada* equally (*RAA-318*). Akbar seems to have followed the same principle. In the reign of Jahangir we notice that the *mazrua*' was reduced to 1/3, thus making *uftada* 2/3 of the total see *RAA-1567, 1556*. Subsequently we notice that those villages which had been abandoned by the *zamindars* for want of realization of the estimated *jama* were assigned to the grantees. See Aurangzeb's *farman* to Muhammad Ashraf (19th R.Y.) in my paper *PIHC*, 1979, pp. 311-14.

suyurghalat) of the old families, as a result of which, he says, Muslim learning suffered very heavily in both Awadh and Allahabad provinces. He does not himself attribute this explicitly to any sectarian motives on the part of the two Awadh rulers; and it is possible to argue that the motives were purely financial. The members of scholarly families had to take to the military profession as a result of these measures, says Azad Bilgrami – a curious statement which suggests that a connection was always maintained between the grant-holders and the army.[35]

The 18th century records of the individual families have not so far supplied any corroboration of Azad Bilgramis statement.[36] Still one can not reject it out of hand.

Our evidence shows that many grants, at least, were confirmed. We have the original *parwanas* issued to the *'amils* and the *mutassadis* of the different *parganas* of the *suba* of Awadh and one *pargana* in *suba* Allahabad by Nawab Safdarjung.[37] A *parwana* was issued to the '*amil* of *pargana* Mahauli *sarkar* Gorakhpur stipulating that 700 *bighas* of land said to have been in *madad-i ma'ash* grant of a *mo'azzin* (attached to the mosque of) Shah Badar Ashraf since the days of Akbar. But now it should be recognised only if the grantees possess the *tashihnama* signed by the *sadr* (of Akbar's reign), otherwise the land should be included in the *Khalisa*.[38] In another *parwana* addressed to the *'amils* of *pargana* Kakori *sarkar* Lucknow, it was ordered that the *madad-i ma'ash* grant of Muhammad Murad, which had been resumed earlier, should be restored to him. But before issuing the confirmatory orders the genuineness of the claims and the papers of the grantee should be scrutinized.[39] Another order was issued to Saiyyed Muzaffar Mahani (probably a *mutaqalli*) instructing him to restore the *madad-i ma'ash* grants of a widow. The widow-grantee had been expelled from her possessions earlier.[40] Similarly, one Raghunath Singh, who was the '*amil* of *mahiat* Azamgarh was directed not to interfere with the *madad-i ma'ash* villages in the possession of one Shaikh Ruh-ul-Amin in *tappa*

35. Ghulam Ali Azad Bilgrami, *Mathirul Kiram*, Vol. I, pp. 221-22.

36. Nevill does record a tradition that all the grants of the Sabzposh family of Gorakhpur were resumed by the early nawabs, however, later on they were restored to the family by Asafuddaulah, who also confessed the title of Sabzposh on the family. The establishment continued to flourish in much better condition after the area was leaded to the English. Cf. H.R. Nevill, *Gorakhpur Gazetteer*, p. 120.

37. Awadhi Lal, *Insha-i Mansur* or *Mansur-ul Maktubat*, MS, Tagore Library.

38. *Ibid.*, ff. 173b-174b.

39. *Ibid.*, ff. 175b-176a.

40. *Ibid.*, f. 182b.

Kadara having an annual *jama'* of Rs 1327.[41] The officials of Sandila were asked by the *nawab* in 1156/1743, not to interfere with the landed possession (*arazi* and *dehat* both) of the *a'immadars* in *pargana* Sandila and the grantees were to be allowed to enjoy the benefits of their grants.[42]

It appears that during the first half of the 18th century – the days of laxity in the Mughal administration – quite a few grants were obtained by the fraudulent means and perhaps the *nawab-wazirs* tried to weed-out such grants and to confirm only the genuine ones. On that account it was always insisted that a full inquiry be made into the credentials of the grantees and into the genuineness of the *farmans* or the *parwanas* held by them. Only after this, were the confirmatory orders to be issued. A natural corollary of this exercise was that the grants were to be immediately forfeited in case of any suspicion. Perhaps to this extent Azad Bilgirami's allegations are true. But in general, as is evident from the above, no particular hostility was shown to the members of the old establishments.

Moreover, the history of the family of the mystics established at Salon traced at the end of this chapter also caste doubt on the allegation of Azad Bilgirami. It appears that the *nawab-wazirs* were fairly tolerant and liberal in giving additional favours to this establishment of the Sunni mystics. The 18th century saw the apex of their fortunes, as the *bayaz* of the family records that in c. 1797 the total number of the villages and *chaks* included in the landed possessions of the family was 40 in all and yielded an annual amount of Rs 40,000; this was in addition to 15 gardens and a number of residential *havelis*.[43] The establishment continued to flourish throughout the period of Awadh kingdom as Buttler (in c. 1837) and Sleeman (in c. 1849) have estimated the annual income of this, "eleemosynary establishment" as between Rs 30,000 to Rs 25,000.[44]

So far as *shite* grants are concerned, the archival material is not very helpful in determining the extent and origin of such grants during the 18th and first half of the 19th centuries. The various District Gazetteers do not also lent any help to us in this respect. The earliest reference in our records comes from 1195/1780 from *pargana* Sandila when an entire village

41. Awadhi Lal, *Insha-i Mansur* or *Mansur-ul Maktubat*, MS, Tagore Library, ff. 182b-183a.

42. *NAI-1349* (1156/1743).

43. This *bayaz* is a manuscript in *nastaliq* script and in very good condition. It is in private custody of the present Sajjada-nasheen of the *Khanqah*. It has about 300 folios c. 1797 (the date of the seal being 1212 A.H.).

44. Donald Buttler, *op. cit.*, p. 139; W.H. Sleeman, *op. cit.*, Vol. I, p. 279.

was granted to one Saiyyid Shah Hidayat Ali in order to meet the expenses of an *Imambara.* The grant is, however, reported to have been an old one.[45] Besides, there are a few *parwanas* preserved at National Archives of India concerning the land and cash grants in *pargana* Sandila for the purpose of the maintenance of *Imambara* and meeting the expenses incurred in connection with *azadari*.[46] But all these *parwanas* date to early 19th century and concern separate individuals as that no connected history can be constructed of any particular *shite* establishments.

Buchanan's survey of the district of Gorakhpur (ceded to the British in 1801) provides some interesting indications of the general policy pursued by the *nawab-wazirs* in relation to the then existing religious establishments. We find, that all the old families were not only tolerated but received additional favours.[47] Indeed Buchanan says, "... nor is there any reason to think that the government of the *nawab-wazirs* was here at least in any degree of intolerant, or gave any preference to those of their own religion.[48]

There existed an *Imambara* in the city of Gorakhpur, whose keeper was known as Miyan Saheb. A large endowment was attached with it. The history of this establishment is quite interesting. The ancestors of the family were said to have settled at Shahpur, *pargana* Dhuriapora in mid-18th century. One of the members of the family (the ancestor of Miyan Saheb) Shah Roshan Ali had adopted *Shism* and had become a devotee of that cult. He sought to establish an *Imambara*, and in this task was helped by nawab Asafuddaulah in the year 1790 AD. A revenue free grant of 15 villages was bestowed upon him by the nawab for the maintenance and upkeep of the *Imambara.* Shah Roshan Ali was exceedingly reserved towards the infidels. He seldom resides in the *Imambara*, but usually supports the 15 to 20 *faqirs*, all unmarried, as he himself was. During the 10 days of the *Muharram* they distributed daily from 25 to 30 *mans* (cash 113 9/10 lb.) of boiled rice and pulse (*khichri*) seasoned with buttler, salt and spices and from four to five *mans* of sugar and molasses in *sherbat*."[49] Shah Roshan Ali died in 1816 and was succeeded by his pupil Ahmad Ali Shah, who received the title of Miyan Saheb. Additional grants were made by the British for the 'loyal conduct' of the family during the course of the Mutiny. Nevill has estimated their landed possession around c. 1900 as consisting of 15 revenue-free villages, with a further 44 villages in

45. *Allahabad documents No. 52* (1195/1780).
46. Acquired collection of Documents, NAI.
47. Martin, *op. cit.*, Vol. II, p. 445.
48. *Ibid.*
49. Montgomery Martin, *op. cit.*, Vol. II, p. 349.

tahsil Padrauna and 17 villages in *tahsil* Gorakhpur.[50] The family has become Sunni, but continues to maintain an *imambara*.

Donald Buttler, while discussing the problem of mendicity in the southern parts of Awadh kingdom,[51] says that there had been a great increase in the number of itinerant beggers as, "now, 100 are being found in a town of 5000 inhabitants where formerly only one or two could be seen." This miserable state of affairs was probably caused due to the impoverishment of the country as a result of the deficiency of the harvest. Little was done by the Government to meet this problem. On the other hand, the old eleemosynary institutions established at the various districts of the Awadh, carried over the work of charity. The keepers of the mystic establishment at Salon used to provide food and shelter to about 100 *faqirs* daily. In Pachhimrath, existed a large endowment known as Bhadarsa having lands yielding Rs 15,000 annually. The sum was distributed among the *faqirs* and *bairagis* by its Saiyyid custodian.

A large Hindu establishment known as *Hanumanjorhi* in the city of Faizabad was patronized by *nawab* Shuja-ud-daulah and "continued in a flourishing condition up to the present time, unmolested by the *chakledar* or *zamindar*".[52] It had a revenue-free grant of Rs 50,000 and no Muslim was allowed to enter its premises. The estate was managed by the *bairagis*, and only a moderate rent was levied per *bigha*. In the city of Ayodhya, there were two Hindu establishments of some importance i.e. *Ram Parsad Khara*, occupied by 200 to 250 *bairagis* and enjoy a revenue of Rs 25,000. The other was at *Bindiya Kund*, having a total rent-free grant of Rs 10,000 and the establishment about 200 *bairagis*.[53] A large *yogi* establishment at Gorakhnath had a rent-free land-grant consisting of three villages in entirety and three detached portions of villages. Martin tells us that, "... from 200 to 250 people go every Tuesday to make offering; some of them are Muhammadans. There are besides two fairs (*mela*) on the Sivratri 10,000 and on the Dasehra of spring 4,000 assemble."[54] Buttler also observed that, "much charity is distributed by the Brahmans out of the small allotment of the lands, granted to them for this purpose by the *zamindars*."[55]

50. H.R. Nevill, *op. cit.*, Vol. 31, pp. 119-20.
51. For this discussion see Buttler, pp. 162-3.
52. Buttler, pp. 162-3.
53. Buttler, pp. 162-3.
54. Mantgomery Martin, Eastern India (the abridgement of Buchanan's report) Vol. II, *op. cit.*
55. *Ibid.*

The autonomous chiefs, paying tribute to the government of *nawab-wazirs*, and the local *zamindars* continued to make grants of revenue-free lands on their own. The beneficiaries were mostly Brahmans, especially men of learning (*Pandits*) and physicians (*baids*). Buttler informs us that, "In Salon and Partapgarh *baids* are found at every six or eight miles and are Brahmans of different denominations. They very frequently are supported by grants of land from *rajas* and other *zamindars*, to the extent of from 20 to 400 *bighas*."[56] Similarly, Bennett while discussing the proprietary rights of the autonomous chiefs (*rajas*) remarks that the "second direct proprietary act was allotment of small patches of uncultivated land chiefly to Brahmans".[57] Grants were also made to astrologers as also family priests.[58] The education of the young among Hindus was almost entirely in the hands of the *pandits*, who were generally maintained by a "Gift of rent-free lands rarely exceeding hundred rupees in annual value from the *zamindars*".[59] Such schools were established in the *chaklas* of Salon, Partapgarh and Akladgunj. These schools were attended by 50 to 100 boys and the *zamindars* similarly granted "the *pandits* allotment which varies from 10 to 100 *bighas* of land".[60]

(b) Revenue Grantees

The numerous documents preserved in various archives and private collections offer us an opportunity to study the class of *madad-i ma'ash* grantees through detailed scrutiny of samples of its units. A number of families have been chosen for this survey, mainly with a view to finding out the main preoccupation of the members of this class and the changes in their fortunes over time. Our records mainly concern succession and inheritance, sale and mortgage of the *madad-i ma'ash* and other rights.

Here and there, however, our subject is also illuminated by the narrative sources and recorded traditions.

(i) The Mystic Family at Salon

The family of the mystics established at Salon claim to be Faruqi Shaikhs and to have come from Yeman whence their ancestors migrated to Nagor, the celebrated Qazi Hamid-uddin of Nagor belonging to this branch. The family is said to have migrated from Nagor to Jaunpur during

56. Buttler, *op. cit.*, p. 175.
57. W.C. Bennett, *The Clans of Roy Bareilly District*, 1871, p. 55.
58. Bennett, *op. cit.*, p. 56.
59. Buttler, *op. cit.*, p. 165.
60. Buttler, *op. cit.*, p. 165.

the period of the Sharqi Sultans.[61] Makhdum Shaikh Addhan became famous as a *sufi* saint, and from him the family members acquired the name of Addhani. One of his descendants, Shaikh Abdul Nabi settled at Salon and here in the year 996 A.H./1578 Shaikh Pir Muhammad was born. After his early education, Pir Muhammad went to Manikpur for higher studies in theology and mysticism. He became a disciple of Shaikh Abdul Karim, the *sajjada nashin* of the *dargah* of Shaikh Husamul Haque.[62] After remaining there for quite sometime under his spiritual guidance and according to his instruction, Pir Muhammad returned to Salon and according to a later tradition took up his abode along with a *sanyasi* hermit.[63]

Shaikh Pir Muhammad soon became celebrated as a holy and pious man to merit the attention of the local officials. Emperor Aurangzeb, on being informed of his fame, asked him to pay a visit to Delhi, but the offer was politely refused. A later family text gives his reply as follows:[64]

> 'O Emperor, the protector of the religion. This servant finds no courage (to attend the royal summons) what can a rustic do at the royal court? If any one comes to my place, the doors are always open, but *karim*[65]

---

61. The families whose history has been reconstructed for the first time, by using the archival materials and records, are the mystics established at Salon, the family of Saiyid Muhammad 'Arif at Bahraich, and the family of Qazi 'Imaduddin of Sandila, *sarkar* Lucknow.
62. Most of the 18th century chronicles and *tazkirahs* either ignore him or refer him in passing. This is obviously because of the fact that his grandson, Saiyid Sadullah of Salon got more prominence as a theologian and a *sufi*. In all his biographical notices, he is always referred as the grandson of Shaikh Pir Muhammad who in turn is called as the great theologian of his times. See Khafi Khan, *Muntakhab-ul-Lubab*, Bib. Ind., Calcutta, 1860-74, Vol. II, pp. 559-60; Ghulam Ali Azad Bilgrami, *Mathir-ul-Kiram*, Hyderabad, 1913, Vol. I, p. 217. For independent references to him see Uhammad Bukhtawar Khan, *Mirat-ul-Alam*, Lahore, 1979, Vol. II, p. 417; Saiyid Shah Ghulam Ali Shah, *Mishkat-un Nubuwah*' Ms., 1212 A.H., *Mishkat*-27 (I owe this reference to Dr Sulaiman Siddiqi, Reader, Department of Islamic Studies, Osmania University, Hyderabad); *A Gazetteer of the Province of Oudh*, Vol. III, 1877, p. 290, Shah Ahmad Husain Jafri, 'Hazrat Pir Muhammad Ki Aayat aur Ta'limat unki Malfuzat ki Roshni main '(Urdu) unpublished paper read at Khuda Bakhsh South Asian Regional Seminar on Significant Manuscripts of Sufism, Aligarh session, March 1985.
63. Abdul Hai, *Nuzhatul Khawatir*, Vol. V, Hyderabad, 1911, pp. 97-8; H.R. Nevill, *District Gazetteer of United Provinces,* Vol. 39, Allahabad, 1923, pp. 100-103; Shah Hadi 'Ata, '*Qasba Salon ka Khandan-e Karimi* (Urdu) *Musannif Quarterly*, Vol. XII, Aligarh, 1945; (iii) pp. 78-80; see also my paper, 'Two *madad-i ma'ash farmans* of Aurangzeb from Awadh; *PIHC* (1979), pp. 302-14.
64. Shah Panah 'Ata, *Rauzat-ul Arwah*, Ms. Private Collection, 1838, f. 248.
65. It is one of the chief attributes of God. Here also it is used in the same sense, but the fact that the name of his spiritual preceptor was Abdul Karim, symbolises the double meaning of the word.

made me dependent upon none. He provides me food when I feel hungry, if I am asleep, He cares, and if (per chance) some sin is committed by me, He helps me out. Hence His favours are sufficient for me and to strive for more will be a useless ambition.'

It is said that on receipt of this letter, the Emperor issued a *farman* on 5th Shawwal 19th R.Y./1086/1676 recognising the land rights of Shaikh Pir Muhammad over 200 *bighas* in the village Mirzapur Bakhtiyar.[66]

The history of the land rights of these mystics begin with this imperial grant and a closer scrutiny of this document leads us to some interesting results. First of all, this grant was not situated in an *a'imma* village, but in a *jagir* territory.[67] The previous authorities (*hukkam*) (presumably the *jagirdars*) of the area had already offered 200 *bigha* of (waste land to the grantee) and the imperial *farman* was issued to confirm the same, so that the grantee might not be harassed by the future *jagirdars* or any of his servants.[68] Secondly, the words, 'an offering to the servants of one knowing mystic truths' (*nazr-i khadiman-i haqaiq-i ma'arif aqah*) which occur in the main body of the *farman* as well as *zimn*, show that the grantee was held in high esteem by the Emperor.

In the lifetime of Shaikh Pir Muhammad, Emperor Aurangzeb issued another *farman* to his son Shaikh Muhammad Ashraf, in 22nd R.Y./1679.[69] This *farman,* too, is in many ways quite interesting. First of all, unlike the usual *madad-i ma'ash* grants, it mentions the total *jama*', and not the area of the grant.[70] Secondly, it confers an entire village in grant. The *zimn*

66. See the translation of the text as well as the *zimn* in Appendix A of my paper in *Two Madad-e Ma'ash farman of Aurangzeb from Awadh,PIHC* (1979), pp. 302-14.

67. Akbar in his 24th R.Y./1578 had issued a *farman* by which he had concentrated all the existing grants in certain villages, and ordered that all the new grants should also be made from the lands of these villages. By this measure, the land rights of the grantees were protected from encroachments by the officials of the *jagirdars* and of the *Khalisa Sharifa, RAA-24*; *Akbar Namah*, Vol. III, p. 240.

68. Since a *jagirdar* could assign a grant only for his term of assignment, which was of a few years' duration, the new *jagirdar* might or might not respect the order of his predecessor. So this class of grantees lived in the greatest insecurity. They were, therefore, always anxious to obtain the confirmation of such assignments from the court to escape eviction by a future *jagirdar*, Irfan Habib, *Agrarian System*, pp. 315-6.

69. See the translation of the text as well as the *zimn* in Appendix 'B' of my paper *PIHC* (1979), *op cit.*, pp. 302-14.

70. All the *madad-i ,a'ash* grants were, as a rule, made in terms of definite area stated in *bigha*. However, there are some exceptions which have been pointed

(*Contd...*)

furthermore gives the *hasil* figures from the 4th R.Y. to 17th R.Y. (which is again unusual), and it contains a recitation to the effect that the grantee had previously settled in the village with the consent (*ba-razamandi*) of the *zamindars*. This seems to imply that the *zamindars* had been unable to meet the revenue demand and so transferred their rights to Shaikh Muhammad Ashraf, who now sought tax exemption from the authorities by way of *madad-i ma'ash*. The village had been nearly abandoned, and its revenue paying capacity greatly reduced, as the figures which appear on the *zimn* of the *farman* show.

The fact that here the grantee was also the *zamindar* of the area, might explain yet another feature of the grant, *viz*. its assignment to the grantee in absolute perpetuity, 'generations after generation and for all time to come' (*naslan-bad naslan wa batnan bad batnan*). This is interesting since it was only in 34th R.Y./1690, that Aurangzeb made all the *madad-i ma'ash* grants hereditary by issuing a general *farman*,[71] whereas the above-mentioned *farman* was issued much before this measure, i.e. in 22nd R.Y./1679 AD.

Shaikh Muhammad Ashraf was granted the revenues of village Singhwal (now renamed Ashraf Gunj). His young age might explain, as to why no spiritual titles are prefixed to his name, contrary to the respectful address used for his father.

Subsequent to these grants, Aurangzeb is said to have assigned the revenues of the village Palhipur to Shaikh Muhammad Ashraf in 1109/1697 as the news-writer (*waqai-i ravis*) of the province informed the court that the present income of Shaikh Muhammad Ashraf was not sufficient to meet his expenses. Probably on similar considerations, Emperor Bahadur Shah too assigned the revenues of village Kishandaspur to him in 1119/1707.[72]

In addition to these grants, it appears that Shaikh Muhammad Ashraf came to possess superior land rights in a number of villages and localities (*chaks*) in *sarkar* Manikpur, *suba* Allahabad as well as in *sarkar* Lucknow

---

out by Irfan Habib, but all such *farmans* relate to other areas of the Mughal empire. For the province of Awadh this is the only reference I could locate. Irfan Habib, *Agrarian System*, p. 301.

71. *RAA-1880*.

72. I have not been able to locate and examine the two *farmans*, however, these *farmans* have been referred in Mr Wood's despatch No. 507 dated 13 July 1861 (from Deputy Commissioner of Partapgarh to the Commissioner and Superintendent of Bainswara division). File No. 1870/1861 (Rae Bareli district), *Board of Revenue*, Lucknow.

suba Awadh. But unfortunately we lack details of these acquisitions. We, however, possess an original *farman* of Emperor Muhammad Shah issued in 10th R.Y./1729 in favour of Shaikh Ashraf. The text of the *farman* carries a recitation in favour of the grantee confirming all his possessions in *sarkar* Manikpur and *sarkar* Lucknow, inclusive of plots of residential and cultivated land, villages and *chaks*. All the officials, present and future, were directed not to interfere with these possessions.[73]

Apart from these early grants, the family possessions were enlarged quite considerably by the local potentates. All such grants were later on confirmed by Emperor Shah Alam in 1175/1761. Fortunately, we possess a number of *wajib-ul arz* documents of the villages. These papers record the nature of the land-rights and the traditional account of the land-holding classes of the villages. These *wazib-ul arz* (petitions regarding the claims and the titles) were made part of the first regular settlement conducted in Awadh after 1860.

Shaikh Muhammad Ashraf nominated his son Muhammad Panah to succeed him (as Sajjada Nashin of the *khanqah)*. He was allotted two tracts of forest land by the *ta'alluqadar* of Bhadri (styled as Raja) for the specific purpose of maintenance of the *khanqah*. The grantee was permitted to cut down forest and get it inhabited by the members of peasant castes (particularly *kurmis*). One tract of the forest land was named Panah Nagar, while the another was named Hayat Nagar (after the name of his deceased brother Muhammad Hayat). Similarly, the Kanhpur's *ta'alluqadars* of Tilain, Raja Balbhadra Singh granted the revenues of the entire villages, Dhankesra and Barwalia, to the establishment for the purpose of the maintaining mosques, *khanqah* and other buildings.[74]

The period of Shah Karim 'Ata (the 4th *sajjada nashin* of the *khanqah*) marks the watershed in the history of this family. He received the grant of the forested area from the *ta'alluqadars* of Kondrajit. The purpose of the grant was to provide for the upkeep of the *khanqah* and for the expenses of the visitors to the *khanqah*. The forested area was brought under cultivation. *Kurmi* being settled there and a village named Karimnagar (after the name of the founder) brought into existence.[75]

---

73. I have not been able to examine the contents of this *farman*, because of it is under the private custody of the family members of Shaikh Muhammad Ashraf who now reside in Pakistan. But a photographic reproduction (obverse side) of the *farman* appears in Shah Hasan 'Ala, *Harir-e Sang*, Nafees Academy, Karachi, 1963, p. 119.

74. See *Wajibul-arz* of villages Panah Nagar, Hayat Nagar, Dhankesra and Barwalia in present *pargana* Salon Distt. Rae Bareli (see para iv).

75. *Wajibul-arz* of village Karimnagar, *pargana* Salon, Distt., Rae Bareli (see para iv).

Emperor Shah Alam II is said to have had great respect for Shah Muhammad Panah. He paid a visit to his *khanqah*. Here Shah Panah requested the emperor for a confirmatory *farman* of the grants he held. He was ordered by the Emperor to submit a full list of the villages held by him in *ma'afi* along with the copies of the *farmans* in his possession.[76] In the 6th R.Y./1193 when Emperor held his *darbar* at Allahabad, the new *farman* was issued in favour of Shah Karim Ata, son of Shah Panah. The *zimn* of the *farman* contained a recitation in favour of all the villages, *chaks*, gardens and *havelies* possessed by Shah Panah. The *farman* was issued during the *wizarat* of nawab Safdar Jung.[77]

In addition, a revenue-free grant of twelve villages was bestowed upon him by Nawab Asafud-daulah. Earlier these villages, "belonged to a family of Kanhpuria Rajputs, who were ousted for contumacy or rebellion".[78] We are also told that the Nawab paid a visit to the mystic at Salon.[79]

We are fortunate in having a complete list of the landed and urban possessions of Shah Karim Ata.[80] It appears that within a span of a century or so this family had acquired a number of villages under various denominations such as *waqf*, *madad-i ma'ash zamindari* and *lambardari*(?) rights. Although the details of all such acquisitions are missing, still one can not rule out the possibility of purchase in some cases. The abstract of the total figures is as follows:

Table - I

Nature of the Possession	*No. of Villages/Chaks*	*Revenue Realization in Rs.*
(i) *Waqf*	23	Rs 25,000
(ii) *Madad-i ma'ash* with *Zamindari*	19	Rs 8,000
(iii) *Lambardari* with *Zamindari*	8	Rs 7,000
Total	**45**	**Rs 40,000**

In addition to these landed possessions, there were 15 orchards (*baghat*) a number of *havelis* and other residential buildings, situated in Salon proper and other *ma'afi* villages under his possessions.

76. For a full history of the landed possessions and the imperial favours, see letter No. 504 dated 13th July 1861, from Mr W.C. Wood, the Deputy Commissioner of Partapgarh to the Commissioner of Bainswara Division. *Board of Revenue, Lucknow, 173/1861-2.*

77. Imperial *farman* of Shah 'Alam dated 15th safar 6th R.Y./1183 A.H. (private custody).

78. *Wajib-ul-arz* of village Karim Nagar, *pargana* Salon, District Rae Bareli.

79. Sleeman, *op. cit.*, Vol. II.

80. This list is appended at the end of a *bayaz* (Ms. in private custody). The *bayaz* belonged to Shah Ashraf Ata and the year on his seal in 1212/1797.

An attempt was made by Shah Karim Ata to divide all these possessions among the three sons equally, reserving only one village for the maintenance of his two daughters in 1823. But the partition had to be annulled as a result of the death of his eldest son Shah Ashraf Ata in his life time.[81] The resultant new scheme of the partition provided that one half of the entire landed property was to be handed over to Shah Panah Ata, who was also nominated as the fifth *Sajjada-Nashin* of the *khanqah* by his father Shah Karim Ata. He was to look after all the charities connected with the *khanqah*, the maintenance of all the buildings and the running of the religious school. The remaining half of the property was equally divided between his son Shah Ghafur Ata and his grandson Shah Ahsan Ata (whose father Shah Ashraf Ata had predeceased Shah Karim Ata). The position of the one village that had been left for his daughters remained unaltered. This scheme of division of *ma'afi* lands was rectified by the court of Lucknow, hence putting a final confirmatory seal on the *waqf* property in the hands of the successors of Shah Karim Ata.[82]

Donald Buttler gives a detailed account of this establishment in 1836.[83] He says that the original proprietors of the town of Salon were the Kanhpuria Rajputs, who were deprived of their estate in Salon *khas* by Nawab Asafuddaulah and it was bestowed upon the ancestors of the family of Shah Karim Ata in *jagir* for the perpetual support of the religious "eleemasynary" or charitable establishment.

The establishment seems to have been the largest of its kind in the southern parts of the kingdom of Awadh. The annual income was estimated by Buttler as at Rs 30,000, all of which was utilised in entertaining *bairagis* and *faqirs* without making any distinction of religion. The visitors use to flock to the *khanqah* in quite large number and at a time there might happen to be about 100 mendicants. These were attended to and looked after by the *sajjada-nashin* of the *khanqah*. The head of the institution (*sajjada-nashin*) was kept in high esteem by the local officials. His reputation is said to have been such that whenever the *chakledar* came Salon, he always paid a visit to the mystic and offered him a few hundred rupees.[84]

The keeper of the establishment did not have any sympathy for the religious zeal of the *wahabis* under Saiyyid Ahmad of Bareilly. He was

81. The *hiba-namah* executed in favour of Shah Ashraf Ata by Shah Karim Ata dated 11th Zilhij 1238/1822.

82. H.R. Nevill, *op. cit.*, pp. 100-103.

83. Although the book was first published in 1839 from Calcutta, but the data were collected in 1837. Buttler, *op. cit.*, pp. 138-9.

84. *Ibid.*

told by the *zamindar* of the area and the *sajjada-nashin* that they considered aiding the poor and lame and the blind as more pious than indulging in holy war. Similarly, they refused to abandon the ceremonies associated with *muharram*.[85]

W.H. Sleeman, while undertaking the tour in the Kingdom of Oudh (1849-50) refers to this Salon establishment as the prime mystic institution of the kingdom.[86] Shah Panah Ata, the then *sajjada-nashin* of the *khanqah* was looked upon with great reverence by both Muslims and Hindus for the sanctity of his ancestors and the institution. He did not go out of the *khanqah* but remained there to receive the homage and distribute food to the needy travellers of all religions. Sleeman estimated the annual income from the grant held by him in 1850 at about Rs 25,000. This amount was utilised by him in meeting the expenses of his family and the needy.

An untoward incident is said to have occurred in the fortunes of the family. In 1834, the head was plundered of all his belongings valued at Rs 25,000 by the *nazim* of Bainswara division, Ehsan Husain. The *nazim* was the son of the powerful minister of the kingdom of Oudh, Subhan Ali Khan. Curiously enough the episode has not been mentioned by Donald Buttler (c. 1836). Similarly, the record of the family papers are also silent over the issue.[87]

In addition to the income from the revenue free-grants assigned by the Awadh rulers, but the local authorities as well as the princes in the remote parts such as Bhopal and Seronge made quite substantial offerings. This way the actual income of the establishment was calculated as to amount about 50,000 rupees a year. The complimentary letters were sent to 'Shah Puna Ata' by the Governor General of India, Lieutenant Governors of the N.W. Provinces and their secretaries, and from the residents at the Court of Lucknow. When W.H. Sleeman was passing through the district of Salon, 'Shah Puna Ata' sent him "letter of compliments and welcome with a present of a tame antelope, and some fruits and sugar". This goodwill gesture was reciprocated by Sleeman, who got the impression that "his character is held in high esteem by all classes of the people, of whatever creed, caste or grade".[88]

---

85. Buttler *op.cit,* pp. 164-5.

86. W.H. Sleeman, *op. cit.*

87. Compare it with the account of Donald Buttler.

88. Sleeman, *op. cit.*, pp. 131-2. Not only this, but the Mughal princes as well wrote complimentary letters to these mystics and few of them have been published from the collections like *Ashraf-ul-insha* and *Muntakhab-ut-i-Saeedi*; see Shah Hadi Ata, 'Muntakhabut-e-Saeed Ka bab dum' (second chapter of *Muntakhab-e-Saeed*), *Musannif* (Urdu) quarterly journal of Majlis-e-Musannifin, Aligarh, Vol. I, 1946, pp. 114-119.

An interesting aspect of the history of this family is the rule of succession that was followed.[89] According to the *Rawaj-e Aam* document of 1861, attested by many *zamindars* of the area, the property of a *sajjada-nashin* was inherited in the following manner:

(a) The lawful heir and the legal representative of the *sajjada-nashin* could only be a *sajjada-nashin*. The latter was to be nominated by the previous *sajjada-nashin* in his life time by observing certain customary ceremonies in a prescribed manner.

(b) All other natural heirs of the *sajjada-nashin* including his widow, were not entitled for any share in the property of the deceased. The sons could claim only a subsistence allowance known as *guzara*, while the widow and unmarried daughters of the deceased were to be looked after by the future incumbent to the office of the *sajjada-nashin*.

(c) The *sajjada-nashin* was only a custodian of the property either held in *waqf* or *ma'afi* and thus was not empowered to affect any change by way of sale or mortgage or by oral gift (*hiba'*).

A close scrutiny of the above provisions of the family *Rawaj-i A'am*, with the help of the records of the Board of Revenue and the litigation, suggests that on a number of occasions the *ma'afi* and *waqf* villages were in fact transferred to the family members in full proprietary rights,[90] thus the customary law was in fact violated.

After the annexation of Awadh an enquiry was instituted to examine the credentials of these grantees. Major Barrow was appointed to conduct it, the then grantee Shah Husain Ata deposited 31 *farmans, parwanas* and *sanads* with the district authorities on 15th June 1856 and obtained a receipt for them. But all these documents were destroyed during the mutiny. The second enquiry could start only after the suppression of mutiny. On the spot enquiry of each and every village was made to ascertain the grantee's

89. The practice still continues Maulana Shah Ahmad Husain Jafri , the present *Sajjada Nasheen* of the *Khanqah*, claims to have been nominated to the said post by his father late Shah Mohammad Husain Jafri, the IX *Sajjada nasheen*, strictly according to the provisions of the *Rawaj-i Aam*. The said claim has been upheld by the Hon'ble High Court of Allahabad (Lucknow Bench) in writ petition No. 1682/1982, Shabbir Ata Vs. District Judge, Lucknow, and others, decided on 12 July 1984 (Hon'ble R.C. Deo Sharma, J.), *A.I.R. 1984*, pp. 737-43.

90. *Iqrar namah* executed by Shah Karim Ata in favour of his eldest son Shah Ashraf Ata dated 11th Zilhij 1238 A.H./1822; *Iqrar-namah* executed by Shah Karim Ata in favour of his son Shah Panah 'Ata dated 6th Jamad I 1248 A.H./1832. (Private Collection).

claim. The details of the enquiry conducted by W.C. Wood, now forms a historical narrative giving the family history, the details of the income and expenditure and the status of these grants.[91] On the basis of this enquiry Lord Canning issued a *sanad* to Shah Husain 'Ata on 26.9.1862 recognizing his allodial rights over the 22 villages of his possession. The confirmation was made upon the condition that it was to continue so long as the income was devoted to the maintenance of the *khanqah* buildings, tombs, mosques, running of a school of 'Muhammadan Education' and continuance of the charities as detailed in the *sanad*.[92]

The history of the family till the time of annexation brings out many interesting points. At the beginning Shaikh Pir Mohammad was assigned 200 *bigha* of cultivable waste in 1676 AD. But in the 18th century after a number of imperial grants and many other favours by the local chiefs, the establishment came to possess a large number of villages and other urban properties. They continued to enjoy this position during the first half of the 19th century as the *nawab-wazirs* and their successors too have been quite liberal in making additions and favours to these mystics. It was on this account that Buttler said that although they call themselves "a *fakir*, though the *malik* (proprietor) of Salon".[93]

(ii) Sayyid Muhammad 'Arif's Family, Bahraich

The *parwana*, sale-deeds and *ijara* papers preserved at Regional Archives, Allahabad relating to the family of Sayyid Muhammad Arif of *sarkar* Bahraich offer an opportunity of studying how the possession of *madad-i ma'ash* rights could be intermixed with a number of other landed rights, such as *zamindari* and *ijaradari*. The family, indeed, had such interests in no less than five *parganas*, viz. *Haveli* Bahraich, Hisampur, Fakharpur, Firozabad and Silak.

If we go by the surviving record, the landed interests of the family originated with a *madad-i-ma'ash* grant by Akbar in 983/1575 to one Sayyid Muhammad,[94] the ancestor of Saiyid Muhammad 'Arif. However, it is difficult

---

91. Copy of the letter No. 504 dated 13th July 1861 from Deputy Commissioner of Partapgarh to Commissioner and Superintendent Bainswara division, *Board of Revenue, Lucknow* (Rae Bareli), 173/1861-2.

92. Justice Saiyyed Mahmood's memorandum on the affairs of *Waqf* Salon 1884.

93. Buttler, *op. cit.*, p. 139.

94. No *farman* of Akbar of 983/1575 regarding this *madad-i-ma'ash* grant could be traced. However, a recitation is always made of this grant in every subsequent *parwana* issued from the time of Jahangir to Aurangzeb. The early history of Sayyid 'Arif's family could be traced out with the help of these *parwanas*.

to reconstruct a genealogy owing to lacunae in our documentary evidence.[95] He was assigned 470 *bigha* land in the village Hasnahra, *pargana* Haveli Bahraich on 2nd shawwal 983/1575.[96] Another grant of 400 *bigha* from village Panyanhari of the same *pargana* was bestowed on him on 24th *Shawwal* 983/1575.[97] It seems that the area of this grant was further raised to 534 *bigha* 8 *biswa* during Akbar's time.[98] The revenue of the villages Sahinda and Panyanhari were assigned to another member of the family, Saiyid Ziauddin, by order of Akbar and Jahangir. This grant was confirmed by a *parwana* issued on 17th *Ramazan* 1028/1618, in favour of Sayyid Ziaullah and others.[99] It is of some interest that this *parwana* bears a small seal of one Neku, styled as *banda-i 'Uluya'* Nur Jahan, the famous Queen of Jahangir.

In *pargana* Fakharpur too, Sayyid Muhammad was granted 40 *bigha* land on 19th Ramzan 983/1575. The grant was confirmed in favour of Mir Sayyid Muhammad 'Arif on 11th Muharram 1074/1666. But now it consisted of only 35 *bigha* and *biswa* 12 after the usual deduction known as *qusur-i Gaz-i Ilahi*.[100] In 1079/1668 Muhammad 'Arif was granted in *hiba* (i.e. free transfer) the *birt* (tax-free grant) rights, designated *milkiyat, zamindari* and *chaudhari*, over the village Damodarjot, *pargana* Firozabad, the granter was Prabhu, who styles himself the *zamindar* and *chaudhari* of that village.[101]

The *zamindari* rights purchased by Muhammad 'Arif were mostly situated in *pargana* Hisampur. The villages purchased by him from time to time were the Pasanjat group of villages, Debidaspur and Inchapur. All these transactions took place between the years 1672 to 1688. Previously these villages were in the *zamindari* possessions of Brahman, Rajputs and Khattris.[102] The various amounts in consideration of which these rights

95. Since we get hardly three names between a period of about hundred years.

96. *RAA-939* (1096/1684).

97. *RAA-897* (1080/1669), *866* (1081/1670), *860* (1074/1663), *864* (1079/1668) and *284* (issued in the reign of Aurangzeb).

98. *RAA-853* (1059/1649).

99. *RAA-849* (1028/1618). In a petition by Sayyid 'Arif (*RAA-1307*), 1107/1695, the name of Sayyid Ziauddin figures prominently and 'Arif claims to have inherited some property from Sayyid Ziauddin.

100. *RAA-861* (1096/1684).

101. *RAA-1271* (1079/1668). It is of some interest that when a free transfer of rights is made by a Hindu *zamindar* to a Muslim, both words, *hiba* and *birt*, are employed.

102. Sale-deeds for Pasanjat (named as Arifpur) are *RAA-1275* (1083/1672), *1301* (1099/1687), *1300* (1099/1687), *1303* (1100/1688); for Debidaspur (named as Ahmadpur), see *RAA-1245* (1092/1681), *1294* (1094/1682); for Inchapur (named as 'Alipur) see *RAA-1284* (1088/1677).

were purchased by Sayyid Ahmad and Sayyid Arif help us to understand the level of *zamindari* prices prevalent in the area.[103]

Table - II

Sl. No.	*Villages*	*Year of Transaction*	*Share of the Village Sold*	*Amount*
1.	Pasanjat group	1083/1672	1/3rd	Rs 405
		1099/1687	1/18th	Rs 57
		1099/1687	1/9th	Rs 127
		1100/1688	1/18th	Rs 61
2.	Debidaspur	1092/1681	1/3rd	Rs 54
		1094/1683	2/3rd	Rs 121
3.	Inchapur	1088/1677	1/4th	Rs 32

A statement of facts submitted by Sayyid Muhammad Arif and attested by three witnesses describes yet another incident. By this time the name of Pasanjat had been changed to 'Arifpur. The village was attacked by the men of Sayyid 'Abdullah of Bahraich joined by certain Hindu residents of four villages and by the servants of one Sayyid Ghulam Mohiuddin of Jarwal. Plundering and destroying the property of the petitioner, they expelled his men, and beat up and troop captive the village headman Kaisav whom they released only on a payment of Rs 10 as ransom. They had now been turned out by the agents of the *jagirdar*, but Sayyid Arif had not recovered any of the property that he had lost.[104]

Saiyid Arif and Saiyid Ahmad possessed *zamindari* rights of villages Kapura and Samanpur, *pargana* Silak.[105] But it appears that in both these places, their position was not secure as the local *zamindars* constantly interfered with their possession and harassed their agents. It was only with the help of the local authorities that their rights and possessions were protected.[106] Other disputes are also recorded. In *pargana* Fakharpur,

103. The revenue figures of the villages in question are not available to us for the years when they were purchased, hence no comparison of the income of *zamindar* with actual revenue could be made. Only the price rise phenomena could be illustrated with the help of these figures. See Irfan Habib, *Agrarian System*, pp. 150-2.

104. *RAA-1304* (1100/1304 (1100/1688). The petition is attested by only three witnesses, while probably one among them had affixed his seal too.

105. In *Ain-I Akbari* and *pargana* of Silak has been recorded within *sarkar* Awadh, but these documents place it under *sarkar* Bahraich. Such adjustment might have taken place for administrative considerations. See *RAA-036* (6th shaban 20th R.Y./1887).

106. *RAA-936* (20th R.Y./1678).

Sayyid 'Arif, Saiyyid Ahmad and Saiyyid Ghyas had inherited 5/6th portion of the village Katurah. Their title was disputed by the local *qazis*. Hence a *parwana* was issued in 1087/1676 recognising their claim.[107]

Apart from these land rights held by 'Arif by way of *madad-i ma'ash* and *zamindari*, he contracted to collect the revenue for a number of *jagirdars*, who held their *tankhwah jagir* in *pargana* Hisampur. These involved the former in further disputes with local *zamindars*. For example, when Saiyyid 'Arif held in revenue farm the *jagir* of Sher Khan in the 20th R.Y. of Aurangzeb/1678 'Arif presented a petition that when, during the term of his revenue contract his men had gone to collect land-revenue from the village Korsama, they were chased out by the *zamindars* of Bhongiri, *pargana* Silak. The *zamindars* looted and destroyed the claimed share of the crop amounting to 2500 mounds.[108]

The *ijara* documents also let us have a glimpse into the relations of the farmer with the *jagirdar*. Between the year 1079 '*amils*/1671 and 1098 '*amils*/1685 Saiyyid 'Arif contracted to collect the revenue for 4 *jagirs* situated in *pargana* Hisampur. In 1079 '*amli* he took on *ijara*, a *haftmaha*' (7-monthly) *jagir* of the value of 1,32,800 *dam*. He had to pay Rs 1934 *bit-muqta* (fixed) to Murtaza Khan and Darya Khan, the *jagirdar*. A *farigh-ul Khati* executed jointly by the *jagirdars* states that the entire amount due to them had been paid, except for Rs 374/12 *anna* which had been withheld by the former on account of *kotal karori*,[109] (perquisites (?) of the *karori* or Revenue Collector) accounts for which were due. A subsequent *parwana* of Darya Khan addressed to the officials, village headmen and the peasants (*muzari'an*) stipulates that Sayyid 'Arif continued to be the *ijaradar* of his portion of the said *jagir* and Abdul Baqi, who had gone there pretending to be the *ijaradar* had nothing to do with the affairs of that *jagir*.[110] Again in the year 1080 '*amli* 'Arif contracted for another *tankhwah jagir* held by Dervesh Beg, Miyan Ilahdad Khan and Muhammad Zaman. Although the total *jama*' of this *jagir* was 4,40,000 *dam*, but because of it was 8-monthly (*hasht-maha*) the *ijaradar* had to pay Rs 7333/4 *anna* in two equal instalments.[111] A receipt issued by Dervesh Beg stipulates that 'Arif had paid him Rs 1833/5 *anna* of his share as an advance.[112] Still another

107. *RAA-899* (1087/1676).

108. *RAA-950* (17th R.Y./1675).

109. *Allahabad-887*.

110. *RAA-867*.

111. *Allahabad-885*.

112. *Allahabad-886*.

qaul-o-qarar (agreement) executed in 1081 '*amli* mentions that Mir Abu Turab, the *mansabdar* leased out a part of his *tankhwah jagir* carrying a *jama*' of 2,10,000 *dams* to Sayyid 'Arif. Since the *jagir* was of 7-month-7 days', the *ijaradar* had to pay Rs 3162 after a deduction of Rs 312 on account of the *nankar* and *muqqaddam* perquisites. The *jagirdar* was thus to get Rs 2850 in two equal instalments.[113] By another *qaul-o-qarar* executed in 1093 '*amli* by Khudadad Khan leased out his *jagir* of village Bandausa to Sayyid Muhammad 'Arif who was the *malik* and *ta'alluqadar* of the said village on a fixed amount of Rs 425.[114]

Sayyid 'Arif also acted as the *wakil* of *diwan* Khudadad Khan at the imperial Court. This implies that for some time 'Arif even left his locality to go to the imperial headquarters at some unspecified time in Aurangzeb's time. One document concerning his dispute with his patron sheds important light on this aspect has been translated and appended as 'A' in Chapter VIII. Suffice it to say, his accounts were subjected to rigorous scrutiny on the termination of his term as the *wakil*.[115]

No further documents are available to enable us to trace the history of this family till modern times. Nevill's *Gazetteer of Bahraich District* is also silent about this family.

(iii) *Qazi* 'Imaduddin's Family, Sandila

Some documents in the acquired collection at the National Archives enable us to study the ecclesiastical offices and the land grants held by a family of *qazis* of *pargana* Sandila during the reigns of Shah Jahan and Aurangzeb. Shaikh Mubarak, the father of Shaikh 'Imaduddin acted as the *qazi*, *muhtasib* and *nirkh-navis* of the *pargana* Sandila and its environs. These offices passed on to Shaikh 'Imaduddin after the death of his father. In remuneration for their discharging the duties, a number of villages and other land grants by way of *madad-i ma'ash* were made over to them. Still some other grants made to them were either on account of some public benefit which arose therefrom or were absolutely unconditional and unrelated to any obligation.

A grant attached to the office of *qazi* Shaikh Mubarak held, in *madad-i-ma'ash*, 200 *bighas* in village Todakpur and 100 *bighas* in village Kasmandi in *pargana* Sandila. Presumably, his son Qazi 'Imad-uddin

113. *Allahabad-884*.

114. *Allahabad-897*.

115. *Allahabad-896* and 1232.

had inherited the title as well as the land grants some times around 1645.[116] He continued to work for a long time in that capacity until 1700 AD. He was succeeded by his son Shaikh Sharafuddin as the *qazi* of *pargana* Sandila in that year. Thereafter, the family disappears from the documents.[117]

The office of the *muhtasib* (Censor of Morals) and *nirkh-nawis* (price-reporter) appeared attached to the office of the *qazi*, first of all, in the *farman* of Aurangzeb issued in favour of Shaikh 'Imaduddin on 11th Rajab 1091/1680. The duties connected with these offices too have been listed. These included the delivering of judgments in matters of disputes and distribution of the (legal) shares among the heirs of the deseased, attestation of the *chaknama* (demarcation papers) and other documents of legal nature, inducing the people to offer the prayers and to follow the religious injunctions, award of punishments, holding of the Friday and other congregational prayers; keeping an eye over the drunkards, miscreants and other bad characters; fixing the prices of essential commodities, standardization of the weights and measures, and despatching the *roznamcha* (daily reports) containing a summary of the prices to the (imperial court?).[118]

Land grants held by the members of the family reveal interesting features. Qazi 'Imaduddin held an annual *qazifa* of Rs 270, but sometimes afterwards the cash-grant was converted into a land-grant, and village Maner, *pargana* Sandila with a total *jama* of Rs 203 was assigned to him by way of *madad-i-mash* grant. This grant was confirmed on 13th safar 14th R.Y./ 1671.[119] The previous officials (*mutassadis*) of the *jagirdars* and *khalisa-i Sharifa'* had in addition made over the revenues of the villages Siya Mao and Maner, *pargana* Sandilah to Shaikh 'Imaduddin. This was confirmed by a *parwana* of 16th Rabi I 16th R.Y./1084/1673.[120] Again, we find him

116. *NAI-1382* (1081 A.M./1670). The document describes how Qazi 'Imaduddin came to possess the title and superior land rights by way of *madad-i ma'ash*. However, Qazi 'Imad was discharging his duties as early as 1645. I have been able to locate one sale-deed attested under his seal of that year (*Allahabad-464* 4 Safar 1055/1645).

117. It seems that some Shahabuddin had disputed the claim of Shaikh Sharafuddin, but the *sadar* upheld the title of later, *NAI-1410*.

118. *NAI-1434* (1091/1681). After Qazi 'Imaduddin, one Ahmad Beg was appointed *qazi*. His connection with Imaduddin's family is not established. He was for some reason removed, and a *farman* was issued on 6th Rajab 44th R.Y./1700 conferring the office of the *qazi* on Sharafuddin, son of Imaduddin with 100 *bighas* as *madad-i ma'ash* on the condition of the service and non-realization of the dues such as *mehrana* and *nikahana*. See *NAI-1385* (1112/1700).

119. *NAI-1381*. The *jama*' was less than the cash grant is perhaps what is to be expected, since the grantee could in time raise the revenue through the extension of cultivation.

120. *NAI-1271*.

receiving 200 *bighas* as *madad-i ma'ash* from village Mahsona. But in case of this grant a condition was imposed that the grantee was to continue in service (*khidmat*) and was not to realise taxes like *mehrana* and *nikahana*.[121] Another *sanad* of 15th Shawwal 22nd R.Y./1680 states that Qazi 'Imaduddin had been assigned the revenue of a village having the *jama' kamil* (maximum assessment) of Rs 200 to Rs 250. This grant too was made in lieu of the service.[122] In the 39th R.Y./1697, the revenues of village Khajari having a total *jama*' of Rs 440 and the village Dhakwar having a *jama*' of Rs 5, were assigned to Qazi 'Imaduddin as *madad-i ma'ash*.[123] From yet another *parwana* village Mirzapur, *pargana* Sandila was included in the *madad-i ma'ash* grant of Qazi Imaduddin; the revenues of this village are said to have been mis-appropriated by others illegally, so that it had to be restored to him and an enquiry was ordered.[124] In 1095/1684, the revenues of village Maini *pargana* Sandila amounting to Rs 270 annually were assigned to Qazi 'Imaduddin as *tankhwah* (salary).[125] This was possibly a temporary assignment.

These grants were made to the Qazi for fulfilling duties of his office. But he seems to have obtained further concessions by claiming to use his land for public benefit. In 1670 he was granted a plot of 8 *bighas* of uncultivated (*banjar*) land in the vicinity of *qasba* Sandila in order to raise a garden or orchard, "for the welfare of the general public".[126] Again on 19th Ramzan 21st R.Y./1679, he was granted 10 *bigha* (cultivated land in the vicinity of *qasba* Sandila for the purpose of raising there an orchard, digging the wells, and planting trees along side the highway for the rest and relief of travellers and destitutes.[127] Interestingly enough such arrangements were resented by the owners (*malikan*) of the land (probably the *zamindars*) and hence the grantee had to request for the transfer of his grant elsewhere.[128] This was done with an increase of 7 *bighas* land, but with the additional obligation of establishing a mosque and *khanqah*. Fortunately, we possess the *chaknama* deed for the demarcation of these 17 *bighas*.[129]

---

121. *NAI-1273*.
122. *NAI-1274*.
123. *NAI-1274*.
124. *NAI-1408*.
125. *NAI-1451*.
126. *NAI-1341*.
127. *NAI-1343*.
128. *NAI-1651*.
129. *NAI-1389*.

A *parwana* issued in the 18th R.Y./1675 confirms a land grant of 294 *bigha* held by Qazi 'Imaduddin in *pargana* Nimkhar, *sarkar* Khairabad. This grant was designed to cover the expenses incurred by the grantee in feeding poor scholars and other destitutes at his *khanqah*.[130] The reference to *khanqah* suggest mystic predilections of the *qazi*, who otherwise should have been an orthodox jurist. Similarly in 24th R.Y./1682 he obtained the revenue free grant of village Mairat, *pargana* Nimkhar, *sarkar* Khairabad. This grant too was made by way of charity.[131] Apparently this family in the 17th century confined itself to income from grants and did not acquire *zamindari* rights of any sort. There is no information as to the fortunes of the family after the 17th century.

130. *NAI-1272*.

131. *NAI-1593*.

Table - I

Suyurghal* in *Parganas* Having Muslim *zamindari

i *Pargana*	ii *Jama*	iii *Suyurghal*	iv *Zamindar*	% iii as to ii
		1 – *Sarkar* Awadh		
1. Ibrahimabad	4,45,417	1,03,806	Ansari	23.30%
2. Inhauna	12,68,470	-	Chauhan Muslims	-
3. Satrikh	11,26,295	92,695	Ansari	8.23%
4. Satinpur	16,60,740	1,09,787	i. Bais Muslim ii. Bachgoti iii. Joshi	6.61%
	45,00,922	3,06,288		6.80%
		2 – Gorakhpur		
1. Utraula	13,97,367	6,935	Afghan Mujanah	0.49%
		3 – Bahraich		
(No *pargana* having Muslim *zamindars*, either exclusive owners or shareholders)				
		4 – Khairabad (Same as in 3)		
		5 – Lucknow		
1. Amethi	30,76,480	3,00,217	Ansari	9.75%
2. Vnam	20,12,372	2,53,747	Saiyids	12.60%
3. Sidhaur	16,92,281	3,12,022	i. Afghan sari ii. Rajput	18.49%
4. Bilgiram	51,24, 113	3,56,892	i. Saiyids ii. Bais	6.96%
5. Fatehpur	31,61,440	2,61,440	i. Shaikhzada ii, Rajputs	8.26%
6. Lucknow Haveli	17,46,771	2,41,195	i. Shaikhzada ii. Zunnardar iii. Kayath (Brahmans)	13.8%
7. Manwi	7,71,372	13,767	i. Musalman ii. Rajputs	1.78%
	1,75,84,829	17,40,280		9.89%

Table - II

Suyurghal* Statistics in *Parganas* having non-Muslim *Zamindars

i *Pargana*	ii *Jama'*	iii *Suyurghal*	iv *zamindar*	% of iii as to ii
		1 – *Sarkar* Awadh		
1. Awadh Haveli	20,08,366	1,58,741	i. Zunnadar ii. Kumbi	7.90%
2. Ambodha	19,98,724	7,318	Bais	0.36%
3. Pachhim rath	42,47,104	38,885	i. Rajput ii. Bachheb iii. Ghelah	0.91%
4. Basodhi	5,05,473	1,505	Bachgotis	0.4%
5. Thana Bhaddon	4,27,5-9	36,172	Bachgohi	8.46%
6. Baktha	3,85,008	3,960	Bachgotis	1.02%
7. Dongbad	53,69,528	2,26,871	i. Rajputs ii. Chauhan iii. Raikwars	4.22%
8. Rudauli	32,48,299	2,49,083	i. Rajputs ii. Chauhans iii. Bais	7.66%
9. Sailuk	47,23,299	2,00,945	i. Rajputs ii. Raikwars	4.25%
10. Sultanpur	38,32,530	98,967	Bachgotis	2.58%
11. Subeha	16,09,293	87,200	Rajputs	5.41%
12. Sarwapati	12,01,835	47,107	Bachgati	0.42%
13. Gworich	37,73,417	3,782	Raikwar	0.10%
14. Kishni	13,39,286	1,23,847	Rajputs	9.24%
15. Mangolsi	13,60,753	86,554	Sambansi	6.36%
16. Naipur	3,08,788	2,940	Different castes	0.95%
	3,63,37,212	13,77,877		3.79%
		2 – *Sarkar* Gorakhpur		
1. Unhaula	2,01,120	2,170	Basins	1.07%
2. Dariyapore	15,17,078	567	Basins	0.03%
3. Rehli	16,18,074	20,873	i. Rajputs ii. Basins	1.28%
4. Gorakhpur Haveli	5,67,385	3,919	Sombansi	0.69%
5. Maghor Ratanpur (2 m)	13,52,585	16,771	i. Bais ii. Basin	0.80%
	52,56,242	99,280		

(*Contd*...)

		3 – *Sarkar* Bahraich		
1. Bahraich Haveli	91,39,141	4,02,111	Rajput	4.39%
2. Husampur	47,47,035	1,601	i. Raikwar ii. Bhali iii. Bais	0.03%
3. Fakharpur	31,57,876	56,035	Raikwar	1.77%
4. Firozabad	19,33,079	4,107	i. Rajputs ii. Tuner	0.21%
5. Khoraunsa	13,15,051	2,628	Bais	0.19%
	2,02,42,182	1,06,482		5.24%
		4 – *Sarkar* Khairabad		
1. Barwar Anjana	43,25,237	1,07,079	i. Rajputs ii. Zunnardar	2.47%
2. Biswa	35,45,643	1,47,916	i. Rajputs ii. Bachheb	4.17%
3. Pali	18,49,270	37,945	Amin	2.05%
4. Bawan	11,61,255	26,488	Amin	2.28%
5. Basrah	2,76,066	4,566	Bacheh	1.65%
6. Chhitapur	17,65,641	41,094	i. Rajput ii. Gaur	2.32%
7. Khairabad Haveli	21,61,234	1,74,191	Zunnardar	8.05%
8. Sandi	30,55,339	1,95,166	Sombansi	0.15%
9. Sora	20,91,983	8,666	Chauhans	0.41%
10. Sadarpur	8,31,175	15,581	i. Bachheb ii. Janwars	1.87%
11. Gopamau	56,20,466	5,62,037	i. Rajput ii. Gaur	9.99%
12. Kheri	32,50,522	50,522	i. Rajput ii. Basin	1.55%
13. Laharpur	30,29,479	2,09,079	Zunnardar	6.90%
14. Machhechta	21,12,176	2,430	i. Rajputs ii. Bachhels	0.11%
15. Nimkher	35,66,055	66,055	Ahir	1.85%
16. Hargaon	2,00,000	26,385	Zunnardar	13.19%
	39,41,541		16,56,100	4.15%
		5 – *Sarkar* Lucknow		
1. Isauli	42,08,046	2,40,846	i. Rajput ii. Bachjoli	5.72%
2. Asiyun	8,30,625	63,421	i. Bais ii. Chandel	7.63%

(*Contd...*)

3. Bangarmau	38,02,122	1,51,481	Ghelot	3.93%
4. Bijlaur	25,05,047	1,93,961	Chauhan	0.12%
5. Bari	12,84,799	51,560	Bais	0.24%
6. Nigawan	4,70,782	12,730	Bais	3.02%
7. Bhitawli	3,40,419	8,194	i. Rajputs ii. Jats	2.40%
8. Jhalotar	11,23,176	21,441	Chandels	1.90%
9. Dewi	19,33,837	1,74,207	Rajputs	9.00%
10. Ranhorpur	24,25,885	79,225	i. Zunnardar ii. Bais	3.26%
11.Sandila	1,05,23,901	8,37,245	i. Bachel ii. Ghetals	7.88%
12. Saipur	26,25,388	27,736	i. Rajputs ii. Chandels	1.05%
13. Sarosi	12,39,767	1,567	i. Rajputs ii. Chandels	0.12%
14. Satanpur	10,28,800	10,192	i. Bais ii. Zunnardar	0.99%
15. Sihali	6,94,707	1,30,216	Rajputs	18.74%
16. Sisandi	3,92,313	13,792	Rajputs	3.51%
17. Sarwar	2,10,316	2,858	i. Rajputs ii. Kumbi	1.35%
18. Fatehpur Chaurasi	9,09,176	6,594	i. Rajput ii. Chandel	0.73%
19. Kursi	16,93,844	62,919	i. Jadwai ii. Rajputs	3.71%
20. Kakori	14,34,430	1,34,430	i. Rajputs ii. Basin	0.93%
21. Kashinda	4,30,596	44,060	Chandels	1.03%
22. Malihabad	44,79,250	1,20,545	Bais	0.37%
23. Mallanwan	35,98,713	2,22,038	Bansi	6.16%
24. Mohan	19,96,673	1,98,484	i. Rajputs ii. Bais	9.94%
25. Mauranwan	16,98,444	14,806	i. Rajput ii. Bais	0.87%
26. Mandiaon	11,36,613	32,900	Jawar Barkosla	2.89%
27. Makraid	5,76,200	5,247	i. Rajput ii. Bais	0.91%
28. Hadha	24,50,522	6,509	Bais	0.26%
29. Hardoi	3,59,748	6,026	Zunnardar	1.67%
	5,34,54,089	28,74,330		5.00%

Table - III

Pargana *having No* Suyurghal *Grants*

	i *Pargana*	ii *naqdi*	iii *Zamindars*
		1 – *Sarkar* Awadh	
1.	Inhauna	12,68,470	Chauhan Muslims
2.	Bihari	8,15,831	Bachgotis
		20,84,301	
		2 – Gorakhpur	
1.	Binnayakpur	6,00,000	Rajputs, Somabansis
2.	Banbhanpora	4,14,194	Rajputs
3.	Bhawpora	1,55,900	Bains
4.	Tilpur	4,00,000	Rajputs, Sombansi
5.	Chilnapora	2,89,302	Rajputs
6.	Dewapora Kotla (2 M)	7,17,840	Basin
7.	Rasulpur Ghasi (2 M)	6,22,030	Somabansi
8.	Ramgarh Gheri (2 M)	4,85,943	Somabansis
9.	Kalihla	40,000	Basins
10.	Kallapora	4,25,845	Bansi
11.	Mahauli	6,18,206	Basins
12.	Mandla	51,100	Not recorded
		42,20,360	
		3 – *Sarkar* Bahraich	
1.	Behra	37,135	Kuhna
2.	Dangdum	4,40,562	Janwars
3.	Raghot	1,66,780	Janwars
4.	Sinjauli	8,77,001	Rajputs and Janwars
5.	Sultanpur	1,66,001	Janwars
6.	Oila Nawagarh	21,40,858	Miscellaneous
		38,28,337	
		4 – *Sarkar* Khairabad	
1.	Barrah	9,86,077	Various castes
2.	Bharwara	4,35,430	Amin
3.	Paila	48,022	Amin
4.	Kherigarh	18,29,328	Bais, Basin, Bachhel and Kuhna
5.	Karkhaila	4,73,727	Amin
6.	Khunkhalmau	2,35,656	Various castes
		41,08,240	

(Contd...)

		5 – *Sarkar* Lucknow	
1.	Asoha	5,90,901	Amin
2.	Unchgaon	4,17,957	Bais
3.	Bahrimau	5.91,409	Bais
4.	Pahhan	2,67,809	Bais
5.	Parsandan	2,37,537	Rajputs and Kumbi
6.	Patan	2,14,256	Kumbi and Zunnardars
7.	Tora Singhaur	1,63,534	Zunnardars
8.	Deorakh	6,89,536	Bais
9.	Dadra	73,737	Rajputs
10.	Ramkot	2,68,099	Rajputs
11.	Sidhupur	5,05,018	Bais
12.	Garh Amethi	18,00,000	Rajputs, Bahmangatis
13.	Kahanjora	8,18,472	Bais
14.	Ghatampur	5,32,561	Zunnardar
15.	Gorinda	3,34,769	Zunnardar
16.	Kumbhi	2,67,809	Rajputs and Bais
17.	Laskar	1,68,529	Bais
18.	Aihar	3,29,735	Bais
		81,91,658	

Chapter-10

Agrarian Conditions in Awadh on the Eve of Annexation

(a) The Impact of British Intervention

The kingdom of Awadh was placed in a peculiar situation during the first half of the 19th century. The excessive interference of the British Resident in day-to-day administration had considerably diminished the authority of the king and his officials. The separate establishment of the Resident was practically as 'alternative seat of power'. According to an authoritative observer (no other than Henry Lawrence), "At Lucknow for years the Resident held public durbar where the grandees attended and pleaded against their own sovereign or his servants. Thus, were the monarch and his subjects arranged against each other, thus was the sovereign degraded in his own capital."[1]

Many of the evils besetting Awadh and the consequent disruption of local agrarian life during the first half of the 19th century arose as a result of British presence (and interference) in the administrative, military and economic spheres of the kingdom though this might not be the only explanation for the distress and miseries to which the peasants in Awadh kingdom were subjected to.

The administrative machinery of the Awadh kingdom was so thoroughly controlled by the British officials as to leave little discretion with its rulers. To quote colonel Southland, "there is no state in India with whose government we have interferred so systematically and so uselessly as with that of Oude .... This interference has been more in favour of men than in favour of measures."[2] Sa'adat Ali, whom even the English recognised as

1. Henry Lawrence, 'The Kingdom of Oudh', *Calcutta Review*, 1845 (111), pp. 414-5.
2. *CR*, 1845, (111), pp. 376-7.

an extremely able and intelligent ruler, suffered from gross interference. The 'dirty hands' of the British were said to be employed against him in the disguise of reforms.[3] After such an 'active survillance of the Resident and his constant 'advice' for the improvement of the administration, things deteriorated to such an extent that by 1836 Donald Buttler was speaking of a virtual collapse of the entire set-up.[4]

The basis of the political and economic structure of the kingdom was the land revenue. It was, therefore, natural for the British to suggest a number of reforms in this sphere from time to time. Such measures were tried by the successive rulers of the dynasty with little or no success. Surprisingly, enough the experiments were always shortlived and seldom lasted for more than a year or so.[5]

The resultant instability in agrarian conditions is well portrayed by Lalji, in a section of his work, *Mirat-ul Auza*. He gives a vivid description for the reasons of the lawlessness and anarchy in the realm. The cruelty and arbitrary manners of the '*amils* and the *mustajirs* and the neglect of their duties by the state officials, were said to be the twin causes of the evils. The chief fault is laid at the faulty nature of the revenue system. The settlement of the revenue upon those who pay it was not made in accordance with their actual portions and shares. Even if it was distributed by the officials between the parties with their mutual consent, the '*amils* and the *mustajirs* never respected the agreement. This naturally resulted in violent protest and reprisals. It so happened that one of two brothers who was the *zamindar* of a *ta'alluqa* submitted the *qubuliyat* for the land-revenue before the '*amil* and the other brother was denied his legal share. The latter began to ravage the estate.[6] Peace would have come, "if the '*amil* had given the half share to the rebel brother ...."[7]

The revenue officials such as the '*amils* and the *chakledars* had the tendency to demand a higher amount of revenue from the *zamindars* and the *ta'alluqadars*. The latter, unable or unwilling to pay the enhanced amount, used to make summary levy and after collecting their retainers and adherents took flight to the neighbouring jungles and offered resistance to the forces commanded by the '*amils* or *chakledar*. Sleeman's diary of

---

3. *CR*, 1845, (111), pp. 385-6.
4. Buttler, *op. cit.*, p. 96.
5. Jagdish Raj, 'The Revenue System of the Nawabs of Oudh', *JESHO*, 1958 (11), pp. 92-104.
6. Lalji, *Mirat-ul-Auza*, ff. 11b-12b.
7. *Ibid.*, f. 13a.

his tour is full of such instances (see Chapter V). Such a policy brought havoc and misery to the rural people. In 1830, Maddock observed, "the *'amils* or his officers finding a yearly decrease of revenue are naturally urged to further exactions until, at length, the Kingdom has arrived at such a crisis that hundred of villages have gone to ruin, the former cultivation is now a waste and the hamlets once occupied are now deserted."[8] With *zamindars* or *ta'alluqadars* fleeing to the jungle with their retainers, the wrath of the revenue officials generally fell on the unarmed peasantry. Buttler comments, "Whenever the *chakledar* pitches his tent, the work of plunder and devastation commences with the uprooting of the neighbouring villages to supply temporary huts for his troops; the *zamindars* and their immediate adherents at the same time flying to the jungles, when they ascertain an intention on the *chakledar's* part to increase their burden."[9] Such a situation forced the *zamindars* to be always at alert. They used to maintain substantial private armies and fire-arms.

It seems that by the time of the Annexation the *chakledar* had come to possess greater liberty in using cannon and fire-arms against the defaulting villages. "During the reign of Sa'adat Ali, a single cannon shot could not be fired by a *chakledar* without being followed by immediate enquiry from Lucknow, as to its causes – now a *chakledar* may continue firing for a month without question."[10] Henry Lawrence once personally witnessed an armed operation by the *chakledar* and speaks of, "the village being carried by storm; 7 or 8 of the inhabitants were killed and wounded, and all the rest were taken captive by the *'amils*."[11] This should not be considered as an isolated case, as such occurrences were quite frequent. "We observe in the daily papers a detailed account of the death in battle of the *'amil* of Burailah, and of the victorious *ta'alluqadar* having in consequence taken to the bush, to be a felon probably for life or at least until he pays the blood money to the court.' In this process several large land-holders were temporarily declared 'outlaws'.

The rise of the banditry was an indirect result of the administrative system established with the help and advice of the British Resident. The main body of the bandits comprised peasants who had suffered because of the inequities of the *chakledars*, the unemployed soldiers, or those whose

---

8. *CR*, 1845 (111), p. 388.
9. Buttler, *op. cit.*, pp. 50-1.
10. *Ibid.*, p. 101.
11. *CR*, 1845 (111), p. 386.
12. Bishap Heber, *op. cit.*, p. 46.

pay was in arrears. Bishop Heber, while he was coming from Kanpur to Lucknow met with what had all the appearances of a state of seize at the very entrance of Lucknow, "because large sum of money, said to be 30,000 rupees, on its way to the treasury at Lucknow, had attracted a number of neighbouring peasants, who were assembled outside the walls with their weapons, waiting for the departure of the treasure."[13] "The sense of insecurity had developed so much among the people, that to Heber's surprise, "all or nearly all the remaining population were as much loaded with arms as the inhabitants of the country but I should apprehend that Lucknow offered at this movement a more warlike exterior than our own metropolis ever did during its most embroiled and troublesome period."[14] Lalji informs us that "because of the prevalence of the acts of depredations throughout the kingdom of Oude, it was necessary for the inhabitants to keep themselves armed, hence every inhabitant carried arms with him even if he had to go outside the house to attend a call of nature."[15] Some places had become quite notorious for the activities of these outlaws. Sarangpur, 10 miles south of Tanda, "has a population of 9000 Hindu thieves, dacoits and thugs, whose depredations extended as far as Lucknow, Gorakhpur and Benares."[16] Still Heber was not ready to think that the people of Oudh were 'habitually ferocious or blood thirsty'.[17]

Apart from the political and military implications of the suppression of law and the consequent rise of the banditry, the entire range of economic activity was dislocated. When the '*amils* and *chakledars* failed to collect the stipulated amount of the land revenue from the defaulting *zamindars* and *ta'alluqadars*, they tried to squeeze the money from the rich merchants and bankers, the latter were forced to, "make advances and take, as security for repayment the receipt of the *zamindar* who was a ruined man, and at the movement a prisoner in the *chakledar*'s camp."[18] Precisely for these reasons many bankers of Rae Bareli district having substantial capital worth up to four lakh rupees left the place and migrated to the neighbouring British districts such as Kanpur, Gorakhpur, Farrukhabad and Benares.[19] On the other hand, the *ta'alluqadars* and the *zamindars* when they fell into arrears in payment of land-revenue and apprehended an intention on the part of

---

13. Buttler, *op. cit.*, p. 46.
14. Lalji, *op. cit.*, f. 75a.
15. Buttler, p. 107.
16. Heber, p. 52.
17. Buttler, p. 86.
18. Buttler, p. 86.
19. Elliot, pp. 135-7.

the *chakledar* or '*amil* to invade their estates, tried to extort money from the family bankers on easy rates to make the payment and thus to effect their escape from the wrath of the government revenue officials. C.A. Elliott has described the machinisation of Rao of Dundeakhera against the family banker Chandan Lal and the way in which the later was forced to change his masters overnight.[20] The banker had carried on his business very well and prospered in such a way that in 1810 he was the owner of only three villages in different parts of the district and in 1825, "his estate has risen to 2½ lac and it continued to fluctuate between this amount and a minimum of 1½ lac till 1850 AD."[21] But his prosperity soon attracted the greedy eyes of the *chakledar*, who thought him to be a "squeezable man and required him to pay more by half a lac than he had done last year (1850)."[22] The banker, foreseeing such an eventuality, had thought it quite expedient to have, "built a house and good deal of landed property in Cownpoor district," so that he could claim protection as a British subject though residing in Oudh."[23] The general feeling of insecurity and mistrust prevailing among the bankers and merchants has been aptly described by Lalji.

> "The bankers and the merchants of (Oudh Kingdom) do not keep their capital at one place due to the fear of the depredations of the *ta'alluqadars* and the *zamindars* – the illegal revenue demands of the '*amils* and the *tehsildars* – there are many who are the owners of property worth two lakhs of rupees and have purchased *zamindaris* and the villages in the British domains. (They) keep their cash and other valuable items at the houses built in (the British) dominions and on getting any idea of the disturbances, send their families to these (houses)."[24]

This flow of capital from Oudh to the adjacent British territories must surely have been a drain on the resources of Oudh.

The drain was not the only economic impact of the British press, but a number of other spheres could be pointed out where the dictates of the Resident undermined the authority of the king in his own kingdom. The Oudh rulers in succession advanced loans to or placed deposits with the East India Company. The interest occurring at the rate of 4 percent or

---

20. Elliot, p. 139.
21. *Ibid.*
22. Elliot, pp. 141-3.
23. Lalji, *op. cit.*, ff. 80b-81a.
24. Aitchinson, Vol. II, Treaty Nos. XLIV, XLVII, XLIX, and L.

5 percent per annum was always earmarked for certain specific charitable purposes. This amount was remitted directly to the beneficiaries and spent on the specified purposes by the Resident himself, who was accountable to none. A number of deeds of such deposits and loans have survived to show who the beneficiaries actually were.[25] The 'bond business' carried out by the East India Company, too implied similar objectives. These bonds carried 5 percent per annum interest. Sleeman estimated that the people of Oudh had approximately invested 3 crores of rupees in these bonds, and many middle class families were entirely depended on the interest of these bonds.[26] The financial as well as the political implications of these transactions were manifold; a large sum of money was drained out of the kingdom, and the payment of annual interest by the Resident to the beneficiaries and to the religious as well as charitable institutions made a large sections of people dependent on British favour.[27]

The merchants of Oudh kingdom who carried their business in the adjacent British districts as well, enjoyed the privilege of seeking the help of the Resident in redressal of their grievances, through the magistrates of the concerned districts. Chandan Lal, to whom we have referred above was assessed for higher amount of revenue by Kashiparsad Tewaree, the *chakledar* of Poorwa. On his refusal the *chakledar* attacked and killed his brother and plundered property worth Rs 25,000. The matter was brought to the prime minister Ali Naqi Khan, who did nothing to punish the culprits. Thereafter, Chandan Lal applied to the magistrate of Cownpoor claiming "protection as a British subject though residing in Oudh". The matter was referred to Sleeman who immediately took up the case and pleaded for justice. At this the king got annoyed with Chandan Lal for defying his authority and ordered his banishment, but through the constant pressure of the Resident, Kashiprasad Tewaree "was dismissed from *chakledarship*, ordered to repay 25,000, banished from the kingdom for two years and (was) declared incapable of entering the "government service again". But it seems that such a course was insisted upon by Sleeman primarily not with a view to seeking justice, but to interfering with the affairs of King. Elliot says, that within 8 years of the action, the British officials had pardoned Kashiprashad Tewaree and made him an honorary Commissioner.[28]

---

25. R.D. Reeves, *Introduction*.
26. *Ibid*.
27. Elliot, *op. cit.*, p.
28. The passengers travelling in such carriages could not be detained by the officials of the state. The privilege, was misused, hence the king strongly protested and also threatened that such carriages would be subjected to checks. Maulvi Masihuddin Ahmad Khan (MMA), *op. cit.*, pp. 140-1.

The erosion of the king's authority during the second quarter of 19th century by a series of systematic acts of omission and commission by the Resident was an important factor for the decline of Oudh. It so happened that some of the notorious and proclaimed criminals found their way into the Residency or to the British cantonement. Similarly, the tenure of the appointment of many high officials of the king depended on the likes and dislikes of the Resident and on occasion the king was forced to dismiss and banish competent officials precisely for this reason. Masihuddin Ahmad, the plenipotentiary of the deposed Wajid Ali Shah to the Queen, cited the instances in some detail – Raja Hunwunt Singh, the *ta'alluqadar* of Dharwapoor and Kalakankar, constantly evaded the payment of the Government dues and put to defiance the authority of the king. But he found his way to the Residency on invitation by the Resident.[29] The remonstrances made by the king were of no avail. His helplessness is depicted when he speaks of "offenders being allowed to find protection in my dominions, without my having the power to bring them to justice."[30] It was also pleaded that if such landholders got protection from the British, others would get encouragement and they too would evade the payment of the revenues. Such a course would ultimately, set forth "mis-government, give rise to innumerable evils, and lead to confusion and anarchy".[31] But in spite of such pleas being made, nothing was done by the Residents to rectify the course they had adopted.

Another incident, cited by Masihuddin Ahmad shows that Sleeman constantly meddled with the authority of the king, disregarded the decisions of the highest native courts of law as well as of the king himself. One Wusee Ully Khan, Under-Secretary to the Prime Minister, was supposed to be a very competent and efficient official of the Oudh kingdom. Unfortunately, Sleeman had developed a prejudice against him. He asked the king to order his banishment from Lucknow as a seditious person. The king declined to act without getting any proof of his 'alleged seditions', as this was likely to "cause considerable disorder in my kingdom".[32] But still Sleeman insisted and balantly declared, "there is no necessity to prove his guilt, as the appointment imposed upon him is not his *jagir* or hereditary property".[33] Wussy Ully Khan was continued to be passed by Sleeman on

29. R.D. Reeves, *Introduction*.
30. MMA, *op. cit.*, pp. 140-1.
31. *Ibid.*, p. 81.
32. *Ibid.*
33. MMA, *op. cit.*, p. 84.

one pretext or another, even after he had proved his fidelity and devotion to the *nawab*'s government. Sleeman's disrespect towards the established norms of the period and his contemptuous disregard to the authority of the king and his highest officials showed them that the "king .....(was) a mere cipher, the resident accounted all in all ..... a real mayor of the palace and the kingly authority feel into utter contempt."[34]

(b) Bengal Army Sepoys as a Factor in Agrarian Instability

The Sepoys formed an important element in the agrarian society of Oudh kingdom. They were generally recruited from a number of powerful Rajput clans and were attached to various British regiments, including those posted in the kingdom of Oudh. It was estimated by a British official in 1845 that, "three-fourths of Bengal's native infantry came from Oudh."[35] The Bengal army, comprised the bulk of the company's forces and if the estimates were accurate, the number of sepoys from Oudh must have been considerable. The people from Oudh were supposed to furnish the best disciplined infantry in India. For these reasons recruiting parties used to come here as far as from Bombay.[36] In round figures, there were some 50,000 Oudh men serving with the East India Company's forces.

An important privilege enjoyed by the sepoys was that, while serving in any part of the country, they could seek the intercession of the British Resident at the Court of Oudh to settle their local disputes. Even if their family members or any of their relatives had some grievance, they too could approach the Resident. In the prevalent conditions of lawlessness such a privilege could be considered very important. The Resident was obliged to take up all pleas of the sepoys with the limitation that civil cases were not to be over 6 years old and criminal cases 3 years old.

It was this privilege that made many Oudh people to join the Company's services as sepoys. An Oudh soldier was entitled to a monthly pay of Rs 5 or 5½ only while a trooper in the British regiment (recruited from leaded and compound provinces) would get Rs 7 per month. Similarly, the Oudh sepoy had no pension benefits and could claim no extra allowance while on march; they were only entitled to avail one month's leave. Of the East India Company, sepoys posted in the Oudh Kingdom enjoyed much greater privileges. Beside being close to home, they got fuel and fodder

34. Cf. Calcutta Review (CR) (1845), Vol. III, p. 380.
35. *Ibid.*
36. Sleeman, *op. cit.*, Vol. I, p. 145.

and often food. Their baggage was always carried for them at public cost. However, these gains were made often at the expense of their fellow peasants and *zamindars*. As Sleeman says, "they (sepoys) were the privileged class who gave much trouble and annoyance and were often terror for their non-privileged neighbours and co-sharers in the land."[37]

The grievances of the sepoys for which they sought redress from the Resident varied in nature and dimensions. There were cases when the near relatives of any sepoy were killed by bandits; or they were robbed off their belongings by dacoits. If the family of the victim was denied justice by the local authorities or the victims were not satisfied with the particular judgment delivered upon a case, the aggrieved family or relatives of the sepoys could approach the Resident. The Resident could order a fresh investigation into the whole matter. Since every individual sepoy could have had no direct access to the Residency, it is quite possible that the petitions were submitted through the Commandant of the concerned regiment. The tour made by W.H. Sleeman in the kingdom provided ample opportunities to every sepoy to approach him directly with a petition.[38] He says, "I have every day scores of petitions delivered to me with quivering lip and tearful eye; by the person who have been plundered of all they possessed, had their dearest relatives murdered or tortured to death and their habitations burnt to the ground by the gangs of ruffians under landlords of high birth and pretentions whom they had never wronged or offended".[39]

The impact of such a privileged class could not but cause bitterness locally behind a façade of submission. The big landholders tried their best to get the sepoys satisfied so as to avoid any unwarranted interference in their affairs. But probably they were never fully satisfied. A British official observed, "the *zamindar* throughout the country will buy, beg, borrow or steal in the name of a British sepoy, in the hope of thus gaining attention to their petty claims .... We are indeed of the opinion that much (of) the Oudh government is molested and degraded by sepoy's claims, true or false, the men themselves are rarely benefited by the Resident's interference. Litigation is promoted; hopes are excited and eventually the party who would, if left to his own resources and the practices of the country, have arranged or compromised his quarrel, is led on to his ruin."[40]

37. It was alleged that Sleeman during the tour of Oudh kingdom, "has been encouraging applications and the receipts of petition from all quarters." Perry Erskine, *Birds-eye view of India*, p. 174 Cf. M. Masihuddin Ahmad, *op. cit.*, p. 84.

38. Sleeman, *op. cit.*, Vol. I, p. 73.

39. Cf. *CR* (1845), Vol. III, pp. 414-5.

40. *Ibid.*

However, it should not be supposed that the sepoys were deliberate victims of any sort of official harassment or that they were the chief sufferers in the kingdom. The period itself was marked by a general deterioration of the law-and-order situation. In midst of such conditions, the sepoys used to create further problems for the local administration by insisting on their privileges, and by invoking Resident's intercession all the time.[41] Often enough, the hollowness of their claims and complaints were exposed and quite known to the British officials themselves. Even Sleeman observed that, "the wrongs of which they (sepoys) complain, are of course such as all men of their class in Oudh are liable to suffer; but no other men in Oudh are so prone to exaggerate the circumstances attending them to bring forward prominently all that is favourable to their own side and keep back all that is otherwise; and to conceal the difficulties which must attend the enforcement of an award when made."[42]

Most often the sepoys preferred their claims against those who had well garrisoned forts and large bands of armed followers. It was practically impossible to subdue them without the help of a large and well equipped British force. Sleeman notes that on an occasion, "thirty lives were lost in attempting to enforce an award in favour of a *sipahee* of our army."[43]

One case cited by Sleeman may well be characteristic. Shaikh Mehboob Ali was a retired *subedar* major. He acquired the possession of a village from his powerful neighbour's estate, in addition to the lands already held by him by invoking the aid of the Resident in his land disputes. But he found it difficult to have the cultivators till the land. Taxed for reasons, he alleged the hostility of his neighbour which prevented the peasants from cultivating that particular village. Such deep rooted hostility existed because of the fact that with Resident's help he had evicted a person who had been the *zamindar* of the village for the last 30 or 35 years. There was no specific statement of the time of the event, nor did the Resident try to ascertain the facts before proceeding with the case. The resulting judgment by the Resident on behalf of the sepoys involved, "the risk of the loss of so many lives, first in obtaining possession and then keeping you (sepoys) in it."[44] It should not be considered as the only instance of the miscarriage of justice as Sleeman himself admits that "cases of this kind are very numerous."[45]

41. Sleeman, *op. cit.*
42. *Ibid.*
43. *Ibid.*
44. Sleeman, Vol. I, p. 165.
45. *Ibid.*

Apart from the big land-lords and the local chieftains, the rural population itself was directly subjected to the high handedness of the sepoys. They perpetuated all sort of atrocities over the peasants under the shadow of British protection wherever the sepoys went all the stocks of grain of the peasants were forcibly taken out by them. While Sleeman himself was passing through the district of Sand , a Bangar and encamped in the village Sakin, the sepoys of his camp had looted all the stock of straw (*bhoosa*) kept by the peasants for the use of their own cattle. The matter was reported to Sleeman by some daring cultivators. On enquiry he was informed that this was the established practice of the day that, "all villages near the road, along which the troops and establishment more are plundered of *bhoosa* and all those, within ten miles of the place when they may be detained for a week or fortnight, are plundered in the same way."[46] Even sometimes the grass-sheds (*chappar*) were removed from the huts of the poor peasants by the sepoys in order to meet the lamp requirements. Sometimes the peasants were duty bound to provide the foodgrains and other necessities to the encamping army of the sepoys. Similarly the army of the state, when on march used to subject the peasants to the same hardships.

46. Sleeman, Vol. I, p. 165.

Bibliography

The documents, books and articles which have been actually cited in the MS are only included in the bibliography. In addition to these sources, much material has been explored but found to contain little information relevant to the present study, and this has not been included here. For abbreviations used here and elsewhere in the MS see the separate list of abbreviations. All manuscripts, printed works and English sources have been arranged in a chronological order. Modern works and articles have been arranged alphabetically, according to authors' surnames.

SOURCES

A – Persian and Urdu

(i) Historical Works

1. Zahiruddin Muhammad Babur (d. 1530), *Babur-nama*, English tr. By A.S. Beveridge, London, 1921.
2. Abul Fazal, *Akbarnama* (1601) ed. Agha Ahmad 'Ali and Abdur Rahim', 3 vols. Bib. Ind. Calcutta, 1873-87.
3. 'Abdul Hamid Lahori (1654-5), *Badshahnama*, ed. Kabiruddin Ahmad and 'Abur Rahim, 2 vols. Bib. Ind. Calcutta, 1867-72. Vol. I is divided into two parts (i) and (ii).
4. Saleh Kambu Lahori, *Amal-i Saleh*, ed. G. Yazdani, 4 vols. Bib. Ind. Calcutta, 1912-16.
5. Muhammad Kazim (1968), *Alamgirnama*, ed. Khadim Husain and 'Abdul Hai, Bib. Ind. Calcutta, 1865-73.
6. Sujan Rai Bhandari (1695), *Khutasat-ut Tawarikh*, ed. Zafar Hasan, Delhi, 1918.
7. Saqi Musta'id Khan (1710-11), *Ma'asir-i 'Alamgiri*, ed. Agha Ahmad Ali, Bib. Indi. Calcutta, 1870-3.
8. Muhammad Bukhtawar Khan, *Mirat-ul 'Alam*, 4 vols. Lahore, 1879.
9. Muhammad Hashim Khafi Khan, *Muntakhab-al Lubab*, 2 vols. Ed. K.D. Ahmad and Haiq, Bib. Ind. Calcutta, 1860-74.
10. Rae Chaturman Saksena, *Chahar Gulshan*, Aligarh, Habibgunj 23/157. The information pertains to the early years of Muhammad Shah.

11. Ghulam Ali Azad Bilgirami, *Ma'athir-ul Kiram*, Hyderabad, 1913.
12. Saiyid Ghulam 'Ali Naqvi, (1808) '*Imad-us Sa'adat*, Lucknow, 1897.
13. Mufti Ghulam Hazrat, *Kawaif-i zila 'Gorakhpur*, A.D. 1810, Aligarh, Subhanullah 954/12.
14. Lalji, *Mirat-ul Auza*, A.D. 1850-5, Aligarh Muslim University Collection, *Farsi; Tarikh* 60. The contents of this work have been described by S.A. Rasheed (No. 103 of this Bibliography).
15. Munshi Muzzaffar Husain Khan, *Nama-i Muzzaffari*, 2 vols. Lucknow, 1917. An Urdu history of the family of Diler Khan and other families of Shahabad with a large number of texts of Persian documents together with some photo reproductions.
16. Kamaluddin Haidar, *Sawanihat-i Salatin Awadh* (Urdu), Lucknow, 1879.

(ii) Official Documents, Manuals, Revenue Statistics

17. Abul Fazl, *Ain-i Akbari* (1595) ed. Blochman, Bib. Ind. Calcutta, 1867-77. I have collated the statistical information with Add. 7652 and Add. 6552 (Microfilm in the Department of History, AMU).
18. *Dastur-ul 'Amal-i 'Alamgiri*, C. 1659. Ms. Br. Mues. Add. 6598; contains *sarkar* wise revenue statistics (Rotograph, Department of History, AMU).
19. *Dastur-ul 'Amal* Aurangzeb : Post 1696 Bodl. Fraser 86 (Rotropraph, Department of History, AMU).
20. *Dastur-ul 'Amal-i Shahjahani*, Br. Mues. Add. 6588 contains *sarkar* wise revenue statistics. From internal evidence Professor Irfan Habib assigns this work to 1701-2 (Rotograph, Department of History, AMU).
21. *Ethe-433* contains *pargana* wise *jama'* (*mal* and *sair*) separately stated) of the Mughal Empire at the close of Shahjahan's reign, alongwith *jama'* and *hasil* figures for Muhammad Shah's period. (Dr Shireen Moosvi kindly allowed me to use her notes of this manuscript).
22. *Zawabit-i 'Alamgiri*, Aurangzeb : post 1691, Add. 6598 (Rotograph, Department of History, AMU).
23. *Kaghzat-i Mutaffariqa*' 18th c. (Br. Mues. Add. 6586 contains *pargana* list with the *jama' dami* for the last years of Aurangzeb's reign (Rotograph, Department of History, AMU).
24. *Akhbarat-i Darbar-i Mu'alla*, newsletters from the Imperial Court, Aurangzeb's reign, 9 vols, in case 47 at the Royal Asiatic Society, London, (Microfilm in the Department of History, AMU).
25. *Akhbarat* in Central Records Office, Hyderabad. Some of these have been published along with English translations by Yousuf Husain Khan, *Newsletters, 1767-1799*, Hyderabad, 1955.

(iii) Insha' Collection and Biographical Works

26. Bhupat Ra'i, *Insha-i Roshan Kalam*, Letters written on behalf of R'ad Andaz Khan, *faujdar* of Bainswara, 1698-1702 and of his son and deputy Sher Andaz Khan, Aligarh, Abdus Salam, 109/339.

27. Santokh Rai, *Insha-i Mansur* or *Mansur-ul Maktubat*, Letters written on behalf of Safdar Jang, addressed to Emperor Muhammad Shah and Qamaruddin Khan, the *wazir*. These were compiled by one Awadhi L'al, 1212 AH/1803. Unique manuscript in Tagore Library, Lucknow University.

28. Munshi In'amullah Raghib, *Ausaf-al Asaf*, MS. Aligarh, Abdul Salam 480/1 *Farsi*, the year of compilation is 1199 AH; Transcribed 1202 AH. The second Chapter of the vol. 2 contains letters, despatches, petitions and *parwanas*.

29. Shah Ashraf 'Ata, *Bayaz*, Ms. 1215/1807 (year on seal). At the end of this *Bayaz*, a list is appended giving the details of the possessions of Shah Karim 'Ata, father of the author (KKC).

30. Shah Panah 'Ata, *Rauzat-ul Arwah*, Ms. 1246/1838 (the date of transcription), contains copies of the letters exchanged between the ancestors of the compiler and the Emperors, princes and notables (KKC).

31. Shah Ghulam 'Ali Shah, *Mishkat-un Nubuwah*, Ms. 1212/1804 (the date of transcription) contains genealogies of mystics, etc. (in the private collection of Dr Sulaiman Siddiqi, Osmania University, Hyderabad).

32. 'Abdul Hay, *Nuzhat-ul Khwatir* (Arabic), VIII Vols., Hyderabad, 1911.

(iv) Documents from Private/Families Collections

33. Documents in the Central Record Office, Allahabad. The documents used by me are those accessioned in the first series, and these have been cited as 'Allahabad with the accession number following. Since these have recently been rearranged the new numbers are prefaced with the letters RAA. These include an original copy of the *sanad* of Sher Shah stipulating the obligations of the *madad-i-ma'ash* grantees (RAA-318). The *farman* of Aurangzeb (c. 1690) relating to rules of succession to *madad-i ma'ash* is RAA-1880.

34. Collection of acquired documents, National Archives of India, New Delhi. These have been cited as NAI, followed by accession numbers.

35. Bilgiram Documents belonging to 16th-18th centuries, Research Library, Department of History, AMU. The 16th century documents have been calendared by Professor Irfan Habib. See No. 81 of this bibliography.

36. Firangi Mahal Documents, Research Library, Department of History, AMU. The collection includes one of Akbar's earliest known *farman* of 1559 confirming *madad-i ma'ash* rights of the ancestors of the Firangi Mahal family.

37. Khairabad Documents belonging to 16th-19th centuries, Research Library, Department of History, AMU. These have been calendared by Dr Iqbal Husain. See No. 85 of this bibliography.

38. Jais Documents belonging to 17th-19th centuries, Research Library, Department of History, AMU.

39. Collection of Documents, Tagore Library, Lucknow University. All these documents belong to a family of *qanungos*, *pargana* Lahorpur, sarkar Khairabad. These have been calendared by me. See No. 93 of this bibliography.

40. Khwaja Yasin, *Glossary of Revenue and Administrative Terms*, Late 18th Century, Br. Mues. Add. 6603.
41. Documents relating to the mystic family of Salon:
    (i) Aurangzeb, *Farman*, granting the revenues of 200 *bigha* of village Mirzapur Bakhtiyar as an offering for the servants of Shaikh Pir Muhammad (KKC). Translation published in *PIHC* (1979), pp. 302-14.
    (ii) Aurangzeb, *Farman*, granting the *jama*' of the village Ashrafgunj Singhwal as *madad-i-ma'ash* to Sheikh Muhammad Ashraf (KKC). Translation published in *PIHC* (1979), pp. 302-14.
    (iii) Muhammad Shah, *Farman*, granting a confirmation to the *madad-e-ma'ash* rights of Shaikh Muhammad Ashraf to all his possessions. Photographic reproduction (obverse side) included in Shah Hasan 'Ata's *Hazir-i Sang*, Karachi, 1963.
    (iv) Shah Alam II, *Farman* confirming all the existing *madad-i ma'ash* rights of Shah Karim 'Ata including a number of *haveli*, gardens, *chaks* and a number of villages (KKC).
    (v) *Iqrarnama*, executed by Shah Karim 'Ata in favour of his eldest son Shah Ashraf 'Ata effecting transfer of the *madad-e ma'ash* holdings in full proprietory rights, dated 11th zilhij 1238/1822 (KKC).
    (vi) *Iqrarnamah*, executed by Shah Karim 'Ata in favour of his second son Shah Panah 'Ata, where an attempt was made to restore the *waqf* character of the properties in question dated 6th jamad I 1248/1832 (KKC).
    (vii) *Wajib-ul arz* of the villages Panah Nagar, Hayat Nagar, Karim Nagar, Dhankesra and Barwalia, *pargana* Salon, district Rae Bareli (KKC). These were compiled in the course of first revenue settlement in Awadh after the mutiny.
    (viii) *Rawaj-e 'am* of *pargana* Parshadepur and Salon, district Rae Bareli (KKC). These were also compiled during the first revenue settlement in Awadh after the mutiny.

B – English

42. Foreign Secret Consultations, 1777 and 1778, *NAI*, Delhi.
43. Foreign Department Secret Consultations, 1780, *NAI*, Delhi.
44. James Rennell, *A Bengal Atlas containing maps of the theatre of war and commerce on that side of Hindustan*, London, 1781.
45. J.V. Valentia, *Voyages and Travel in India, Ceylon, the Red Sea, Abbysiniya and Egypt 1802-6*, 3 vols, London, 1809.
46. Francis Buchanan, *District Reports* (1806-12), ed. And abridged by Montgomery Martin, *The History, Antiquities, Topography and Statistics of Eastern India*, 3 vols. London, 1838, Indian reprint, 1976, 5 vols. London, 1838, Indian reprint, 1976, 5 vols. The Survey of Gorakhpur is from Montgomery Martin's abridgement (Vol. II, has been used).

47. Bishop Reginald Heber, *Narrative of a Journey through the Upper Provinces 1824-25*, London, 1828.

48. Walter Hamilton, *The East India Gazetteer*; containing particular descriptions of the empires, kingdoms, principalities, provinces, cities, towns, districts, fortresses, harbours, rivers, lakes, etc. of Hindostan and the adjacent countries, 2 vols. London. 1828.

49. Donald Buttler, *Outlines of the Topography and Statistics of Southern District of Oudh and Cantonment of Sultanpur*, Calcutta, 1839.

50. W.H. Lawrence, 'Kingdom of Oudh', published in *Calcutta Review*, 1845 (iii).

51. Edward Thornton, *A Gazetteer of the Territories under the Government of the East India Company and of the Native States on the Continent of India*, 4 vols. London, 1954.

52. Masih-ud-din Ahmad, *Oude : Its Princes and Its Government Vindicated*, London, 1857, edited by Safi Ahmad, under *British Aggression in Awadh*, Meerut, 1969.

53. W.H. Sleeman, *A Journey through the kingdom of Oudh during 1849-50*, 2 vols., London, 1858. R.D. Reeves' introduction to an abridgement of this work (No. 104 of this Bibliography) is indispensable for understanding the background to the original Diary.

54. Board of Revenue Papers, Lucknow. The files of Rae Bareli district relating to 1861-2 and of Oudh general relating to 1858 have been used.

55. Karl Marx, 'Lord Canning's Proclamation and Land Tenure in India *New York, Daily Tribune* No. 5344 of 7th June 1858. The article is included in *The First Indian War of Independence*, Progressive Publishers, Moscow (English version), 1952.

56. C.U. Aitchinson, *Collection of treaties engagements and sunnuds relating to India and neighbouring countries*, 6 vols. Calcutta, 1876 (Vol. II has been used).

57. Report from the Select Committee on East India finances with Proceedings, minutes of evidences 1873, *British Parliamentary Papers; Colonies East India*, Vol. XXI, IUP, Shannon, Ireland, 1970.

(ii) Modern Works

58. M. Athar Ali, *Mughal Nobility under Aurangzeb*, Bombay, 1966.

59. A.A. Azmi, '*Ta'alluqadars* in the kingdom of Awadh, paper read in *Indian History Congress* (1965), Cyclostyled.

60. A.A. Azmi, 'Position of Agriculture and Economy of the Nawabi Oudh', *PIHC*, 1967 (Patiala) Session.

61. Ashok V. Desai, *Population and standard of Living in Akbar's Times,* IESHR, *IX (ii),* Delhi, 1972.

62. Shah Hadi 'Ata, 'Muntakhabat-e Sa'adi ka bab dum' (Urdu), *Mussanif Quarterly*, Vol. XIII, Aligarh, 1946 (1). The author reproduces Persian texts of the letters addressed to the mystics of Salon by the Mughal princes

and other notables during the 18th and 19th century, along with a short summary in Urdu.

63. Shah Hadi 'Ata, 'Qasba Salon ka Khandon-i Karimi' (Urdu), *Mussanif Quarterly*, Vol. XII, Aligarh, 1945 (iii), pp. 78-80. The author reproduces the statement of Shah Mehdi 'Ata given before some Law Court in 1880.
64. Darogha Haji Abbas Ali, *An Illustrated Historical Album of Rajas and Ta'alluqadars of Oudh*, Allahabad, 1880.
65. Richard B. Barnett, *North India Between the Empires*, Berkeley, 1980.
66. Purnendu Basu, *Oudh and the East India Company*, Lucknow, 1980.
67. W.C. Benett, *A Report on the Family History of the Chief Clans of Roy Bareilly District*, Lucknow, 1870.
68. John Beams, 'On the Geography of India in the Reign of Akbar', Part I, Subah Awadh *Journal of Asiatic Society, Bengal*, LIII, (1884), pp. 215-32, with map.
69. *Cambridge Economic History of India*, ed. Tapan R. Chaudhary and Irfan Habib, Delhi, 1982.
70. *Patrick Cornegy,* Notes on the Land-Revenue Assessment of Upper India, London, 1874.
71. *Census of India* (1911), Calcutta, 1913. This volume contains figures from the earlier censuses (beginning with those of the 1872 census).
72. Bernard S. Cohn, 'Structural Changes in Indian Rural Society, 1595-1885' in *Land Control and Social Structure in India*, ed. R.E. Petursburg, Madison, 1969.
73. W. Crooke, *The Tribes and Castes of North Western Provinces*, 1896.
74. Department of Revenue and *Agricultural Statistics of India* (Calcutta, Issues of 1884-5 and 1885-6).
75. C.A. Elliott, *The Chronicles of Onnaoo,* Allahabad, 1862.
76. *A Gazetteer of the Province of Oudh*, 3 vols, Allahabad, 1877.
77. Ibn Hasan, *Central Structure of the Mughal Empire*, and its practical working up to the year 1657, London, 1936.
78. Irfan Habib, *Agrarian System of Mughal India*, Bombay, 1963.
79. Irfan Habib, *An Atlas of the Mughal Empire*, OUP, Delhi, 1982.
80. Irfan Habib, '*Zamindars* in the *Ain*', *PIHC* (1958).
81. Irfan Habib, 'Aspects of Agrarian Relations and Economy in a Region of Uttar Pradesh during the 16th Century', *IESHR*, IV (iii), 1967.
82. Irfan Habib, 'Colonialization of Indian Economy', *Social Scientist*, No. 32, 1972.
83. Irfan Habib, Note on Population, 1800-1872, Presented in a Seminar on *Transformation of Mughal Indian Economy into Colonial Economy*, Aligarh, 1975 (Cyclostyled proceedings).
84. Irfan Habib, 'Studying a Colonial Economy without perceiving Colonialism', *Centre of South Asian Studies*, University of Cambridge, 1984, (Cyclostyled). However, this article has been published in *Modern Asian Review* (iii) and *Social Scientist*, No. 139.

85. Iqbal Husain, 'A Calendar of Khairabad Documents: 16th-19th Centuries', *Islamic Culture*, Vol. LIII, No. (i) and (ii), Hyderabad, 1979.

86. Shah Ahmad Husain Jafri, 'Hazrat Pir Muhammad ki *hayat* aur t'alimat unki *malfuzat* ki Roshni men' (Urdu) paper presented at *Khuda Bakhsh South Asian Regional Seminar on Significant Manuscripts of Sufism*, Aligarh Session, March 1985. The author had made use of the manuscripts like *Bahre-Anwaj-e Karimi* and *Fawaid-e Karimi* extensively.

87. S.Z.H. Jafri, 'Two *madad-e ma'ash farmans* of Aurangzeb from Awadh', *PIHC*, (1979).

88. S.Z.H. Jafri, 'Administration of the *Jagirs* in Awadh during 17th century', *JUPHS* (1984).

89. S.Z.H. Jafri, '*Zamindars* in the Kingdom of Awadh' paper read in *Indian History Congress*, (1980), Cyclostyled.

90. S.Z.H. Jafri, 'Bais *Zamindars* of Awadh', Paper read in Indian History Congress (1981), Cyclostyled.

91. S.Z.H. Jafri, 'The Land Controlling Classes in Awadh – A Study of Changes in their Composition 1600-1900' Paper read in *Indian History Congress* (1982), cyclostyled.

92. S.Z.H. Jafri, 'Origin and growth of *ta'alluqadari* tenures in Awadh', Paper read in *Indian History Congress* (1984), cyclostyled.

93. S.Z.H. Jafri, 'Side Lights on Administrative Structure and Agrarian Relations in Awadh – A Study of Laharpur Documents (16th-18th Centuries)', Paper read in *Seminar on Sources of Socio-Economic History of North India*, University of Allahabad, 1985.

94. Shireen Moosvi, 'Production, Consumption and Population in Akbar's India', *IESHR* X (ii), 1973.

95. Shireen Moosvi, 'Formulations of Land-Revenue Rates Under Akbar', *IHR* (1976), Delhi.

96. Shireen Moosvi, 'Magnitude of Land Revenue Demand and the Income of the Mughal Ruling Class Under Akbar', *Medieval India – A Miscellany*, IV, Aligarh, 1977.

97. W.H. Moreland, *India at the Death of Akbar*, London, 1920.

98. W.H. Moreland, 'The Agricultural Statistics of Akbar's Empire', *Journal UP Historical Society*, 11(I), 1922.

99. Zahiruddin Malik, 'The problems of *faujdari* jurisdiction in Bainswara', Paper read in *Indian History Congress* (1973), cyclostyled.

100. H.R. Nevill, *District Gazetteers of the United Provinces of Agra and Oudh*, various vols. One for each district, Lucknow.

101. *Report of the UP Zamindari Abolition Committee*, 2 vols, Allahabad, 1950.

102. Jagdish Raj, 'The Revenue System of the Nawabs of Oudh', *JESHO*, 1959.

103. S.A. Rasheed, 'Mirat-al-Auza', *IHRC*, 1954.

104. R.D. Reeves, *Sleeman in Oudh*, Sleeman's diary of his tour of Oudh, edited and abridged with introduction and notes, London, 1971.

This volume has been used for the informative introduction by Reeves. For Sleeman's own work, see No. 53 of this Bibliography.

105. A.L. Srivastava, *First two Nawabs of Awadh*, first edition 1933, IInd edition, Agra, 1954.

106. A.L. Srivastava, *History of Shuja-ud-daulah*, 2 vols, First edition, 1939, IInd edition, Agra, 1961.

107. K.K. Trivedi, 'Changes in Caste Composition of the Zamindar Class in Western Uttar Pradesh, 1595-c. 1900', *Indian Historical Review*, 11(I), 1975.

108. J.A. Valuker, *Report on the Improvement of Indian Agriculture*, London, 1893.

109. G. Watt, *The Dictionary of Economic Products of India*, 6 vols, London, 1889.

110. Albert T. Walker, *Memoirs of the Indian Meterological Department* (from Records up to 1920), Calcutta, 1924.

111. H.H. Wilson, *A Glossary of Judicial and Revenue Terms of British India*, London, 1875.

Index

Q

R

S

W

Z